Open Computing Guide to UnixWare

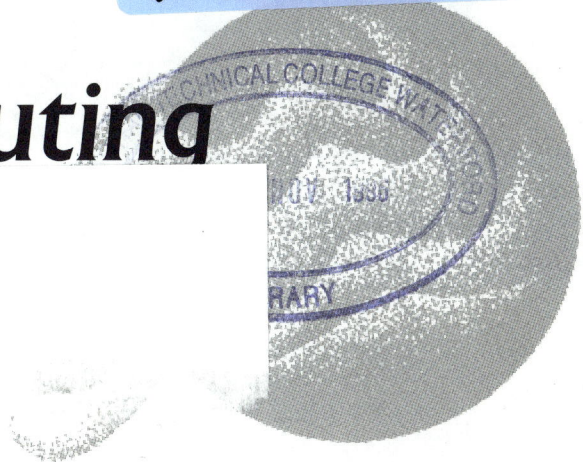

Joseph Radin,
Levi Reiss,
and Steven Nameroff

Osborne **McGraw-Hill**

Berkeley New York St. Louis San Francisco
Auckland Bogotá Hamburg London Madrid
Mexico City Milan Montreal New Delhi Panama City
Paris São Paulo Singapore Sydney Tokyo Toronto

Osborne **McGraw-Hill**
2600 Tenth Street
Berkeley, California 94710
U.S.A.

For information on translations or book distributors outside the U.S.A., or to arrange bulk purchase discounts for sales promotions, premiums, or fundraisers, please contact Osborne **McGraw-Hill** at the above address.

Open Computing Guide to UnixWare

1234567890 DOC 998765

ISBN 0-07-882027-8

Publisher
  Lawrence Levitsky

Acquisitions Editors
  Joanne Cuthbertson
  Jeffrey Pepper

Copy Editor
  Ann Spivack

Proofreader
  Pat Mannion

Computer Designer
  Peter Hancik

Illustrator
  Rhys Elliott

Series Design
  Jani Beckwith

Quality Control Specialist
  Joe Scuderi

Cover Design
  EM Design

We dedicate this book to our wives and children:

Sara, Gal, and Nurit Radin;
Noga, Sami, and Maya Reiss; and
Michael Ann and Micah Nameroff

Contents At A Glance

PART III
Networking

Contents

PART II
System Administration

Acknowledgments

What do we have in common with the Academy Award winners for best screenplay? Perhaps not the wordsmithing, but the heartfelt need to acknowledge the efforts of others to put it all together. May we have the envelope, please?

Jeff Pepper, Editor-in-Chief and Acquisitions Editor, as always, you got us started and followed the project closely to the not-so-bitter end. Joanne Cuthbertson, Acquisitions Editor, on a day-to-day basis you made it happen. Kelly Vogel, your meticulous attention to the little and not-so-little things helped so, so much. Ann Spivack, you filled the cutting room floor to our (and our readers') gratification. Andy Yaros, for catching those oh-so-little glitches that would have been oh-so-frustrating for everyone. Richard Wallis, for your valuable input during the early stages.

We appreciate the support received from David Hacking, NetWare Services, and Garry Perry, Unix Systems Group, Novell Inc. Special thanks go to the UnixWare developers for their outstanding product. Without them, this book would not exist.

Final appreciation goes to our wives and children—Sara, Gal, and Nurit Radin; Noga, Sami, and Maya Reiss; and Michael Ann and Micah Nameroff—for their infinite patience. We will enjoy being with them once again.

As is customary, the authors acknowledge their full responsibility for any errors.

Introduction

If you are reading this, you most likely fall into one of these categories:

- You've never heard of UnixWare, and you wonder what it is.
- You have used UnixWare, or are about to use UnixWare at your home or office, and you want to use it more effectively.
- You are responsible for maintaining a UnixWare system and you are wondering whether this book contains enough information to guide you through the details of system administration.

These next few pages are designed to help you decide whether this book (or possibly even UnixWare itself) is right for you.

Unleash the Power of Your PC

As the hardware behind personal computers becomes more and more powerful, the software has started falling further and further behind. Just how fast can those cards zip off the screen after you've won a game of solitaire? With UnixWare, you can harness the raw power of Pentiums by letting many users do many tasks simultaneously on the same machine. This *multitasking* capability is just one of the many advantages of UnixWare, as you'll discover while you study this book.

Another advantage of UnixWare is consistency. People who use Unix on a workstation at the office can have UnixWare on their PC at home and not only be comfortable with the command set, but get full connectivity over a modem line to their office network. People who understand Unix system administration will easily transition to UnixWare system administration, making it much easier to find and hire administrators. Plus, if you have a heterogeneous network of PCs and Unix workstations, UnixWare will make all the machines communicate with each other using standard protocols and commands.

If you are an avid DOS or Windows fan, have no fear: UnixWare can run both DOS and Windows programs. This book will show you how.

How This Book is Organized

Open Computing Guide to UnixWare is divided into three parts, plus several appendices.

Part One
Part One gets you started as a UnixWare user. Chapter 1 gives you some background on Unix and outlines some of its advantages. Chapter 2 shows you how to use the UnixWare desktop most effectively. In Chapter 3 you learn about the standard UnixWare applications. Finally, Chapter 4 describes how to install and execute DOS and Windows programs within the UnixWare environment.

Part Two
Part Two covers system administration for UnixWare. If you do not consider yourself a system administrator, you will be surprised at how many administrator-like tasks you will be required to do, such as installing applications, setting file permissions, and backing up files. Also, if you think your system is not tuned well, you can go to your system administrator armed with proof about performance problems. If you are a system administrator, this part of the book will be indispensable to you.

Chapter 5 introduces you to system administration terms and tasks. Chapter 6 guides you through installing new UnixWare applications. Use Chapter 7 when you are changing the hardware configuration of your computer. In Chapter 8 you learn how to add and remove users, and manage passwords and groups. Chapter 9 covers printing and printer management. For file systems management, including backup and restore, study Chapter 10. Finally, Chapter 11 describes how to diagnose and correct system performance problems.

Part Three

Any time you have more than one computer accessing the same data, or two computers communicating with each other, you have some sort of network. Part Three covers networking as it relates to UnixWare. Chapter 12 gives you an introduction to the fundamentals of networking. Chapter 13 shows you how to configure your computer to support network protocols such as TCP/IP. If you have NetWare, Chapter 14 will help you use your UnixWare machine as a NetWare server. Chapter 15 shows you how to set up and use electronic mail.

Appendices

The appendices are designed to be references that you use in specific circumstances. Appendix A covers physical device management. Use Appendix B if you find errors running **fsck**, UnixWare's file system checking utility. Appendix C steps you through the installation of UnixWare and Windows. If you use your modem or serial port for a network connection, refer to Appendix D to help you set it up.

PART 1
Getting Started

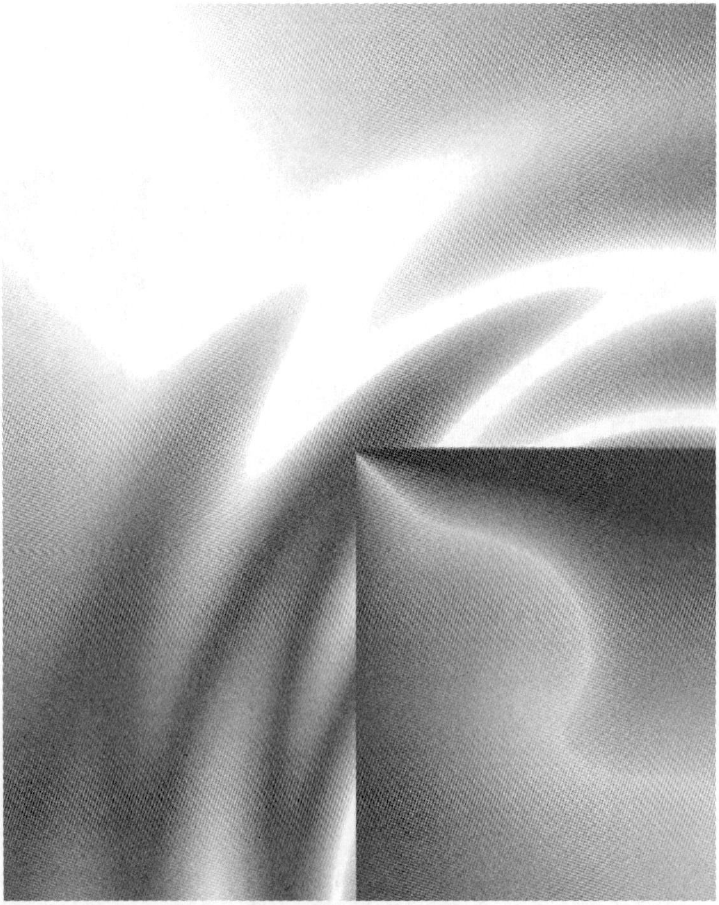

CHAPTER 1

Introduction

Welcome to UnixWare. This software combines in a single package the power of Unix, the ease of use of Windows, and access to the multitude of applications for the Novell/DOS/Windows environments. This book shows how you can benefit from UnixWare's unique capabilities whether you are running a single computer or a network of hundreds of computers executing different operating systems. Before rolling up our sleeves let's take a quick look at UnixWare's family history and its advantages over other operating systems. Then we'll introduce its two basic configurations.

The History of Unix

Unix is an *operating system*. An operating system is the control program that manages the hardware and software resources of a computer system. This program provides the interface between the computer hardware and those who use the computer, from novices doing data entry to expert programmers and system administrators. Every time a hardware advance is made, such as CD-ROM technology, the operating system must be updated. Vendors of operating systems also enhance their programs to make them more powerful and easy to use. Unix is no exception. Fig 1-1 shows the evolution of the Unix operating system.

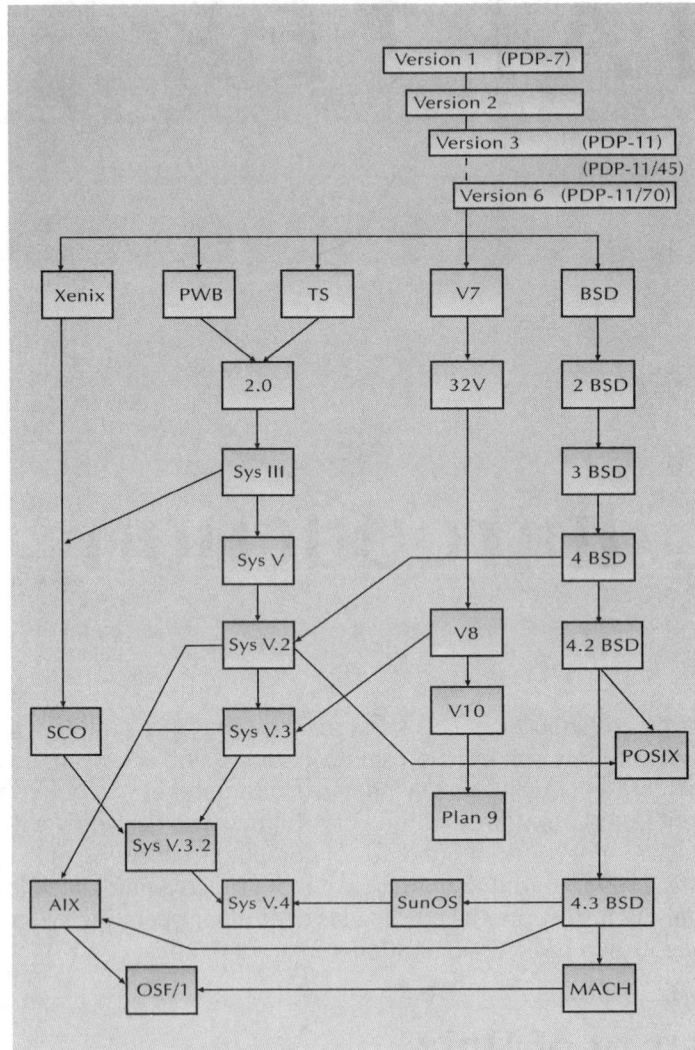

FIGURE 1-1. *The evolution of Unix*

In 1965 Bell Telephone Laboratories, commonly known as Bell Labs, the research arm of AT&T, joined General Electric and Project Mac of the Massachusetts Institute of Technology to develop an operating system called Multics. Multics was designed to enable large numbers of users to access the computer simultaneously and share data. As is so often the case, the system took much longer to build than had been originally planned. In 1969 Bell Labs withdrew its representatives from the Multics team and went on to develop its own system called Unix.

Unix was originally programmed in assembly language, a programming language intimately linked to the particular platform on which it runs. Reprogramming an operating system written in assembly language to run on an even slightly different computer is a major task. In 1973 designers rewrote the major portion of Unix in the C programming language to give it portability, a feature no other operating system existing at that time had. *Portability* is the ability to move software from one hardware platform to another, without major recoding. Eventually, Unix was running on widely divergent computer hardware. The developers of Unix have always claimed that their program is an open system, one that encourages the development of compatible vendor products.

Two major versions flourished, the AT&T Unix (now called System V) and Berkeley Unix (BSD), developed at the University of California, Berkeley, in the mid-1970s. Over the years the two versions have grown closer together, sharing each other's technological advances. However, it is clear to all but a few diehards, mostly concentrated in the scientific and academic communities, that System V has won the Unix wars. As of early 1995 the current version is Release 4.2.

The Advantages of Unix Systems

It is no surprise that Unix has become such a popular operating system in many competitive marketplaces. In terms of sheer power and flexibility, it outstrips both MS-DOS and MS-Windows. At the same time, Unix can be easier to use than the proprietary minicomputer and mainframe computer operating systems. Besides being easily ported, Unix is both *multitasking*, meaning it can perform several tasks at the same time, and *multiuser*, meaning it can simultaneously serve multiple users. In addition, Unix gives you extensive software including the X Window system, which allows for display of graphics interfaces, and sophisticated networking capabilities. Let's look at these important advantages in greater detail.

Portability

Previous operating systems were intimately linked to a single computer or narrowly defined family of computers. Changing computers meant changing operating systems and heavily modifying or abandoning existing applications. Unix broke new ground by being portable. You can move Unix and applications running under Unix from one computer to another with relative ease, even if the two computers have widely divergent architecture. This portability enables installations to acquire a computer running Unix without worrying about becoming a prisoner of the manufacturer. When an installation outgrows the computer, your existing Unix applications can be adapted to run on the new hardware (assuming, of course, that Unix itself has been ported to the new hardware).

Multitasking

Unix was designed to multitask. Multitasking means that the computer system can perform several tasks simultaneously. Even on a stripped-down version of Unix, users can answer their electronic mail, calculate travel expenses with an electronic spreadsheet, and pop the results of these calculations into an expense report using a word processor. Such multitasking is not readily available with MS-DOS but is available with MS-Windows and OS/2.

A Multiuser Environment

Unlike MS-DOS, MS-Windows, or OS/2, Unix is a multiuser system. It allocates resources and protects them, but allows users to share data when desired. Whereas a single-user system may not require a system administrator, every multiuser system must have a system administrator to function effectively.

Beyond DOS Compatibility

Many DOS users are hesitant to switch to Unix because they don't want to give up their familiar applications such as WordPerfect and Lotus 1-2-3. They needn't worry. Popular DOS programs are available on Unix, often in keystroke-compatible versions. Most Unix implementations run in a DOS-compatible mode. This provides full access to all familiar services including executing programs and formatting diskettes. However, Unix software often goes beyond the DOS versions. For example, the Unix version of Lotus lets a user display and process more than two dozen active spreadsheets at any given time; it also allows access to most Unix databases. Finally, once they get accustomed to Unix, many DOS devotees will switch to Unix applications.

The X Window System

Ever since the introduction of the Apple Macintosh, numerous computer specialists and nontechnical users have preferred a graphical user interface (GUI) to the uninformative character interface supplied by MS-DOS and the Unix shells. The most widely used GUI on DOS computers is MS-Windows, a product of the Microsoft Corporation. Unix has adopted a standard for GUIs, the X Window system, which was developed at the Laboratory for Computer Science at the Massachusetts Institute of Technology. Unlike MS-Windows, which is a commercial product, the heart of the X Window system is essentially free to all.

Sophisticated Networking Capabilities

Unix offers a wide range of networking functions and facilities. Unlike local-area networks, Unix networks are not limited to a small geographical region; they may span the globe. When properly implemented, Unix networks provide virtually seamless access to almost any existing computer system. Unix is a common way to access the Internet, the global networking system providing services such as electronic mail to over 20 million people.

Microcomputer Versions of Unix

Microcomputer Unix is not a recent phenomenon; in 1980 Microsoft released XENIX 2.3, which was originally restricted to a single user. Today's microcomputer users can choose from several variants of Unix, most of which are based on System V. For example, the Santa Cruz Operation distributes SCO Open Desktop UNIX based on the older Unix System V: Release 3.2. UnixWare is based on the current version of Unix System V: Release 4.2.

UnixWare

In April, 1991, control of Unix System V was transferred from AT&T to Unix System Laboratories (USL), whose major stockholder was AT&T. Other investors were Novell, Inc., whose main product—NetWare—has dominated local-area networking for microcomputers, and Sun Microsystems, Inc., the most important manufacturer of engineering workstations, whose operating system was based on BSD Unix. In December, 1991, Novell and USL announced a joint venture called Univel to develop a NetWare-enhanced version of Unix. In November, 1992, Univel released UnixWare 1.0, and shortly thereafter Novell announced its purchase of USL from AT&T. Novell continues to develop and market both Unix and UnixWare. Release 1.1 of UnixWare appeared in late 1993, and Release 2.0 appeared in January, 1995.

What UnixWare Can Do—An Overview

UnixWare provides an up-to-date, System V Release 4.2, version of Unix that runs on microcomputers. It offers an easy to use graphical interface that makes many operations a mouse-click away. In connectivity UnixWare surpasses all other Unix versions, in particular NetWare. In fact, it is easier to hook up UnixWare to a Novell server than to connect a NetWare DOS client to a Novell server. For those of us still in the DOS or Windows world, it can run these applications, often—but not always—without a hitch. UnixWare is no stranger to the information highway; it seamlessly accesses the Internet, popular electronic mail services such as MHS, and on-line information services such as CompuServe. Everybody is talking about "client-servers." UnixWare, with its excellent connectivity and wide range of applications, is designed to perform client-server applications with maximum efficiency. UnixWare also excels in backing up and managing networks, and accessing print, communication, and database servers.

The Two Configurations of UnixWare

UnixWare comes in two basic configurations, the Personal Edition (PE) and the Application Server (AS). The Personal Edition is basically a single-user networked platform for running applications. The Application Server is a multiuser system. Both the PE and AS may be enhanced by add-on products to help meet specific needs.

The Personal Edition

The UnixWare Personal Edition is fairly inexpensive, and can run thousands of Unix applications for SCO, System V, BSD, and other systems. Version 2.0 includes

TCP/IP (a major networking protocol), enabling a PE system to connect to other Unix systems, in addition to its superb facilities for connecting to NetWare. The Personal Edition runs with as little as 100MB of disk space and 8MB of memory, but 12MB is recommended.

The basic system package includes the Unix System V Release 4.2 Operating System. Other features include basic system administration capabilities and a core Unix command set. A full-screen text editor is included. The Graphical Desktop Manager includes support for both OSF/Motif and Open Look GUIs, icon and file class definitions for application integration, printer setup program GUI, and an on-line hypertext help system. The Merge package includes support for MS-DOS 3.x, 4.x, or 5.0, DR DOS 6.0, and all standard DOS-based NetWare utilities. The Desktop Manager recognizes and executes DOS *.BAT, *.EXE, and *.COM files so that DOS applications can be executed directly.

The Application Server

The moderately priced UnixWare Application Server (or AS) licenses an unlimited number of users and includes all features provided with the Personal Edition. Univel recommends 16MB of memory and 200MB of disk space to accommodate the AS.

The Application Server platform provides distributed access to traditional transaction-oriented commercial applications as well as emerging client-server and groupware applications. The Applications Server is a true multitasking operating system that can function as both a server and a client and can run thousands of Unix applications for SCO, System V, BSD, and other systems. It also provides integrated support for DOS and optionally MS-Windows applications as well as new services to NetWare clients, including multiple concurrent login sessions, network installation, and print services. The AS includes standard Internet utilities as well.

Add-on Products

Both the Personal Edition and the Application Server are considered basic models of UnixWare, and can be enhanced to meet specific needs. You can upgrade your UnixWare with any of these additions:

- A more powerful version of TCP/IP (available for both the PE and AS)

- The (NFS) Network File System (available for the PE)

- Server Merge for Windows allows several users to run MS-Windows and MS-Windows and DOS applications simultaneously (available for the AS)

■ The Software Development Kit for programming in the UnixWare environment (available for both the PE and AS)

■ System auditing, file system performance tools, and data encryption, for more enhanced system security (available for both the PE and AS)

You should now have an understanding of what UnixWare is and what its benefits are. In Chapter 2 you will start to confirm the advantages as you learn about the UnixWare Desktop.

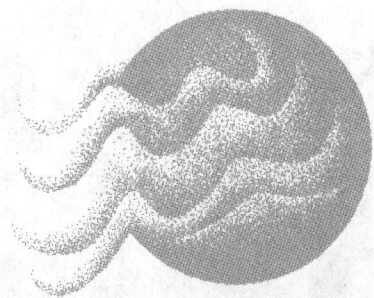

CHAPTER 2

Getting Around on the Desktop

The UnixWare Desktop (shown in Figure 2-1) is a proprietary, easy to use Graphical User Interface (GUI) that provides even inexperienced users with extensive access to Unix, DOS, and NetWare. Whether you are a complete neophyte or a seasoned Unix guru, you'll usually communicate your needs to UnixWare via the Desktop. In later chapters you'll see when you must use the command line and when you may want to use it instead of using the Desktop.

This chapter is devoted to the Desktop. After a brief discussion on manipulating windows, you'll learn how to log in to UnixWare and exit gracefully. In the heart of the chapter we examine Desktop features in detail. You will then learn how to customize the Desktop for maximum efficiency and ease of use.

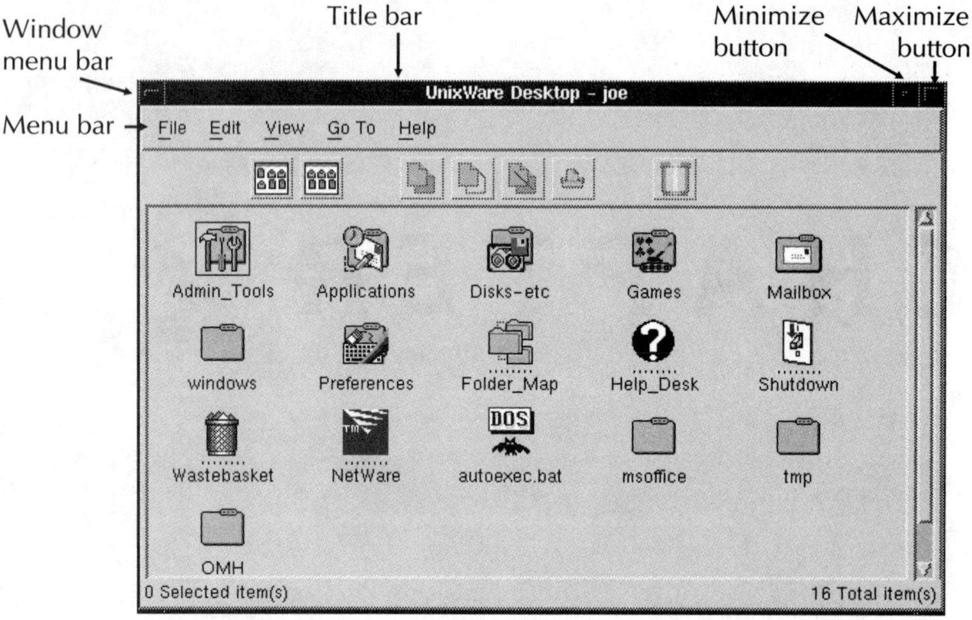

Window menu bar

Title bar

Minimize button

Maximize button

Menu bar

FIGURE 2-1. *The UnixWare Desktop*

Manipulating Windows

UnixWare is a window-based system. The Desktop shown in Figure 2-1 contains basic window features including the title bar showing the window name, a menu bar allowing you to make selections via the mouse or the keyboard, and several buttons. If you are familiar with any windowing system, you need only skim this section. If this is new to you, get ready to enter the 1990s. After reading this section and the next one, you'll be able to log in and practice these basic manipulations.

Opening and Closing Windows   Open a window by double-clicking on its icon. To close it, select File from the menu bar and click on Exit, press ALT-F4, or click on the Window Menu button in the upper-left corner of the window.

Activating Windows   Activate a window by moving the mouse pointer to it and then clicking anywhere within the window. When you do so, the window frame changes color and its icons become available for selection.

Moving and Resizing Windows   To move a window, place the mouse cursor anywhere in the title bar and drag it to the desired location. The window outline moves but the window itself remains in its original location until you release the mouse button. Resize a window by dragging its side or corner. Release the mouse button when finished.

Minimizing and Maximizing Windows   The two buttons at the right of the title bar are the Minimize button (with an arrow pointing down) and the Maximize button (with an arrow pointing up). Selecting the Minimize button reduces the window to an icon. Minimize a window to reduce screen clutter without closing the window. Selecting the Maximize button enlarges the window so that it occupies the entire screen, making it easier to see its contents. Maximize a window when you intend to work with it for a period of time.

Logging In

Prior to logging in to UnixWare you must have an active user account, known to your particular installation. (Chapter 5 describes the specific process for creating a user account.) UnixWare provides several types of user accounts, depending on user sophistication and administrative policy. The root user (usually the system administrator) has full control over the system; for example, he or she can examine all files and can remove other users. The root user accesses the system via the command line rather than the Desktop. The system owner has special privileges when working from the Desktop. For example, he or she can start applications and grant or revoke system privileges for other users. However, in command line mode the system owner is just another regular user. UnixWare provides for several special users such as the sysadm (short for system administrator). These special users log on directly to the command line rather than to the Desktop. As you'll see in Chapter 5, a busy system administrator can offload noncritical activities to one or more special users. However, the root user still has full system privileges.

The UnixWare login process is simple. The login window appears on the monitor shortly after you start the computer. Type your username in the Login ID box and press the ENTER key. Next type in your password. (For security reasons the password is not displayed on the screen.) Then click on the Login box. After the system confirms your username and password, it displays the characteristic UnixWare Desktop.

Press the Exit button to leave the system via the login prompt. One of the first things that DOS users learn when they move up to Unix is to never turn off the power, except in extreme circumstances such as fire. Although UnixWare is designed to recover when a user improperly exits, get in the habit of following proper logoff procedures, especially if you will be using other Unix systems.

The UnixWare Desktop

Get to know the UnixWare Desktop; you'll be using it often. The Desktop contains a menu bar and icons. Menu commands and icons often overlap; which one you use depends to a large extent on your own style. But in order to use UnixWare efficiently, you should know how to access both the menu bar and the icons.

Before learning more about the Desktop, you'll need to understand one UnixWare term, the *folder*. A folder is simply a collection of files. Folders in UnixWare are the same as directories in DOS or Unix.

The Menu Bar and Toolbar

The Desktop menu bar contains the following menu items, File, Edit, View, Go To, and Help. Select a menu item by clicking on it or by holding down the ALT key while pressing the underlined letter (either uppercase or lowercase). Table 2-1 summarizes the commands available through the menu bar. Many of these commands will be covered in more detail later in this chapter.

MENU NAME	COMMAND NAME	COMMAND DESCRIPTION
File	New	Creates a new folder or file located in the currently open folder.
	Open	Opens the selected icon, which may represent a folder, an application, or a data file. Opening a data file icon automatically launches the associated application.
	Open-New	Creates a new file or folder and opens it.
	Print	Prints the selected file on the default printer.
	Find	Searches for designated files by name, last modification date, type, or contents.
	Exit Desktop	Ends your Desktop session.
Edit	Undo	Rolls back the last Copy, Delete, Link, Move, or Rename command.
	Copy	Copies a selected file or folder.
	Move	Moves a selected file or folder.
	Link	Links a file or folder, making it available from a different location without physically copying it.

TABLE 2-1.   *Desktop Menu Commands*

MENU NAME	COMMAND NAME	COMMAND DESCRIPTION
	Rename	Changes the name of a file or folder.
	Convert	Changes the file format from Unix to DOS or vice versa.
	Delete	Deletes the selected icon, transferring it to the Wastebasket. Deleted icons may be restored within a given time period (the default period is seven days).
	Select All	Selects all icons in the current folder. After selecting icons you may move or copy files to them.
	Unselect All	Unselects selected icons in the current folder.
	Properties	Displays the File Properties window showing designated specifications for the selected icon.
View	Align	Aligns current folder icons in neat rows and columns.
	Sort	Sorts current folder icons by name, size, type, or date of last modification.
	Format	Changes the presentation of current folder icons. Choices include Icon (default), Short (displays icon and filename), and Long (displays icon, filename, size, date created, etc.).
	Customize	Specifies visibility of current folder icons and displays the View: Customize window.
Go To	Desktop Window	Returns to the Desktop.
	Parent Folder	Places the user in the parent folder of the current folder, which becomes the new current folder. Selecting this icon repeatedly accesses the home folder.
	Other Folder	Opens a designated folder and displays the Folder: Open window.
	Folder Map	Displays a graphical representation of the file system. Click on a displayed icon to open a new folder.
Help	Folder	Displays help for any menu option or window accessible from the selected folder.
	Table of Contents	Lists all available help topics for folders.
	Help Desk	Displays the Help Desk window, the starting point for accessing available UnixWare help.

TABLE 2-1.   *Desktop Menu Commands* (continued)

In many cases the fastest way to initiate an operation is by clicking a toolbar icon. Toolbar icons available from the Desktop include: Align Items, Sort Items by Type, Copy, Move, Link, Print, and Delete.

Desktop Icons

The initial UnixWare Desktop contains numerous icons. Clicking on an icon selects it, and double-clicking opens it. The following paragraphs briefly describe the most common Desktop window icons.

The Applications Folder Window   The Applications Folder window contains icons for standard applications that are provided as part of UnixWare. Table 2-2 describes each of these icons.

ICON NAME	DESCRIPTION
Clock	Displays an alarm clock in digital or analog format.
Calculator	Opens an onscreen calculator.
Icon_Editor	Allows you to design an icon to represent an application, file, or folder.
Mail	Provides a mail service for the local and remote systems.
DOS	Opens a DOS session to run DOS-based applications.
Win	Opens a MS Windows session to run Windows-based applications.
Win_Setup	Allows you to define Windows startup parameters.
Msg_Monitor	Allows you to view messages from the operating system that you cannot easily view while the Desktop is running.
Remote_Access	Allows you to log into a remote system.
Remote_Apps	Provides access to applications on remote computers.
Terminal	Opens a terminal window to access the (shell) command line.
Text_Editor	Opens an editor for creating and modifying ASCII text files such as those used in shell scripts.
Online_Docs	Lets you view the UnixWare documentation online.

TABLE 2-2.   *Icons in the Applications Folder Window*

The Disks-etc Folder   The Disks-etc folder shown here contains icons representing drives associated with removable media:

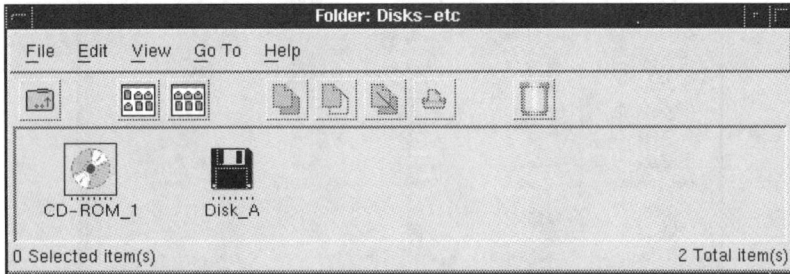

Depending on your physical system these may include floppy drives, tape drives, and CD-ROM drives.

The Folder Map Window   The Folder Map window shown here displays the names and dependencies of two levels of your folders:

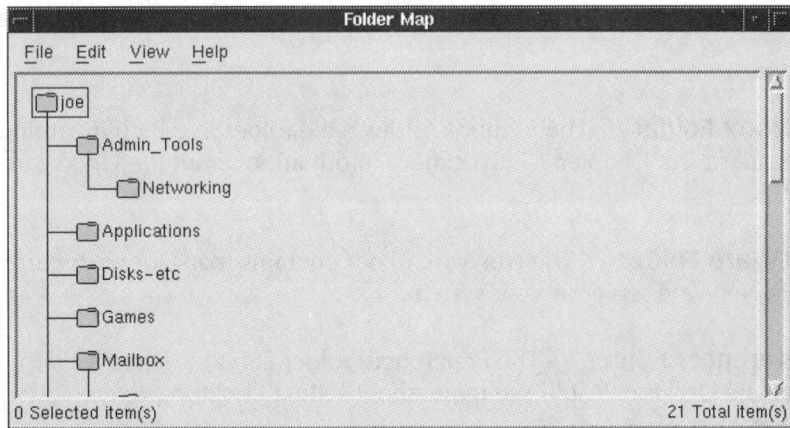

Use this window to navigate your file system.

The Games Folder   UnixWare comes with two games: Puzzle and Xtetris. If you load more games you will probably want to create icons for them in this folder.

The Help Desk Window   The Help Desk window, shown in Figure 2-2, contains icons that, when you click on them, supply information about invoking UnixWare or third-party applications.

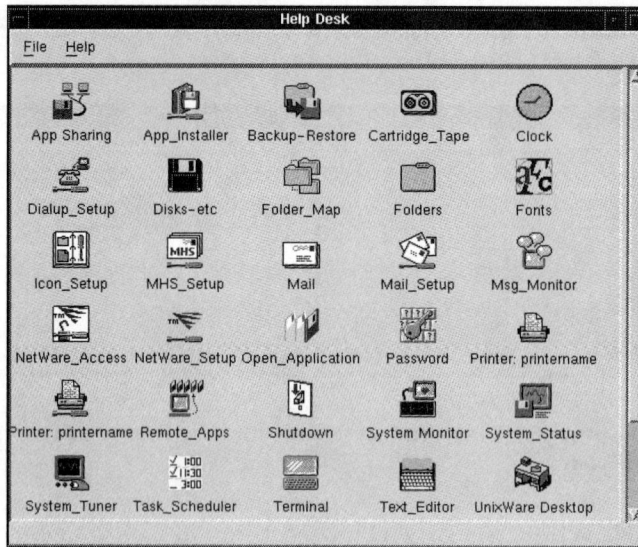

FIGURE 2-2.   *The Help Desk window*

The Mailbox Folder   The Mailbox folder is the folder in which incoming mail messages are saved. Chapter 15 gives more information about the UnixWare mail system.

The NetWare Folder   The NetWare folder contains icons for each currently accessible NetWare server in your system.

The Preferences Folder   The Preferences folder contains icons used to customize the Desktop. You'll see more about setting Desktop preferences later in this chapter.

The Admin_Tools Folder   The Admin_Tools folder contains icons used to configure the system. Table 2-3 summarizes these icons.

The Wastebasket Window   The Wastebasket window contains your deleted folders and files. This window is empty at system installation. You'll learn how to use the Wastebasket later in this chapter.

The Shutdown Icon   System shutdown is restricted to the root user who is the system administrator. This icon may be used to shut down the system in an orderly

ICON NAME	DESCRIPTION
Networking	Accesses networked systems.
Appl_Installer	Installs or removes applications.
App_Sharing	Provides the mechanism for sharing applications with remote systems.
Backup-Restore	Creates backups or restores from these backups.
Display_Setup	Configures the monitor.
Extra_Admin	Launches the sysadm account, which carries out designated system administration functions from the command line. This icon is only available with the Application Server.
Hardware_Setup	Configures system hardware including CD-ROM and the hard disk.
Icon_Setup	Specifies the actions associated with icons and assigns icons to files and applications.
MHS_Setup	Installs a Message Handling System mail gateway to access a remote NetWare system.
Mail_Setup	Configures the mail utility.
Printer_Setup	Installs printers.
System_Monitor	Configures the system owner console.
System_Status	Displays information such as the amount of memory and the presence of a math coprocessor.
System_Tuner	Enables authorized personnel to fine-tune the system.
Task_Scheduler	Enables authorized personnel to schedule programs.
User_Setup	Adds and manages user accounts.

TABLE 2-3. *Icons in the Admin_Tools Folder*

fashion. As a normal user you should use the Exit command from the File menu to exit the system.

Understanding the File System

Unlike in DOS, UnixWare file and folder (directory) names are case-sensitive; UnixWare distinguishes between the filenames **myfile** and **Myfile**, whereas DOS

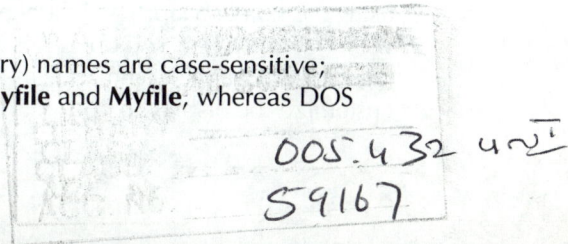

does not. The UnixWare file system is hierarchical, starting from the root folder (designated as "/"). An individual's personal files are kept in his or her *home folder*. Folder icons resemble a cut folder with a label tab. File icons typically look like a dog-eared piece of paper.

Just as with DOS, files and folders are created with a pathname that specifies their location in the file system. Pathnames are absolute or relative. The *absolute pathname* specifies the file's full pathname starting from the root. A *relative pathname* specifies the file's location relative to the current directory, not from the root.

A sample absolute pathname is **/home/myfiles/games/gameabc**, in which the file **gameabc** resides in the **/home/myfiles/games** directory.

One relative pathname for this file is **games/gameabc**, which resides in the current directory **/home/myfiles**.

The absolute pathname for the file **NWfile** in the folder **NWfolder** residing on the NetWare server **servername** in the volume **volnum** is **/.NetWare/servername/volnum/NWfolder/NWfile**.

Opening and Creating Files and Folders

When an icon appears somewhere in a window, you can't tell just by looking at the picture whether that icon represents a file, folder, or executable program. Of course over time, assuming no one makes massive changes, you will become familiar with certain icons and their associated actions.

Opening an Existing File or Folder

When you double-click on an icon, you *open*, or activate, that icon. For a folder, this means the current window will be replaced by the contents of the folder. For a file, it means different actions depending on the file type. Opening a text or datafile displays the file contents and starts the Text Editor. Opening a special datafile locates the datafile and starts the application that manipulates the data file. Opening a system resource (printer, remote system, or diskette) causes an action such as displaying the printer queue. Finally, opening an application icon displays the application window and starts the application.

In most cases opening an icon creates a new window. Opening a folder, however, normally affects the current window. If you want to create a new window when you open a folder, choose the Open New command from the File menu.

Using the Folder Map

If you don't see the icon you want to open in the current window, you might try using the Folder Map. The Folder Map gives you a tree-like view of the folders in your system. When you open this application you will see a window similar to Figure 2-3. Use the commands in the View menu, summarized in Table 2-4, to customize the display to your liking.

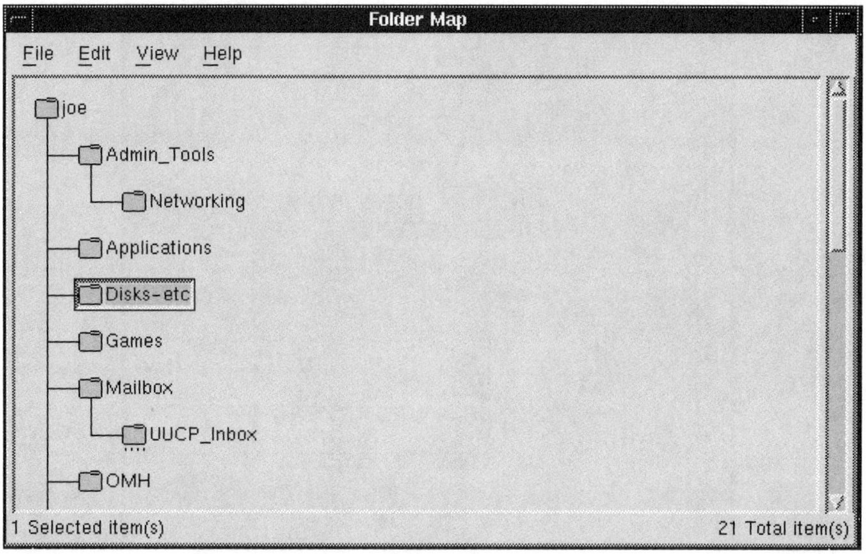

FIGURE 2-3. *A typical Folder Map window*

Finding a File or Folder

If the folder map doesn't help, and you know that a file exists somewhere in the system, use the Find command in the File window. UnixWare will generate the window shown in Figure 2-4. Use Table 2-5 to help set the options needed to find the file, then click Find.

COMMAND NAME	DESCRIPTION
Show Folders	Displays folders one level below the selected folder.
Hide Folders	Hides all folders below the level of the selected folder.
Show Entire Branch	Displays all levels of folders under the selected folder.
Start Map Here	Sets the selected folder as the display starting point.
Start at <login>	Sets your home folder as the display starting point.
Start at Other	Selects another path as the display starting point. In the ensuing Open window, click on folder names or the Parent Folder until you locate the folder, or enter the full pathname to the folder in the folder text box.

TABLE 2-4. *View Commands in the Folder Map Window*

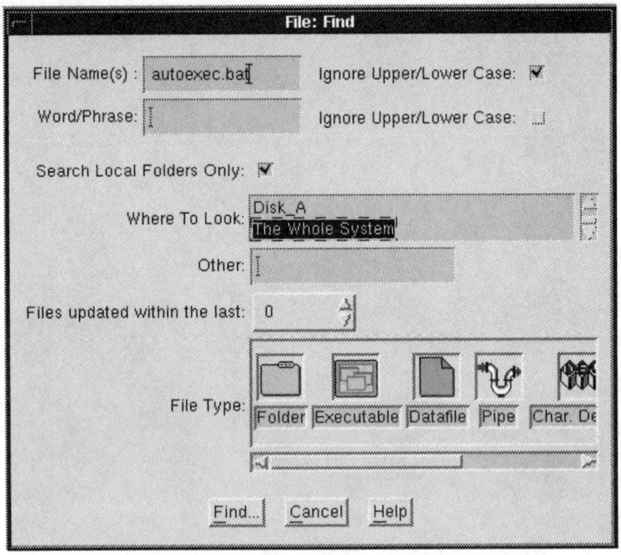

FIGURE 2-4. *The File: Find window*

FIELD	DESCRIPTION
File Name	Enter the filename. The metacharacters * and ? are defined as in DOS.
Ignore Upper/Lower Case	Specify whether to ignore the case of the filename. Remember that Unix filenames are case-sensitive, whereas DOS filenames are not.
Word/Phrase	Enter a word or phrase to find text files containing that item.
Where to Look	Click on the folders in the list to indicate where you want to search.
Other	Enter the name of a folder not included in the Where to Look field.
Files updated within the last ? days	Enter a number between 0 and 365 or use the arrows to select a number to restrict the search to files updated within this time period.
File Type	Click on the file type. The default is all file types.

TABLE 2-5. *The File: Find Window Options*

After a search is completed, the Found Files window appears as shown here:

```
┌─────────────────────────── Found Files ────────────────────────┐
│  File   Edit   Help                                             │
│ ┌────────────────────────────────────────────────────────────┐ │
│ │ 📄 /home/joe/autoexec.bat    rw-r--r-- joe      other    209 20:53:34 Tue │
│ │ 📄 /autoexec.bat             rw-rw-r-- bin      sys      149 18:01:07 Sun │
│ │                                                            │ │
│ └────────────────────────────────────────────────────────────┘ │
│ Search Completed.                                              │
└────────────────────────────────────────────────────────────────┘
```

This window displays the file or list of files meeting the search criteria. Use the Edit and File selections in the menu bar to process these files.

Creating a New File or Folder

To create a new text file or folder, choose New from the File menu to generate the New window shown here:

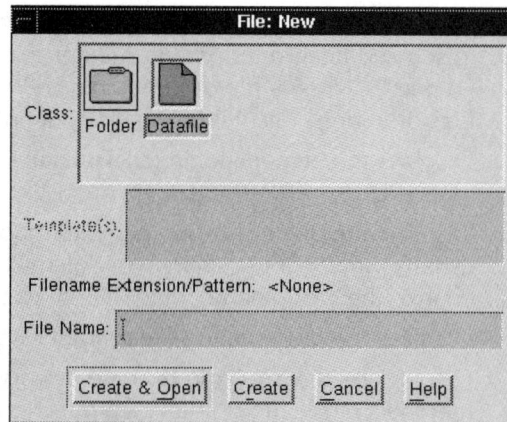

```
┌─────────────────── File: New ──────────────────┐
│                                                 │
│            ┌────┐  ┌────┐                        │
│   Class:   │    │  │    │                        │
│            └────┘  └────┘                        │
│            Folder  Datafile                      │
│                                                 │
│   Template(s):  ┌────────────────────────────┐   │
│                 │                            │   │
│                 └────────────────────────────┘   │
│   Filename Extension/Pattern:  <None>            │
│   File Name: ┌────────────────────────────────┐  │
│              └────────────────────────────────┘  │
│       ┌────────────┐ ┌──────┐ ┌──────┐ ┌────┐    │
│       │Create & Open│ │Create│ │Cancel│ │Help│    │
│       └────────────┘ └──────┘ └──────┘ └────┘    │
└─────────────────────────────────────────────────┘
```

Set the following options as needed:

■ **Class**   Click on Folder to create a folder. Click on Datafile to create a text file. Icons for other class types are displayed if they were created using Icon Setup. See the manual for more details.

■ **Templates**   Click on a template if available. A *template* is a file containing the model of commonly used formats like memos or reports.

■ **File Name**   Enter the filename or folder name. Some applications require specific filename extensions, as specified in the File Name Extension/Pattern field.

When you click on Create & Open at the bottom of the window, the file or folder opens and its icon appears on the Desktop.

File and Folder Properties

Every file and folder has certain properties associated with it. You can change many of these properties. When you create a new file or folder, you should check its properties immediately. For example, when you create a file or folder, you are its owner and automatically have permission to perform certain operations on it such as reading, writing, and executing it. If you want to limit those permissions (that is, allow other users to perform only the operations that you see fit on your files and folders), you set the properties. Table 2-6 lists the properties that you can set.

OPTION	DESCRIPTION
File Name	Displays the selected filename or folder name. To change it, simply enter a different name.
No. of Hard Links	Displays the number of hard links associated with the file (discussed later in this chapter under "Linking Files and Folders"). When a file or folder has no hard links to other files or folders, this field displays 1, denoting the file itself.
Owner	Displays the owner's login ID. To change the owner, enter a new ID.
Group	Displays the owner's group name. Group members may usually view, but not change or delete the file or folder. To change the group name, enter a new name.
Modification Time	Displays the last time the file or folder was modified.
Owner Access	Displays read, write, and execute permissions for the members of the file or folder's group. To change owner permissions, click on the new settings.
Group Access	Displays read, write, and execute permissions for the group. To change group permissions, click on the new settings.
Other Access	Displays read, write, and execute permissions for other users. To change permissions, click on the new settings.

TABLE 2-6.   *File Preferences Options*

NOTE
The Properties window for DOS files and folders lists fewer options than for Unix files and folders.

Moving, Copying, and Linking Files

When you move a file, you are changing the folder where the file is located. When you copy a file, you are duplicating it in another folder. When you create a link, you are making a reference to a file in another folder. The following sections describe each of these actions.

Moving Using the Drag-and-Drop Mouse Operation
Use the following procedure to move one or more files or folders:

1. Select the file you want to move. To move several files at once, hold down the CTRL key while clicking on each file or folder icon you wish to move.

2. Drag and drop any selected icon onto the destination window if open or onto the folder's icon if the destination window is closed.

Moving Using the Menu
Use the following procedure to move a file or a folder from one window to another using menu operations:

1. Select the file you want to move. To move several files at once, hold down the CTRL key while clicking on each file or folder icon you wish to move.

2. Choose the Move command from the Edit menu.

3. Either locate the target folder using the Folder list, or enter the full destination pathname in the As field.

4. Click on Move at the bottom of the window to move the selected file or folder and close the window.

Copying Using the Drag-and-Drop Mouse Operation
Use the following procedure to copy one or more files or folders:

1. Select the file you want to copy. To copy several files at once, hold down the CTRL key while clicking on each file or folder icon you wish to copy.

2. Hold down the CTRL key again, and drag and drop any selected icon onto the destination window if open or onto the folder's icon if the destination window is closed.

Copying Using the Menu

Use the following procedure to copy a file or a folder from one window to another using menu operations:

1. Select the file you want to copy. To copy several files at once, hold down the CTRL key while clicking on each file or folder icon you wish to copy.

2. Choose the Copy command from the Edit menu.

3. Either locate the target folder using the Folder list, or enter the full destination pathname in the As field.

4. Click on Copy at the bottom of the window to copy the selected file or folder and close the window.

Renaming a File or Folder

When you move a file to another location in the same folder, you are essentially renaming that file. Use the Rename command from the Edit menu in this instance instead of the Move command.

Linking Files and Folders

CAUTION
Linking files and folders is an advanced UnixWare feature. If you are not sure how it works, get help. For additional information refer to the Command Reference that comes with the software.

Linking a file or folder is similar to copying a file or folder. However, linking does not create a duplicate of the selected file or folder, but only gives another name for it, enabling you to access the same file or folder from more than one location. Using links instead of copies saves space.

To create a link, select the icon you want to link, and choose the Link command in the Edit menu. The Link window gives you the following options:

- **Link**   Displays the name of the selected file or folder.

- **To**   Indicates the path to which the file or folder will be linked.

- **As**   Lets you enter the name assigned to the link for the file or folder.

- **Link Type**   Allows you to choose Soft to create a *soft link* or Hard to create a *hard link*. Soft links are represented by icons with a dotted line underneath. A soft link can reside on different file systems (for example the UnixWare file system and the NetWare file system). Deleting the original file removes the soft link. Hard links can reside on the same file system. If you delete a hard link to a file but other hard links to that file exist, you can still access that data through the other hard links.

CAUTION
Hard links cannot point to a folder name.

Deleting and Recovering Files and Folders Using the Wastebasket

Use the Wastebasket to delete files and folders. The Wastebasket manages deleted files and folders, permitting recovery under certain conditions as described in this section.

Deleting a File or Folder
To delete a file or folder, drag and drop the file or folder icon onto the Wastebasket icon on the UnixWare Desktop window or onto the open Wastebasket window. Or, use the Delete command from the Edit menu.

NOTE
Each file and folder in the Wastebasket includes a version number, for example, **myfile:1** and **myfile:2**. If two files with the same name exist, deleting a file first deletes the one with the lowest version number; in other words **myfile:1** is deleted before **myfile:2**.

Recovering a File or Folder
If you delete a file accidentally, you can recover it by dragging and dropping the file from the Wastebasket back to a permanent folder. You also can recover files by selecting them and using the Put Back command from the Edit menu.

Emptying the Wastebasket
You have complete control over determining when, or how often, the files in the Wastebasket are removed (known as *emptying* the Wastebasket). You can have the Wastebasket emptied every time you exit the system, or when a file has been in the Wastebasket for a certain time period, or only when you empty it yourself explicitly.

To set the option you need, open the Wastebasket, displaying the window shown here:

Now choose Options from the Actions menu, and select one of the following:

- **Clean Up Method**   Click on By Timer, On Exit, Immediately, or Never to specify whether files and folders are removed from the Wastebasket after a specified time period, whenever you quit or close UnixWare, as soon as an item is put into the Wastebasket, or never.

- **Remove Items After**   This option is only used with the By Timer option specified above. Select a number between 0 and 31 to correspond to your selection of Minutes, Hours, or Days and enter the number of minutes, hours, or days to pass before the Wastebasket automatically deletes its contents.

Using Files and Folders with Diskettes

Floppy disks play an important role in the UnixWare environment—they let you back up data, copy data to other machines, and install new programs. UnixWare supports several types of floppy disk formats, including the traditional DOS format.

The Disk-etc folder provides access to diskettes, as well as cartridge tapes and CD-ROMs. When you open a floppy disk icon in this folder you will see the contents of that diskette. From there you can use drag-and-drop operations or menu commands to copy files to and from the diskette. When you open a diskette in any supported format, UnixWare automatically opens the appropriate type of window. For example, when you open a diskette containing backup files, UnixWare starts the Restore application.

Special DOS Considerations

Although UnixWare handles DOS files and DOS formatted diskettes just as it handles UnixWare files and formatted diskettes, you should be aware of several differences:

■ When you open a DOS diskette, DOS filenaming conventions take precedence. Whereas UnixWare allows spaces, special characters, and unlimited characters in filenames and does not restrict the location of the period, DOS allows only eight characters to the left of the period and three to the right. Filenames are truncated to fit this rule when UnixWare files are transferred to a DOS diskette.

■ You cannot create either a hard link or a soft link to a DOS file.

■ The Properties window displays different options for DOS files.

Formatting Diskettes

To format a new diskette, right-click on the appropriate floppy drive icon and choose Format. You will see the following Format window:

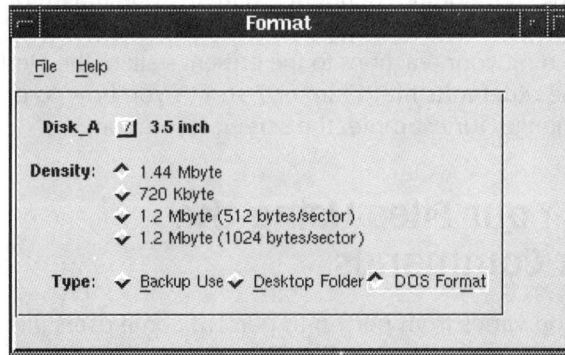

Choose your desired format. The Type field gives you these three options:

■ **Backup Use**   Formats the media for archiving files. Chapter 10 gives more information on backing up and restoring.

■ **Desktop Folder**   Creates on the media a file system that can be used as any other Desktop folder. For example, you can drag and drop files and folders from the diskette window into any UnixWare folder.

■ **DOS Format**   Formats the media for use with DOS files. The assigned filenames must obey DOS filenaming conventions.

Once the formatting starts, you can choose Format from the File menu to display the Format in Progress window, which has a sliding bar indicating the progress of the format operation. You'll receive an appropriate message when formatting is completed.

Customizing the Desktop

Although the UnixWare Desktop has been designed with user convenience in mind, not all users have the same preferences; in other words, one size does not fit all. These are just a few of the features that you can customize: the actions associated with mouse buttons; background and window colors; the alignment of icons on the screen; keystroke definitions; the application launched at system startup; and internationalizing the system by modifying language, date, and number formats.

TIP
Once you start to play with desktop customization you will see that settings are not independent: changing one may require changes in others. Therefore, it's important to keep a logbook of your changes, including your reactions to the present state of the Desktop, contained in the **.Xdefaults** file. Chapter 7 shows you how to modify this file to change, for example, the screen resolution.

Organizing Your Files Using the View Menu Commands

The optimal Desktop varies from person to person. Some users like to see very few icons at a time, whereas other people like to see the entire screen filled with icons. The commands in the View menu let you customize your desktop to suit your needs.

The Sort command changes the order of files and folders. You can choose from the following menu options:

- **By Type**   Lists files and folders by file type (folder, data file, executable, etc.).

- **By Name**   Lists files and folders in alphabetical order (ASCII alphabetical order, capital letters before lowercase letters).

- **By Size**   Lists files and folders from smallest to largest.

■ **By Age**   Lists the files and folders by time and date of latest change, starting with the newest.

The Format command changes the file and folder representation. Format has the following menu options:

■ **Icons**   Displays files and folders as unique icons, whose name appears below the icon. This is the default view.

■ **Short**   Displays files and folders as identical miniature icons; each icon's name appears to the right of the icon.

■ **Long**   Displays the names, permissions, owner, group, size, last modification date, and links (if any) for each file and folder.

Customizing Your Display Using the Filter Command

You can suppress the display of certain files and folders by ordering the display of specific icon types or defining the display pattern. The Filter command, from the View menu, lets you define precisely which files and folders are displayed within a folder.

> **NOTE**
> By default all icons are displayed.

If you want to specify exact names, use the Name field. Enter the names of files that you wish to display, separated by a space. Use metacharacters to indicate the files and folders you want to display. The * and ? metacharacters are familiar to DOS users: * indicates 0 or more characters and ? indicates one character.

The File Type field lets you filter by type rather than name. The following selections are available:

■ **Folder**   Folders only.

■ **Executable**   Programs.

■ **Datafiles**   Files associated with a given application.

■ **Pipe, Char, Device, Block Device, Semaphore, and Shared Memory** Special file types used internally by UnixWare and other applications.

Setting Desktop Window Preferences

Individual users set their preferences such as redefining mouse actions by accessing the Preferences folder, shown in Figure 2-5, and then selecting the appropriate icon and completing the information. Each group of preferences is set independently. The process for redefining settings and then confirming them or canceling them is similar for various window preferences, but details vary.

Mouse Preferences

Because of its importance in running UnixWare, set the mouse to your taste before indicating your other preferences. The left button functions—clicking, double-clicking, dragging, and dragging and dropping—are rarely redefined. However, the right button of a two-button mouse is often redefined. As UnixWare comes out of the box (with its factory settings), the right button of a two-button mouse invokes the Paste function (as in the word processing Cut and Paste operation), which isn't used in most other UnixWare applications. You'll probably find that you'll use the right mouse button more often if you set it to the Menu function, which displays the menu associated with the selected icon. To do so, select the Mouse Preferences window and then click on Three in the Number of Mouse Buttons option at the top of the screen. You'll no longer have the Paste

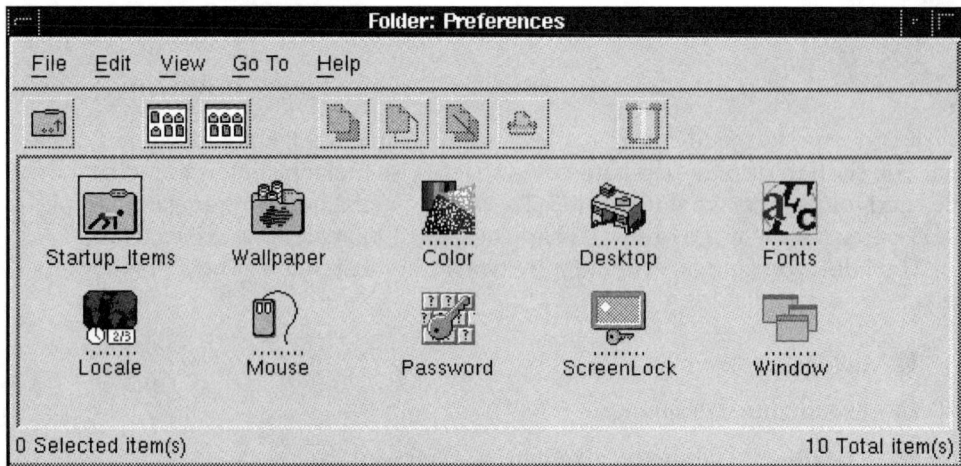

FIGURE 2-5. *The Preferences folder*

function but setting the very useful Menu function to the right mouse button in effect renders a two-button mouse and three-button mouse compatible.

Users who prefer it may simulate a left-handed mouse by accessing the Mouse Preferences window and then clicking on R for each option set to L and vice versa. This effectively interchanges the left and right buttons. Righties simply reverse these changes to return to what they perceive as the normal situation.

NOTE
To avoid confusion, make the Paste-Menu change before making the Left-Right change.

The mouse Preferences window is shown here:

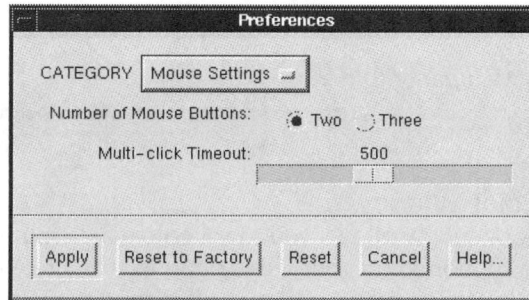

Once you have completed your redefinitions, confirm them by clicking the Apply button at the bottom of the Preferences screen. Click on the Reset button to return to the previous Desktop settings. Click on the Reset to Factory button to return to the settings in place at installation time.

The Wallpaper Folder
The Wallpaper folder shown in Figure 2-6 contains the Wallpaper installer icon and several wallpaper icons representing GIF (graphics image format) files. A vast variety of GIF files are available commercially and on bulletin boards. Once the desired GIF file is installed on your system, invoke it by dragging and dropping it onto the Wallpaper installer icon.

The Startup Items Icon
The Startup Items icon allows you to designate the applications activated at Desktop initialization. This makes it just a bit easier for users to start their favorite applications such as WordPerfect.

FIGURE 2-6. *The Wallpaper folder*

The Preferences-Color Window

The Preferences-Color window allows you to set colors that you like, depending on the number of colors supported by your video adapter. The Preferences-Color window shown here is used to create custom colors for different Desktop areas:

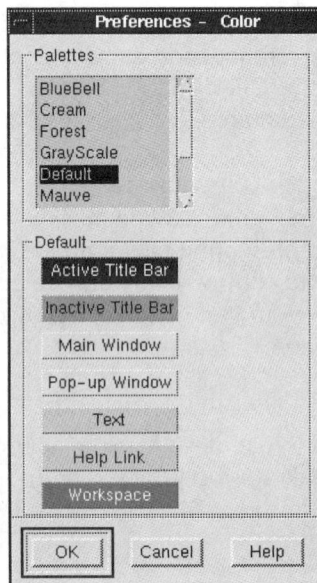

The Desktop Preferences Window

The Desktop Preferences window allows you to customize the appearance of the Desktop. Options include Start Desktop at login, Show Path in Window Titles, File Window Grid Spacing, and Default Folder Window Size specifications, Application's Working Directory, Open Folders in, and Keep Remote Folders Current. Table 2-7 describes each of these briefly.

The Fonts Window

The Fonts window, shown in Figure 2-7, allows you to install or delete fonts. Fonts are identified by family (such as Courier), by style (such as bold), and by point size (such as 12).

The Password Window

The Password window allows you to change your password. UnixWare requires that the new password differ from the old password by at least three characters.

FIELD	DESCRIPTION
Category	Specifies that you will select Desktop preferences.
Start Desktop at login	Specifies whether the Desktop (default) or the command line appears at system startup.
Show Path in Window Titles	Specifies whether or not the full pathname of a window is displayed in the window title bar. The default is no, in which case only the window name is displayed.
Folder Window Grid Spacing	Specifies the number of pixels placed between icons.
Default Folder Window Size	Specifies the number of rows and columns of icons displayed in a given window. The default value is two rows and three columns.
Application's Working Directory	Specifies whether the working directory is in the Home folder or the application's folder (the default).
Open Folders in	Specifies whether to open folders in the same window or a new window. The default value is same window.
Keep Remote Folders Current	Specifies whether to update remote folders automatically. The default is no.

TABLE 2-7. *Desktop Preferences Fields*

FIGURE 2-7. *The Fonts window*

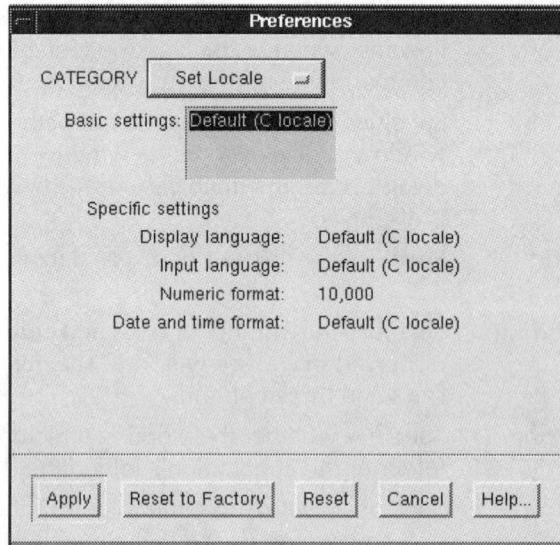

FIGURE 2-8. *The Locale Preferences window*

The Locale Preferences Window

The Locale Preferences window, shown in Figure 2-8, allows you to internationalize the desktop by setting language, date/time, and number formats. For example, you may create separate settings for Belgium (French), Canada (French), France, and Switzerland (French), as well as Canada (English), to name just a few possibilities.

The Window Preferences Window

The Window Preferences window, shown in Figure 2-9, allows you to set preferences for the options described in Table 2-8.

The ScreenLock Window

The ScreenLock window, shown here, allows you to lock the screen after a predetermined time period between 2 and 60 minutes:

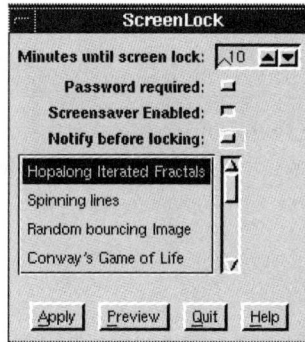

```
┌─────────────────────────────────┐
│ ░░│      ScreenLock              │
│ Minutes until screen lock: │10 ▲▼│
│       Password required:  ⌐      │
│      Screensaver Enabled:  ▆     │
│      Notify before locking:  ⌐   │
│ ┌─────────────────────────────┐  │
│ │ Hopalong Iterated Fractals │▲│ │
│ │ Spinning lines             │▒│ │
│ │ Random bouncing Image      │▒│ │
│ │ Conway's Game of Life      │▼│ │
│ └─────────────────────────────┘  │
│                                  │
│ │Apply│ │Preview│ │Quit│ │Help│  │
└─────────────────────────────────┘
```

This facility is useful for protecting against screen burnout and reducing the threat to system security.

Options in the ScreenLock window include:

- ■ **Password Required**   Used for security.

- ■ **Screensaver Enabled**   Lets you choose whether or not to blank the screen, or which screensaver to invoke.

- ■ **Notify Before Locking**   Invokes chimes 30 seconds before locking the screen.

Press the SHIFT key to reset the timer and keep the screen from locking.

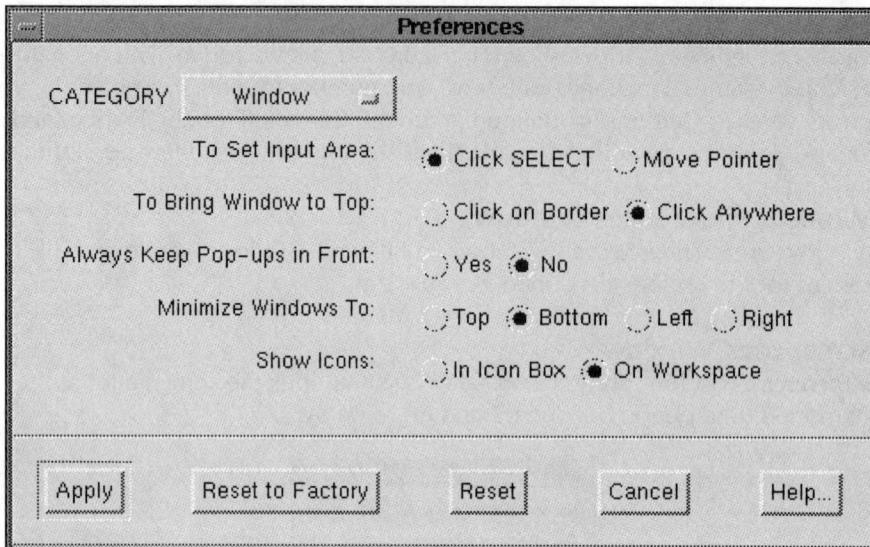

FIGURE 2-9. *The Window Preferences window*

OPTION	DESCRIPTION
To Set Input Area	Specifies how to set the input focus. Choices are Click SELECT (default) and Move Pointer.
To Bring Window to Top	Specifies how to bring a window to the top of the window hierarchy. Choices are Click on Border (the default) and Click Anywhere.
Always Keep Pop-ups in Front	Specifies whether or not to keep pop-up windows in front of the main window. The default is No.
Minimize Window To	Specifies where minimized windows will be placed on the screen. Choices are Top, Bottom (the default), Left, and Right.
Show Icons	Specifies whether to place icons in a special window known as an icon box or on the desktop background, the default selection.

TABLE 2-8. *Options in the Window Preferences Window*

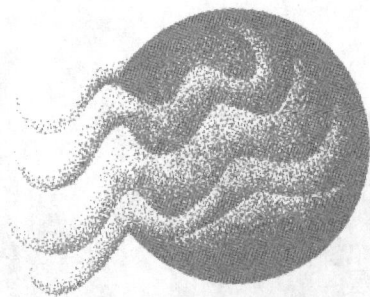

CHAPTER 3

Using UnixWare Applications and NetWare

Now that you know your way around the Desktop, it's time to start applying UnixWare. The first step is using UnixWare applications such as the Text Editor and the Clock. Next you'll see the more sophisticated applications contained in the Utilities folder including the Internet Browser and the Remote Access application, which, respectively, provide access to the Internet and applications running on remote computers. Finally, this chapter shows you how to access NetWare servers and authenticate them.

Using UnixWare Applications

Some of the most commonly used UnixWare applications are the Text Editor for creating and modifying (ASCII) text, the Terminal window for entering commands, and the Clock accessory. The following sections discuss each of these applications.

The Text Editor

You'll use the Text Editor to process ASCII text files, for example to create and modify startup files that customize a given host environment as discussed in Chapters 5, 7, and 13.

The Text Editor is a full-screen editor, meaning you can use arrow keys and navigational keys such as PGUP and PGDN. The HOME key will take you to the start of the current paragraph and the END key will take you to the paragraph's end.

Start the Text Editor by double-clicking on the Text Editor icon in the Applications folder. This generates a Text Editor window, ready to receive text or commands from the keyboard or mouse. If you are creating a new file, you can start typing immediately. If you want to modify an existing file, use the Open command from the File menu, and select the name of the file you wish to load into the editor. You will see the window shown in Figure 3-1.

Selecting and Manipulating Text

Like most modern word processors, the Text Editor lets you manipulate blocks of text. Selecting the amount of text you wish to work with is very easy; use any of the procedures described in the following table:

TO SELECT	PERFORM THIS ACTION
All text	Choose the Select All command from the Edit menu.
A paragraph	Triple-click on the paragraph.
A word	Double-click on the word.
Several words	Drag on the words.
Unselecting text	Click anywhere within the document.

Once you have selected text, you can copy it to the clipboard. The *clipboard* is a temporary section of memory reserved for holding text. The clipboard makes it easy to copy or move data from one place in a file to another, or from one file to another file. If you are moving text, use the Cut command from the Edit menu to copy the text into the clipboard and clear it from the editor. If you want to keep the text, but make a copy of it, use the Copy command. Then move the cursor to the

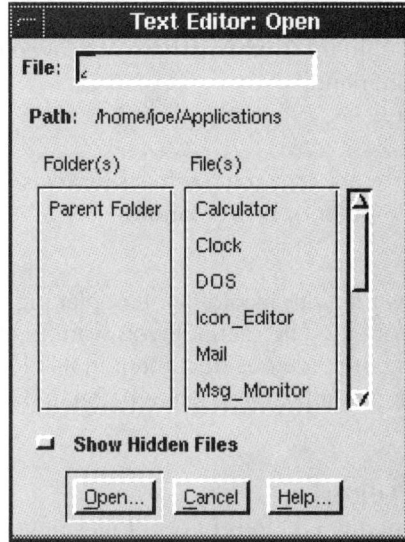

FIGURE 3-1. *The Text Editor: Open window*

new location for the text, and choose the Paste command to copy the clipboard contents at the cursor location.

Searching for Text

The Text Editor includes a search feature that is much faster and more accurate than hunting through your document for a specific word or phrase. To use this feature, choose the Find command in the View menu. The window you see here will be displayed:

Fill in the Text field with the text to be located. This field is case-sensitive, which just means the system considers RON, Ron, and ron to be different entities. Metacharacters such as * are allowed. As you click Next or Previous repeatedly the system will show you each occurrence of the text in the current file.

Saving Files

The changes you make within the Text Editor are not saved to disk until you explicitly use the Save command.

> **TIP**
> Saving your work on a regular basis protects you from losing work due to a computer or power failure.

If you want to save the file with its old name, replacing the previous version, use the Save command from the File menu. If you want to change the filename as you save it, thereby saving the previous document in its old format, use the Save As command. Enter either a relative or absolute pathname in the File field, and choose Save.

Customizing the Text Editor

The Text Editor lets you modify all kinds of ASCII files. If you are using it to write a letter, however, you might want it to work differently than when you are writing a computer program. The Preferences command in the View menu lets you modify two characteristics of the editor: word wrapping and line numbering.

The Wrap at: field in the Preferences window determines whether words are wrapped or split when text reaches the right margin. You can set wrapping to one of these three options:

- ■ **Words**   Select this to wrap words (let the whole word flow to the next line) when text reaches the right margin.

- ■ **Characters**   Select this to wrap characters to the next line when text reaches the right margin.

- ■ **No Wrapping**   Select this to force you to break up lines explicitly by using the ENTER key.

The Number on: field specifies whether there are line numbers in the left margin.

If you want to change properties for all future Text Editor sessions (until you change them again), choose the Set button at the bottom of the window; otherwise, choose Apply.

The Terminal Window

The Terminal window provides access to the UnixWare command line. Primarily privileged users, such as system administrators, use this feature. Most of the time

you can use Desktop applications for any changes you need to make, but occasionally
you might find yourself needing to use the Terminal window.

Start the Terminal window by double-clicking on the Terminal icon. The $ or #
prompt indicates a root user. At this point you may enter any of dozens of available
Unix commands, many of which are described in later chapters of this book. When
you finish, use the right mouse button to display the pop-up menu, and choose
Hangup. Table 3-1 provides a summary of all the commands available from the
pop-up menu.

Copying and Pasting Text in the Terminal Window

To copy or paste text in the Terminal window, first select the text, then right-click
on the Terminal window, and select Edit. Then choose from these menu selections:

- **Stay Up**   Maintains the Edit menu on the Desktop. The Edit menu
  becomes a window from which you can send, paste, or copy text, or close
  the window.

- **Send**   Places the selected text at the cursor location, as in the Copy and
  Paste operation.

- **Paste**   Places clipboard text at the cursor location.

- **Copy**   Copies selected text to the clipboard.

COMMAND	DESCRIPTION
Edit	Sends, pastes, and copies text.
Redraw	Redraws the Terminal window.
Soft Reset	Resets the scrolling region and the Terminal window.
Full Reset	Clears the screen and resets the Terminal window, including its properties.
Terminate	Stops the application running in the Terminal window.
Properties	Changes certain characteristics of the Terminal window.
Kill	Sends a kill signal to stop the task or application running in the Terminal window and exits the Terminal window.
Hangup	Sends a signal to stop the task or application running in the Terminal window and exits the Terminal window. Hangup is a lower priority signal than Kill.
Interrupt	Interrupts the application running in the Terminal window.

TABLE 3-1.   *Terminal Window Commands from the Pop-Up Menu*

The Clock Accessory

UnixWare provides an onscreen clock that can do more than merely track the time. Display the clock by double-clicking on the Clock icon. If the time is incorrect, you must have system administrator privileges to reset it. Chapter 11 gives more information.

Setting the Alarm

The following procedure sets the alarm and displays an optional message. To avoid surprises, remember that it's a 24-hour clock, so 13:00 stands for 1 P.M.

1. Right-click on the Clock and select the Set Alarm command.

2. Set the Message: field to the text you want displayed when the alarm rings. Set the Time: field by typing or using the arrow keys.

3. Click on Set Alarm to activate the alarm, which will display the message at the specified time.

Customizing the Clock

The Properties command from the Clock pop-up menu lets you customize how the clock is displayed and how it acts. Select from these options:

- **Chime** Specifies if and when the clock chimes. Choose Traditional to chime the time every hour (for example, three chimes at 3 P.M.) and once on the half hour. Select Ship's Bells to chime once each half-hour.

- **Mode** Specifies the clock appearance, either analog or digital.

- **Tick** Specifies how often the time is updated, either every second or every minute.

The UnixWare Utilities Folder

The UnixWare Utilities folder includes the System Status utility, the Internet Browser, the Remote Access utility, and the Remote Applications window. These items are described next.

The System Status Utility

The System Status utility tells you about your UnixWare session and your computer's hardware. Specifically, it displays the following information:

- The current Unix version.

- Your computer's network node name, used by linked computers.

- Your UnixWare login name.

- The current date and time.

- The time zone.

- The size of installed memory.

- The math coprocessor chip installed, if any.

- The size of installed drives, both floppy diskettes and cartridges.

- The size in megabytes of the UnixWare and NetWare file systems.

- A slider bar showing the size of disk space actually in use for both
  file systems.

Chapter 11 shows how to change some of these values.

The Internet Browser

The Internet Browser allows you to find and display documents located anywhere
on the Internet by clicking on *hyperlinks*, highlighted words and phrases, icons, or
images. If the Browser is already installed on your system, you can double-click the
icon to start the application.

If the Browser is not installed, you must use the Install Browser application in
the Networking folder under Admin Tools. This icon is only active if you have a
connection to the Internet and have configured your system for access to a Domain
Name Service (DNS) server.

NOTE
You cannot install the Internet Browser unless your user account has
the appropriate permissions assigned to you.

Installing the Internet Browser
Use the following procedure to retrieve the Internet Browser from the Novell FTP
Server and install it on your system:

1. Double-click the Networking icon in the Admin Tools folder.

2. Double-click on Install_Browser to generate the Install Internet
   Browser window.

3. Click on Install. After the installation is complete, UnixWare displays a window requesting you to designate users whose Applications folder will contain the Internet Browser icon.

If you aren't sure how to use the Internet Browser, you can get additional information in either of two ways. The Info command in the Install window displays information on the screen. You also can use the Get Documentation command to retrieve (and eventually print) a PostScript file describing how to use the Internet Browser.

The Remote Access Utility

Use Remote Access to log into a remote system, or copy files to a remote system.

NOTE
You can also use Dialup Setup and Internet Setup to copy a remote system icon to a folder.

Before using Remote Access, your system must be configured for TCP/IP networking via a modem or direct connection, and you must have an account on the remote system.

Logging In to a Remote System
Use the following procedure to log in to a remote system:

1. Double-click on Remote Access in the Applications folder, or on any other remote system icon previously copied from Internet Setup or Dialup Setup.

2. Enter the name of the remote system and your login ID.

NOTE
If your system is configured for TCP/IP networking, click on the Remote System Lookup window to display a list of systems defined in your **/etc/hosts** file, or a list of systems in your domain (if you have DNS configured on your system).

3. Click on Connect at the bottom of the window to log in to the remote system. To store the current options (and have them reappear whenever you need them by double-clicking on the Remote Access icon) click on Save before exiting.

4. Exit the window.

Copying Files to a Remote System

Use the following procedure to copy files to a remote system:

1. Open the folder containing the file you wish to copy to a remote system.

2. Drag and drop the file to a Remote System icon. The Remote System - File Transfer window appears, as shown in Figure 3-2.

3. Enter the system name and a login ID (in the User Receiving Files field), if the defaults are invalid.

4. Click on Send to copy the file to the remote system. If you'll use these settings in the future (by simply double-clicking on the Remote Access icon when you wish to apply them), click on Save.

By default, files are transferred using the UUCP protocol. If you want to use Local System Access instead, click the Show Other Options button. Then select Remote Copy in the Transfer Files Using field, and enter the pathname in the Copy Files To field.

NOTE
Remote copy requires permission from the remote user.

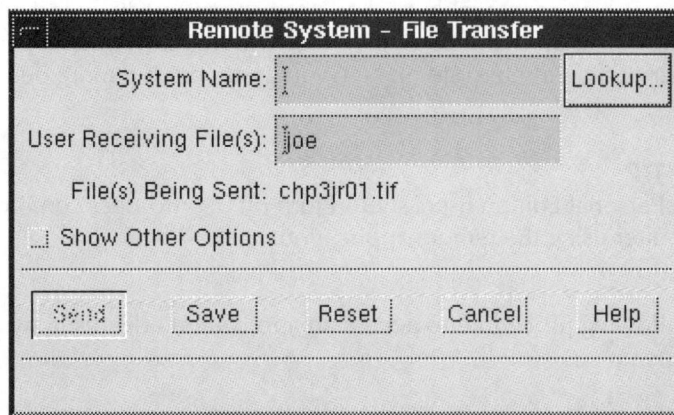

```
┌─────────────────────────────────────────────────┐
│            Remote System – File Transfer          │
│  ┌───────────────────────────────────────────┐   │
│        System Name: │           │  │ Lookup... │   │
│                                                    │
│  User Receiving File(s): │joe              │      │
│                                                    │
│     File(s) Being Sent: chp3jr01.tif               │
│  ▢ Show Other Options                              │
│  ─────────────────────────────────────────────    │
│  │ Send │   Save    Reset   Cancel    Help         │
└─────────────────────────────────────────────────┘
```

FIGURE 3-2.   *Remote System - File Transfer window*

Changing Remote Access Connection Properties

As you get more comfortable with UnixWare, and you use Remote Access more frequently, you can customize the properties associated with your access. Choose Properties from the View menu to view a list of options similar to those displayed when you copy files. Set the defaults to the ones you use most often.

One field, called Always Confirm, lets you bypass certain windows when you no longer need them. Turn off Connections to suppress the display of the Remote System - Access window whenever you double-click on the Remote Access icon. And you can turn off File Transfers to suppress the display of the Remote System - File Transfer window whenever you drag and drop a file onto a Remote System icon.

The Remote Applications Window

The Remote Applications window allows you to access applications that are advertised on a UnixWare Application Server. The applications actually run on the remote system, but are displayed on your system.

NOTE
The Remote Applications and Application Sharing tools require the presence of NetWare servers.

Use NetWare_Access to enable peer-to-peer communication and add yourself as a new user on the remote screen (provided that you have permission from the owner of the remote system). NetWare is covered in more detail later in this chapter.

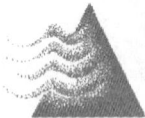

TIP
Personal Edition users should turn off peer-to-peer communication after using the remote application.

Use the following procedure to access an application advertised by another UnixWare system.

1. Double-click on the Remote_Apps application in the Applications folder.

2. Select the UnixWare server containing the application you wish to access from the displayed list. A window may request your user ID (login name) and password for that server, unless your login and password are the same for multiple UnixWare servers.

3. After a successful login, the Remote Applications box displays a list of applications advertised by the selected remote system. Select one. Although the selected application will display on your system it actually runs on the remote system.

4. Choose either Open to start the application, or Make Icon to create an icon for the selected application. If you used the NetWare Access utility icon for the remote system, make an icon for it as well. Clicking on Make Icon generates an icon in your Application folder. This icon uses the UnixWare servername and the application name with a **.rem** extension (for remote).

Double-clicking on a remote application icon (one with a **.rem** extension), may generate a window in which you enter the login name and password as entered in the Remote Access window previously described. After entering this information, click on Open to start the application.

Accessing NetWare

Perhaps the biggest advantage of UnixWare compared to other Unix systems is the ease with which you can access NetWare. Given the fact that the same company developed NetWare and UnixWare, this should hardly come as a surprise. This section shows how to access and authenticate NetWare servers. In NetWare terminology, *authenticate* means to convince the server that you are an authorized NetWare user. Chapter 14 returns to the subject of UnixWare-NetWare connectivity, examining the role of the system owner. In contrast, the procedures in this chapter are available to regular users.

Use the NetWare Access icon, located in the Networking folder under Admin Tools, to perform the following activities:

- Log in and log out of NetWare servers attached to your system.
- Change your NetWare password.
- Access files remotely.
- View information about a server.

Logging In to a NetWare Server

You need a valid ID to log in to a NetWare server. When you try to access an unavailable NetWare server, a clock is displayed onscreen for 45 seconds. Then you see the message "Cannot attach to server."

CAUTION
A UnixWare user can log in to a given NetWare server only once per session. To access permissions associated with another login, log out and log in again with a new ID.

Logging In with Your Login ID

To log in to, or authenticate, a NetWare server, do the following from the NetWare Servers for *<login ID>* window:

1. Click on the desired server.

2. Click on the Login at the bottom of the window to generate the Authentication Panel.

3. Enter your login name for this NetWare server and the appropriate password.

4. Click on Apply to log in and close the window.

If the login is successful, your login ID appears in the Authenticated column in the NetWare Servers for *<login ID>* window.

Logging In with Another Login ID

To log in to a NetWare server with a valid UnixWare login ID other than your own, start from the NetWare Servers for *<login ID>* window and do the following:

1. Click on Actions in the menu bar and select New User. The Choose User window appears, as shown here:

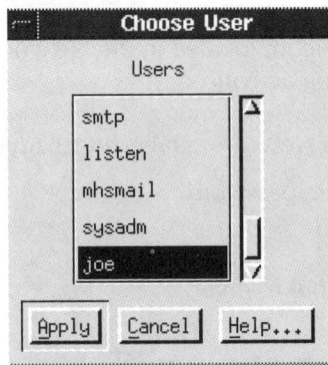

2. Click on a login ID from the displayed list of valid UnixWare users. (Chapter 14 describes how to add another user to the system.)

3. Click on Apply to select the login ID.

4. At the prompt, type in the associated UnixWare login password.

5. Click on Apply to close the Password window.

6. Click on Cancel to close the Choose User window.

At this point you can log in as if you were using your own ID.

Changing Your NetWare Password
To change the NetWare password of an authenticated user, start from the Network folder in Admin Tools and follow these steps:

1. Double-click on the NetWare Access icon. The NetWare Servers for *<login ID>* window appears.

2. Click on the server associated with the password you want to change.

3. Click on the password at the bottom of the window. You'll see the Change Password window.

4. Enter your old password at the prompt (if you had one) and click on Apply.

5. When prompted again, enter your new password.

6. Click on Apply.

7. At the final prompt, enter your new password a second time. Then click on Apply to confirm that your password is correct and close the window.

Logging Out of a NetWare Server
When finished accessing a server, it is a good idea to log out of the NetWare sessions. From the NetWare Servers for *<login ID>* window, click on any servers you want to log out of. Then choose Logout at the bottom of the window to confirm the logouts. Your login ID is no longer in the Authenticated column of the NetWare Servers for *<login ID>* window.

Accessing Files and Folders via the NetWare Icon

You will probably access or print NetWare files and folders regularly. However, before you can access or print them, you may need to change permissions. Chapter 8 gives details on permissions.

Accessing Files and Folders on a NetWare Server

From the Desktop, use the following procedure to access files and folders located on a NetWare server linked to your UnixWare system:

1. Double-click on the NetWare icon to generate the NetWare Folder window. In this window you'll see an icon for each available NetWare server, as shown in Figure 3-3.

2. Double-click on the NetWare server whose files you want to access. At this point you may see an Authentication Panel requesting you to enter a valid login ID and a password for the NetWare server.

> *TIP*
> Contact your NetWare system administrator if you don't have an account for this NetWare server.

3. If your login was successful, you'll see a list of available volumes. Double-click on the volume containing the folder you want to access. You'll see a window of available folders.

4. Double-click on a folder. You'll see the files and folders that you have permission to see.

5. Double-click on a file to open it and display its contents.

After opening a NetWare file or folder, you can process it via the File and Edit menu options in the UnixWare menu bar.

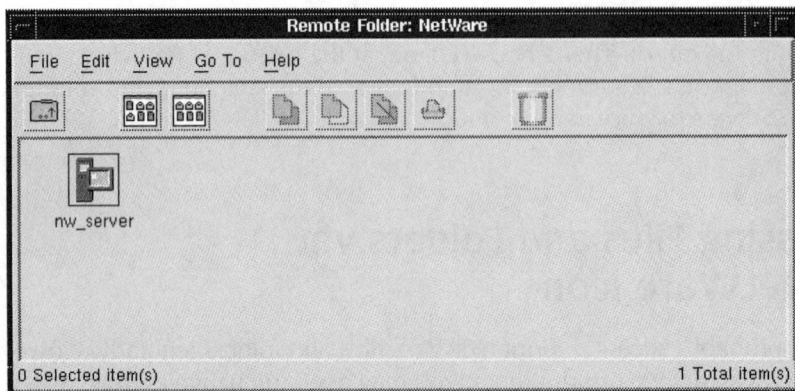

FIGURE 3-3. *NetWare Folder window*

> **CAUTION**
> Verify your permissions for processing files and directories on the
> NetWare server. See your NetWare system administrator to obtain
> adequate permissions.

Opening Files Using a Remote Application

To open a file residing on a NetWare server using a selected remote application,
you must use a combination of the NetWare Access application and the Remote
Applications window. First, log into the proper NetWare server, as described in the
previous paragraph, and close the NetWare Servers for <*Username*> window. Then
go to the Remote Applications window, and double-click the desired application.

Viewing Control Information

UnixWare makes it very easy to obtain control information about NetWare servers.
Seeing what is going on in the system can be done with a few mouse-clicks. You
can get a list of NetWare servers, your network and node address, and a list of
users and a list of volumes for a given server.

Viewing the List of NetWare Servers

To display the list of NetWare servers for a given network, simply open the
NetWare Access window from the Networking folder. You'll see a window with a
list of NetWare servers that are or can be connected to your UnixWare system. To
refresh the server list, choose the Update Servers command from the Actions menu.
Now the server list is refreshed and you can see the changes made since the
NetWare Servers for <*login ID*> window was opened.

Viewing Your Network Address and
Node Address

In the default Short view, the NetWare Access window puts server names in the
File Server column and login IDs in the Authenticated As column. You can add
network addresses and node addresses to the display by activating the Long view.
To do this, start in the NetWare Servers for <*login ID*> window, and choose
Format from the View menu. Choose Long to include the file server name, the
authenticated user name, and the server's network address and node address.

Viewing the List of Users or Volumes on a Server

When the NetWare Servers for <*login ID*> window is active you can obtain more
information about a particular server. The User List button at the bottom of the
window displays the Users Information for <*servername*> window with a list of
currently logged in users. The Volume List button shows the Volume List for
<*servername*> window with a list of volumes available on that server.

CHAPTER 4

Using DOS and Windows Within UnixWare

Not surprisingly, UnixWare has made a major commitment to supporting the Microsoft environment, or MS-DOS (DOS) and MS Windows. It does so via the Locus Computing Corp.'s DOS Merge (hereafter referred to as Merge) and a subset of Novell's own DR DOS 6.0, an operating system compatible to MS-DOS. Merge allows you to run DOS, MS Windows, and UnixWare applications simultaneously. Users will find that UnixWare's access of DOS and MS Windows is transparent.

After a brief discussion on DOS disk drive names and search paths, this chapter introduces you to the DOS window, and demonstrates several DOS commands and DOS applications. The last section describes how to use MS Windows on your UnixWare system or on a remote server.

DOS As Seen By UnixWare

This section shows those who are comfortable using DOS on a standalone microcomputer how to master DOS in the UnixWare environment. It describes UnixWare's drive mappings, which distinguish between personal and shared files, tells how to set the search path so that you can access your DOS programs and files, and gives the naming conventions to follow so that UnixWare doesn't modify your DOS filenames unnecessarily (and unintelligibly).

Users of standalone DOS systems are accustomed to having full control of all their DOS files; they can access, change, and delete all files they have created. UnixWare allows users full control of all their personal DOS files. In addition, it accords them access to shared DOS files. UnixWare's DOS drive mappings distinguish between personal and shared drives.

DOS Drive Mappings

To make effective use of DOS in the UnixWare environment, you must know how UnixWare identifies DOS and NetWare drives. Most DOS users will be familiar with at least some of the drive identifiers but others are specifically designed for UnixWare.

- **Drive A:** Just as for standalone DOS, **A:** refers to the first floppy disk drive on the UnixWare system.

- **Drive B:** Just as for standalone DOS, **B:** refers to the second floppy disk drive on the UnixWare system.

NOTE
Drives A: and B: may not be shared.

- **Drive C:** This drive refers to the entire UnixWare file system, including the user's home directory. Its root is the root of the Unix file system. Regular users have restricted permissions to files and directories on **C:**, except for their home directory.

- **Drive D:**   This drive, which is unique to each user, refers to part of the UnixWare file system. The user's (Unix) home directory is the root directory for **D:**. Use this drive to install personal applications that must be installed in a root directory. Regular users have restricted permissions to files and directories on **D:**, except for their home directory.

- **Drive E:**   This shared drive refers to the first physical DOS partition on a hard disk. This partition must be formatted.

CAUTION
A DOS partition is a segment of your hard disk configured to run DOS. It is not DOS itself. Under UnixWare, DOS is located in the Unix partition.

- **Drives F: to I:**   Additional DOS partitions on the hard disk. These drives must be manually assigned to partitions as discussed later in this chapter under the "Configuring DOS" section.

- **Drive J:**   Refers to part of the UnixWare file system. The directory **J:** is a synonym for the DOS directory **C:\USR\LDBIN**, equivalent to the shared UnixWare directory **/usr/ldbin**. Use this drive to install public applications that must be installed in a root directory, such as shared MS-Windows 3.1. Regular users have access to files and directories on **J:**.

- **Drives K: to LASTDRIVE**   Refers to other DOS devices, such as NetWare volumes.

NOTE
The default value of **LASTDRIVE** is **N:**.

- **Drive O:**   Refers to the NetWare login drive.

Setting the Search PATH

The PATH statement specifies a list of directories in which to search for applications that do not appear in the current directory. The UnixWare default search PATH is defined in the **C:\AUTOEXEC.BAT** file. It includes the directories **C:\USR\DBIN** and **C:\USR\LDBIN** that respectively contain UnixWare-supplied standard DOS commands and user-supplied DOS commands and applications.

Users should modify the PATH statement in their personal boot file, **D:\AUTOEXEC.BAT**, to access personal applications that are not referenced in the

C:\AUTOEXEC.BAT file. (Chapter 3 shows how to use the UnixWare text editor to modify files.)

Naming Conventions

Recall that DOS filenames have from one to eight characters, an optional period, and from zero to three characters following that period. Spaces and multiple periods are forbidden in filenames. DOS converts lowercase characters to uppercase.

UnixWare filenames are much less restricted. For example, the period may be placed anywhere within the filename, and UnixWare allows multiple periods. The length limitation is so great (255 characters) as to be irrelevant in practice. Like other versions of Unix, UnixWare distinguishes between lowercase and uppercase characters. Whether or not you use the European Language Supplement, UnixWare allows more non-alphabetic characters than DOS. UnixWare, more precisely Merge, converts UnixWare filenames into legal DOS filenames, where necessary.

TIP
Wherever possible, compose UnixWare filenames according to DOS naming conventions to avoid filename conversions. In particular, limit special characters in filenames to the period (.), the hyphen (-), and the underscore (_), and use only lowercase letters.

Using the DOS Window

To create a DOS window, double-click on the DOS icon in the UnixWare Desktop (Applications folder). If you have created an icon for a DOS application (one where the extension is .EXE, .COM, or .BAT), you can double-click on that icon. This starts the DOS Window and then the application.

Alternatively, you can run DOS commands from the Terminal window application (described in Chapter 3). At the Unix prompt, type **dos +x**. Or, from the command line (Korn and Bourne shells) type **XMERGE=***display_type*, where *display_type* is VGA or CGA, and then type **export XMERGE**. After testing, add these lines to your **.profile** file. C shell users should type **setenv XMERGE** *display_type*. After testing add these lines to the **.login** file.

The DOS Menu

Once you have activated a DOS window, you may access the DOS menu to modify the window. To do so, right-click in the DOS Window or press the

SCROLL-LOCK key. The DOS menu offers the following options: Zoom, Focus/Unfocus, Refresh, DOS Colors/Desktop Colors, DOS Keys/Desktop Keys, Autofreeze, and Quit.

Zoom   The Zoom option maximizes a DOS window to fill the entire screen, so that UnixWare looks like a traditional DOS computer.

> **TIP**
> Some DOS applications such as MS Word operate in graphical mode and require the Zoom option. In these cases, the system will notify you to activate the Zoom option.

Press the SCROLL-LOCK key to reverse the Zoom option.

> **NOTE**
> The Zoom option is not available for X terminals.

Focus/Unfocus   Select the Focus option to use a mouse in a DOS application that supports a mouse. It restricts the mouse to the DOS window. Select the Unfocus option to use a mouse in another Desktop window.

Refresh   The Refresh option redraws the DOS window to show changes that have occurred.

DOS Colors/Desktop Colors   Merge uses the standard UnixWare Desktop colors; however, the color palette does not always match the DOS palette. You can force the window to display the correct DOS colors with the DOS Colors option.

> **NOTE**
> If your system automatically uses DOS colors, this menu item is dimmed (inactive).

DOS Keys/Desktop Keys   This option lets you toggle between the DOS operation and Desktop operation of the function keys. By default, the Desktop functions are disabled when you are in a DOS window. If you want access to these function keys, choose Desktop keys.

Autofreeze   The Autofreeze option prevents DOS applications from continually monitoring the keyboard buffer. Invoking this option may increase system performance.

Quit   The Quit option closes the DOS window and returns to UnixWare.

Printing Under DOS

Chapter 9 describes the procedure for installing printers under UnixWare. Once you have completed the procedure to install the **doslp** printer, you have access to a DOS printer. UnixWare routes LPT1 port print requests to **doslp**. To change this routing, from the DOS window enter a **printer** command such as the following:

```
printer lpt1 unix "lp -duw5"
```

This command sends LPT1 print requests to the UnixWare printer designated as uw5. The **printer** command also can redirect requests to LPT2 and LPT3.

> ***TIP***
> If your printout contains incompletely printed pages, you may need to increase the default printer timeout of 45 seconds. To double this timeout for a printer attached to port LPT1, enter the following command from the DOS command line: **printer lpt1 unix /t90**.

Quitting DOS

Use *any* of the following methods to exit from DOS:

- Type **quit** at the DOS prompt.
- Click on Quit in the DOS menu.
- Press CTRL-ESC and then CTRL-K.

Configuring DOS

The DOS Options window lets you customize your DOS Window. In particular, you may specify the video type, the DOS drive used, the COM ports for communication, the memory, and the LPT ports for printing. Generate the DOS Options window by right-clicking on the DOS icon in the Applications window or right-clicking on an icon associated with a DOS application and selecting Options.

After configuring DOS, click on Start to launch either the next session of DOS or the designated application.

CAUTION
Configuration changes last only until you restart the computer. To make them permanent (until you change them again), click on Apply.

Video Configuration
By default, UnixWare starts DOS sessions in 16-color VGA mode (640 × 480). Other video choices are CGA, EGA, and Hercules (monochrome monitors).

Drive Configuration
Click on drive letters E: through I: to assign additional DOS partitions. DOS drive letters are designated as "dosE" through "dosI".

NOTE
For the first DOS partition, dosC and dosD are DOS drives C: and D: under DOS. C and D are DOS drives under UnixWare. To copy the file TEMP.XYZ from the UnixWare partition to the DOS partition, enter the following command:

```
COPY D:\TEMP.XYZ dosD:\TEMP.XYZ
```

COM Port Configuration
Select either COM1 or COM2 for the communications port. To access a communications port (which you can do only if nobody else is using it), you must have read/write permission. COM1 references the UnixWare device **/dev/tty00**, and COM2 references the UnixWare device **/dev/tty01**. Before DOS can access them, these ports must be assigned read/write permissions for all users, which the root user does with the following code before closing the Terminal window:

```
chmod +rw /dev/tty00
```

or

```
chmod +rw /dev/tty01
```

CAUTION
Because they are non-shareable devices, do not save COM port configurations with the Apply option. Instead, use Start to attach the specified ports to the application for a given session.

Memory Configuration

The default is 640KB of conventional (standard) memory. You may add up to 15MB of extended memory for applications such as MS Windows 3-1 or up to 8MB of expanded memory for applications such as WordPerfect.

Click on either standard (if you have up to 640KB of memory and extended memory) or EMS (for LIM EMS 4.0 compatible expanded memory). Select standard memory if you want to start an MS Windows 3.1 session manually from a DOS session. Novell recommends 3MB of standard memory for systems up to 8MB of memory and 120MB of hard disk assigned to UnixWare. Novell recommends 4MB of standard memory for larger systems.

> **CAUTION**
> Selecting more memory than available may degrade performance or prevent DOS from starting. If so, close any other open windows or select less memory.

LPT Port Configuration

As discussed in Chapter 9, output to ports LPT1, LPT2, and LPT3 defaults to the UnixWare spooler called **doslp**. To access an LPT port for a nonprinting application, attach it to the LPT1 port using the Start button.

> **CAUTION**
> Because they are non-shareable devices, do not save LPT port configurations with the Apply option. Instead, use Start to attach the specified ports to the application for a given session.

Viewing Current Configuration Settings

To view the current DOS configuration settings, press CTRL-ESC followed by CTRL-I from the DOS command line or any DOS application. To view these settings from MS Windows, open the Main window, double-click on the MS-DOS prompt icon to display the DOS command line, and then press CTRL-ESC followed by CTRL-I. Press the SPACEBAR to return to MS Windows.

Installing and Accessing DOS Applications

Installing personal and public (shared) DOS applications on UnixWare is usually straightforward. To install copy-protected and protected-mode applications, refer to the system manuals. After presenting general suggestions, this section shows you step by step how to install personal and public DOS applications, and then how to configure and "play with" DOS, once it is installed. The section concludes by showing you how to change the DOS version, for example, if you are upgrading from the DR DOS subset supplied with Merge.

Installing Personal DOS Applications

Personal applications are available to individual users in their home directory. Install a personal DOS application by logging into UnixWare, double-clicking on the DOS icon in the Desktop Applications folder, and then following the package's installation procedure. The following information may be requested during installation:

- **Installation Drive and Directory**   The installation drive is **D:**, the directory is your home directory, followed by the program subdirectory; for example: **D:\WORD**.

- **Printer Port**   Specify LPT1, LPT2, or LPT3 as the printer port, and indicate your printer type.

- **Display Type**   If your applications cannot automatically detect your display type (most can) specify VGA, Hercules, or CGA.

- **Mouse Type**   UnixWare supports a two-button Microsoft bus mouse. The application must not install its own mouse driver.

    CAUTION
    When installing MS Word version 5.5 do not select the mouse installation option from the menu. If you do, the mouse will not function properly. The Merge mouse driver was saved as **mouse.old**. Log in as root (if you can't, get the system administrator to do so) and enter the following:

    ```
    cd /usr/lib/merge
    mv mouse.sys mouse.msw
    mv mouse.old mouse.sys
    ```

    Of course, this advice might well apply to other software packages.

- **AUTOEXEC.BAT and CONFIG.SYS Files**   Do not let the application modify the system files AUTOEXEC.BAT and CONFIG.SYS automatically. If necessary, modify your personal AUTOEXEC.BAT and CONFIG.SYS files according to the product documentation. To do so use the DOS or Unix text editor as discussed in Chapter 3.

■ **Specific Processor** For DOS applications UnixWare supports only the 8086 processor. If a given DOS application requires a different processor, you may be able to install it on a DOS partition as described in the system manuals.

Installing Public DOS Applications

Public applications are available to multiple users in a shared directory subordinate to **C:\USR\LDBIN** or **J:**; however, all users must respect the manufacturer's licensing agreement. The following procedure describes how the root user installs public DOS applications and modifies the system startup files **C:\AUTOEXEC.BAT** and **C:\CONFIG.SYS**.

1. Enter **chown *username* /usr/ldbin /autoexec.bat /config.sys** on the command line, where **username** is the appropriate system owner login ID.

2. Access UnixWare and, if you are the system owner, double-click on the DOS icon.

3. Type **CD C:\USR\LDBIN** to access the directory that will contain the shared application area. This directory is also known as drive **J:**.

4. Follow the package's installation instructions, installing it on a subdirectory of **C:\USR\LDBIN**, or equivalently, a subdirectory of **J:**.

5. If necessary, modify the system AUTOEXEC.BAT and CONFIG.SYS files according to the product documentation.

CAUTION
Do not allow the application to modify these files.

6. If you have modified file permissions, reset them by typing the following command: **chown bin /usr/ldbin /autoexec.bat /config.sys**.

7. Close the Terminal window.

Installing Applications on a DOS Partition

Some copy-protected DOS applications cannot be installed on the shared file system, and therefore must be installed in a DOS partition. If you have no DOS partition, you must first create one as described in Appendix C. Then start a DOS

window, move to the drive letter assigned to the DOS partition, and install
the application.

Occasionally a copy-protected DOS application cannot be installed from the
UnixWare Desktop. In this case use **fdisk** from a Terminal window to make the
DOS partition the active partition. Then shut down your system and reboot the
computer under DOS. Once in DOS you can install the application on the DOS
partition. To boot UnixWare again, run **fdisk** within DOS and make the Unix partition the active partition. When you reboot, UnixWare will boot instead of DOS.

> ### *CAUTION*
> Use a bootable DOS floppy diskette to boot DOS on your system. A
> DR DOS 6.0 diskette, which includes **fdisk**, is provided with your
> original UnixWare media.

Installing an Application on Drive E:

Some DOS applications must be installed and run under the same drive letter. The
applications note the drive letter on which they are installed and will not run from
any other drive. When you run under DOS on your DOS partition, DOS usually
identifies the DOS partition as drive C:. When you run under DOS on UnixWare,
the same partition is referred to as drive **E:**, causing such applications to fail. You
can resolve this problem by typing the command **SUBST E: C:** at the DOS prompt.

Once you've made the substitution you can install the application on drive **E:**
according to its documentation. Whenever you run this application from DOS on
UnixWare, the drive is automatically referenced as drive **E:**. To run this application
from DOS on your DOS partition, after booting DOS type the command **SUBST E:
C:** at the DOS prompt and then run the application from drive **E:**.

> ### *NOTE*
> Merge does not support the DR-DOS 6.0 SUBST command.

Installing a Different DOS Version

As discussed in the chapter introduction, UnixWare accesses DOS via the
proprietary Merge package. This package provides a subset of DR DOS 6.0, similar
to MS-DOS. The subset does not include all DR DOS commands, such as BACKUP
and RESTORE, and does not come with documentation. Therefore, you may wish
to install another version of DOS.

With the following steps you can install under UnixWare the full DR DOS 6.0,
MS DOS 5.0, MS-DOS 6.0, MS-DOS 6.21, or reload the subset of DR-DOS 6.0. (At
the time of this writing, Novell DOS version 7.x is not supported.) Merge only

works with bootable diskettes. If your DOS diskettes are already bootable, start with step 2.

1. In the case of DOS 5.0 Upgrade Package or other nonbootable diskettes, create bootable diskettes as described in the product manual.

2. Start UnixWare and double-click on the Terminal icon in the Applications window.

3. Access the root mode by typing **su** followed by the root password (if you can't, get the system administrator to do so).

4. When requested type **dosinstall**, and follow the instructions to remove the old DOS version and install the new one. Because the actual physical partitions are not touched, this command does not affect files.

Using MS Windows

UnixWare provides full access to MS Windows in a standalone (personal), shared, or network environment. If MS Windows is not installed on your UnixWare system, follow the steps outlined in Appendix C. Once MS Windows 3.1 has been installed correctly, start it by double-clicking the Windows icon in the Applications folder. From then on you can use Windows the same way you did with DOS.

TIP
If the screen briefly displays a DOS window and does not launch MS Windows, you have probably forgotten to add the MS Windows directory to your PATH statement, as explained in the procedures for installing MS Windows in Appendix C.

Occasionally the Windows screen may get jumbled. If this happens, refresh the Windows screen by either pressing the SCROLL LOCK key and selecting Refresh from the DOS menu or pressing ALT-TAB to activate the next Windows application, which automatically refreshes the screen.

To quit Windows, access the Program Manager, and then choose the Exit Windows command from the File menu.

CAUTION
Do not log out of the UnixWare Desktop without exiting Windows correctly.

The following sections describe how to install Windows applications and how to access MS Windows remotely.

Installing New Windows Applications

For the most part installing a Windows application within UnixWare is the same as installing one in a DOS environment: Choose Run from the File menu and enter the appropriate name. This section describes some points to check if installation doesn't work as planned.

To install the application in your UnixWare home directory specify **D:** as the installation drive.

When you install a communications program for a modem or other communications equipment, first configure DOS for the port to which your modem is connected. Right-click on the Windows icon in the Applications folder and set the desired COM port as described in the "Configuring DOS" section earlier in this chapter.

Windows under Merge supports Windows applications designed for Standard (80286) mode. DOS applications requiring 80386 or 80486 processors or that require DPMI/VCPI protected modes are not supported.

> *CAUTION*
> Before opening Windows applications by clicking on their icon, first associate them through Icon Setup.

Accessing Remote MS Windows

Sometimes you want to run MS Windows from a host computer that doesn't have Windows installed, but is attached to a remote computer that does. This section shows how to access a remote Application Server on which MS Windows was installed, and then run it from a local host running either the Application Server or the Personal Edition of UnixWare. In both cases the local host must have a login account on the server.

Accessing a Remote MS Windows Host
Use the following procedure to access MS Windows 3.1 residing in a remote Application Server:

1. Double-click on the System Setup icon from the Desktop.

2. Double-click on the Application Sharing icon, and double-click on the ensuing Applications icon. This opens the Applications folder.

3. Drag and drop the Windows icon from the Applications folder into the Application Sharing window. This creates an MS Windows entry.

4. Click on the MS Windows entry to highlight it, and then click on the ensuing Change Type button to change its application type to X Application.

5. Click on the Edit button to display a Text Editor window.

6. At the end of the file, change the line:

```
"X_Application")"/home/login/Applications/Win";;
```

to this line:

```
"X_Application")"/home/joe/Applications/Win""+x";;
```

by adding **+x"** to the end of the line, before the semicolons, and replacing *login* with your login ID, such as **joe**.

7. Save the file and exit the editor.

CAUTION
To access MS Windows from a remote server, there must be an AUTOEXEC.BAT file on the server containing a PATH statement that references the user's MS Windows directory.

Running MS Windows Remotely

This procedure executes remotely installed MS Windows from a local host running either the Applications Server or the Personal Edition of UnixWare.

1. Start UnixWare and double-click on the Applications Setup icon from the Desktop.

2. Double-click on the Remote_Apps icon, and then specify the Servers with Applications option.

3. Locate the name of the remote host (server) running MS Windows and click on it.

4. If the Authenticate window is displayed, enter your login ID and password, and click on Authenticate.

5. Locate MS Windows in the Remote Applications window, and click on it.

6. Click on the Make Icon button, and then click on Cancel.

7. Double-click on the MS Windows icon appearing in the Applications folder.

Learning System Administration

This is the end of Part One of this book, where you learned UnixWare from the user's point-of-view. In Part Two, you will begin learning system administration tasks. Even if you are not the system owner or administrator, you will benefit from mastering the concepts presented in the chapters that follow.

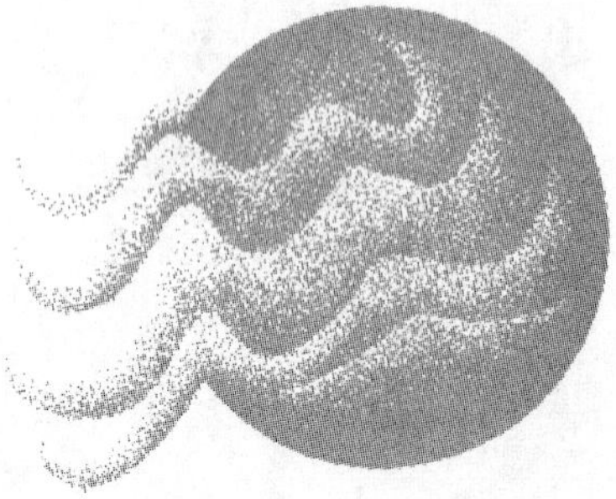

PART 2

System Administration

CHAPTER 5

Introduction to UnixWare System Administration

Successful computer systems don't maintain themselves, especially when two or more people compete for computer resources. Part II of this book, which begins with this chapter, presents UnixWare system administration in great detail. This chapter introduces system administration and the related network administration. It distinguishes among UnixWare's four user categories and the interfaces available to each user category. Although UnixWare offers extensive facilities from the Desktop, system administrators or their trusted assistants may have to customize their installation by writing automated procedures called scripts (similar to MS-DOS batch files). These scripts can simplify tasks and reduce the frequency of errors.

UnixWare Account Categories

One of the things that sets off UnixWare from previous versions of Unix is its extended set of account categories. Traditional Unix systems defined two formal account categories, the root account reserved for the system administrator or superuser, and regular user accounts. The root account conferred complete system privileges, whereas regular accounts had strictly limited privileges. In practice such systems permitted intermediate account types. UnixWare defines four user categories: owner, for the system owner; root, for the system administrator or superuser; sysadm, for trusted assistants; and regular accounts with no special privileges. An individual with access to a privileged account can access a less privileged account. For example, the root account can access both the sysadm account and regular user accounts.

The System Owner Account

The system owner is the person who installs UnixWare, setting the original owner, root, and sysadm passwords. Sometimes the same person installs and administrates UnixWare. The system owner may be employed by an outside company such as Novell (UnixWare's distributor). In this case the system owner installs and tests the system, and then delivers it to the system administrator whose first act is to change the root password, rendering the system private. The owner can run any of the utilities in the Admin Tools window to configure UnixWare—for example configuring the user environment or TCP/IP.

Once an owner leaves the Desktop interface by opening a Terminal window or by logging in as a non-Desktop user, the traditional Unix system permissions take place. For example, editing a restricted file from a Terminal window requires at least the sysadm level of permission.

After installing UnixWare, the system owner can shut down the system. For added security remove this capability by coding the following two lines at the shell prompt:

```
cd /home/system_owner_name
rm shutdown
```

Restore this capability by coding the following two lines at the shell prompt:

```
cd /home/system_owner_name
ln -s /usr/X/Desktop/Shutdown Shutdown
```

> ***TIP***
> The system owner may access the root account via the **su** (superuser command) from the Terminal window, provided that he or she knows the root password.

The root Account

The root account is the account associated with the superuser, a person such as the system administrator who has been accorded full system privileges. By default, the root account does not work via the Desktop but via the command line, as in traditional Unix systems. The following activities are restricted to the superuser:

- Setting up and configuring hardware using the device configuration utility (DCU).

- Increasing or decreasing resource usage limits.

- Specifying the network interface.

- Modifying system peripherals.

- Tuning the system by changing UnixWare system parameters.

These privileges come at a cost. Because superusers are allowed to do anything, their errors can have major consequences. The system will not stop them as it stops mere mortals. Therefore system administrators should perform routine work using a regular account, not their superuser account. They also should use existing scripts and utilities wherever possible.

The sysadm Account

The sysadm account is a privileged account that is not associated with any particular user. You create this account during the initial installation of UnixWare. The sysadm user accesses the system via a series of menus known as the Operations, Administration, and Maintenance interface or more simply, the sysadm interface.

Regular Accounts

Regular accounts have limited system privileges. They are refused access to many files and commands, and work primarily from the Desktop.

System Administration Tasks

A single person, or occasionally a team of people, must have the final say on allocating resources among users and resolving the inevitable conflicts. If one individual is responsible for system administration and another for network administration, the two must work closely together to maximize system effectiveness and efficiency. Sometimes a single individual is responsible for both system and network administration. This may lead to a sorely overworked administrator. For help in deciding how many people should administer your system, consider the following system and network administration duties as they apply to your particular installation.

Administrative Duties

The UnixWare system and network administrator is the person or people ultimately responsible for keeping UnixWare users happy. Although we refer to the singular system administrator in this book, often several people perform both system and network administration.

Successful administration requires both technical competence and a mastery of interpersonal skills. The following list of administrative duties is not exhaustive, but does serve as a starting point. Depending on installation policy and the magnitude of the system, the administrator may be assigned all or just some of these duties, but in the long term must assure that everything gets done. Would-be system administrators need not despair. Although this list is long, several tools can help. UnixWare itself automates key system administration tasks. Often administrators need only push the right buttons.

> **NOTE**
> The superuser (system administrator) always has access to the root account. The system administrator can also use the sysadm account and the Desktop

Adding and Removing User Accounts

The UnixWare system is too precious a resource for just anyone to access it on demand. The system administrator is responsible for creating accounts for authorized users and removing accounts for users who are no longer authorized. Like many system administration tasks, adding and removing user accounts is partially technical and partially political. Should a student lose computer privileges for playing a game, sending a dirty joke to other users, or attempting to crash the system? The system administrator must decide. Chapter 8 addresses the theory and practice of adding and removing user accounts.

Communicating with Users

The system administrator must communicate the installation's UnixWare strategy and tactics to the users, usually through electronic mail. If policy states that users must change passwords every six months, the system administrator should warn them reasonably in advance. Many systems display the latest news bulletin the first time the user logs in on any day. Chapter 15 gives more information about electronic mail and its uses.

Backing Up and Restoring Files

The three certainties of life in the computer age are death, taxes, and losing files, but generally not in that order. The system administrator must institute and enforce an effective file backup policy, including network files. The system administrator can select hardware and software to aid in this process. Different levels of backups should be executed on a daily, weekly, and monthly basis. Chapter 10 discusses the basics of UnixWare file organization, and how to customize file organization for maximum performance. It then presents scripts that smooth the backup procedure, reducing manual errors.

Starting Up and Shutting Down the System

UnixWare is not the same as MS-DOS. When an MS-DOS system crashes you can simply turn the computer off and on again. When a UnixWare system goes down, it may have to be painstakingly rebuilt. The process should not be attempted by untrained individuals. From time to time the system must be shut down—for example, to perform scheduled hardware maintenance or to add a new peripheral.

Changing the Hardware Configuration

The system administrator plays a key role in hardware selection and installation. He or she monitors system performance and documents the need for new hardware. When new hardware is acquired, the system administrator is responsible for its physical installation and subsequent testing. Chapter 7 discusses a variety of hardware devices and presents the device configuration utility (DCU).

Installing Applications

As you have seen in the previous chapter, it is often easy to install external applications (under DOS or MS Windows) once the shells are installed and running.

Installing UnixWare applications can be just as easy, albeit time-consuming, as you will see in Chapter 6. The UnixWare system administrator may spend a lot of time installing applications for users; this makes sense, particularly in a networked system, for both efficiency and cost considerations. Centralizing the installation reduces the problems caused by having multiple versions of the same applications.

System Troubleshooting and Tuning
A major portion of a system administrator's time and effort is spent troubleshooting and fine-tuning the system. Typically, when tuning is required, the users will complain. Perhaps the new laser printer has trouble recognizing input from such-and-such a location. Perhaps the latest version of a manager's favorite graphics program is just too slow. Whatever the problem and whatever its cause, the system administrator is expected to find the answer, and fast. Numerous chapters in this book contain tuning and troubleshooting tips and point out common pitfalls.

Network Troubleshooting and Tuning
System administrators must constantly troubleshoot and fine-tune the network. Both UnixWare commands and a multitude of third-party tools explain in great detail what is happening in the network, provided the system administrator knows what to look for. Several chapters in Part III of this book help administrators understand these tools and their use.

Administering the X Window System
The X Window system is a complicated client-server-based system. Successful implementation of the X Window system demands a unified user interface, across multiple applications. Such interfaces do not evolve by accident; they require detailed planning and coordination. Despite the technical and administrative demands of X Window systems, more and more UnixWare-based systems are installing them. Network administrators will spend much of their time and energy getting X Window up and running and then optimizing its performance.

Communicating with Other Systems
The days of the personal computer sitting isolated in its corner are over. Computers running the UnixWare operating system are rarely used alone. These systems may be connected to other Unix-based computers or to computers running other operating systems such as DEC's VMS and Macintosh's System 7.

UnixWare Interfaces

One of UnixWare's strengths is its multiple interfaces. For many users, UnixWare *is* its graphical user interface, the Desktop. The Operations, Administration, and

Maintenance interface, commonly known as the OA&M or sysadm interface, is a character-based interface consisting of predefined forms and menus. Finally, the command line provides full access to all UnixWare programs and files, but only for authorized users.

The Desktop Interface

Chapter 2 presented the UnixWare Desktop in great detail. When most users think about UnixWare, they think of the Desktop. Many administrative procedures, such as creating user accounts, may be performed via the Desktop, in particular the System Setup folder. Using the Desktop may be the quickest, simplest way to perform routine system and network administration tasks, but it offers a limited number of options. Chapters 6 through 11 cover specific Desktop applications for system administration.

The sysadm (OA&M) Interface

The Operations, Administration, and Maintenance interface, commonly known as the OA&M or sysadm interface is a character-based interface consisting of predefined forms and menus. This interface has been designed to facilitate administrative procedures, many of which are not available via the Desktop. To activate it first access the Desktop and then select the Extra_Admin icon in the System_Setup folder. The OA&M interface is part of the optional Advanced Administration package for the Applications Server version only. You may also access this interface by typing the command **/usr/sbin/sysadm** from the shell (but only if you have a valid sysadm password).

Although the OA&M interface is not as easy to use as the Desktop, it does give you more options. For example, with the OA&M interface you can configure a wider variety of peripherals than you can from the Desktop. Navigating among the interface's menus and forms is fairly easy. Figure 5-1 shows a typical OA&M menu. Figure 5-2 shows a typical OA&M form.

Backup Scheduling, Setup, and Control
The backup_service menu lists functions for scheduling, setting up, and controlling backups. These functions include starting backups automatically, displaying reports of successful backups, scheduling reminders to do backups, and reporting on the status of backups. Chapter 10 discusses file backup in greater detail.

File System Creation, Checking, and Mounting
The file_systems menu provides several file system management tasks. These tasks include checking for and repairing errors on a specific file system, monitoring disk

```
┌─────────────────────────────────────────────────────────────────┐
│ ░░░              Extra_Administration                          ░ │
├─────────────────────────────────────────────────────────────────┤
│ UnixWare 2.0 Operations, Administration and Maintenance        ▲ │
│ ▓▓1▓▓▓▓▓▓▓▓▓▓▓▓▓▓UNIX System V Administration▓▓▓▓▓▓▓▓▓▓▓▓▓▓▓▓▓▓ │ │
│ >applications█  - Administration for Available Applications    │ │
│  backup_service - Backup Scheduling, Setup and Control         │ │
│  file_systems   - File System Creation, Checking and Mounting  │ │
│  machine        - Machine Configuration, Display and Shutdown  │ │
│  network_services - Network Services Administration            │ │
│  ports          - Port Access Services and Monitors            │ │
│  restore_service - Restore From Backup Data                    │ │
│  schedule_task  - Schedule Automatic Task                      │ │
│  software       - Software Installation and Removal            │ │
│  storage_devices - Storage Device Operations and Definitions   │ │
│  system_setup   - System Name, Date/Time and Initial Password Setup │
│  users          - User Login and Group Administration          │ │
│                                                                ▼ │
│ Move the cursor to the item you want and press RETURN to select it. │
├─────────────────────────────────────────────────────────────────┤
│ HELP       ENTER   PREV-FRM      NEXT-FRM  CANCEL  CMD-MENU       │
└─────────────────────────────────────────────────────────────────┘
```

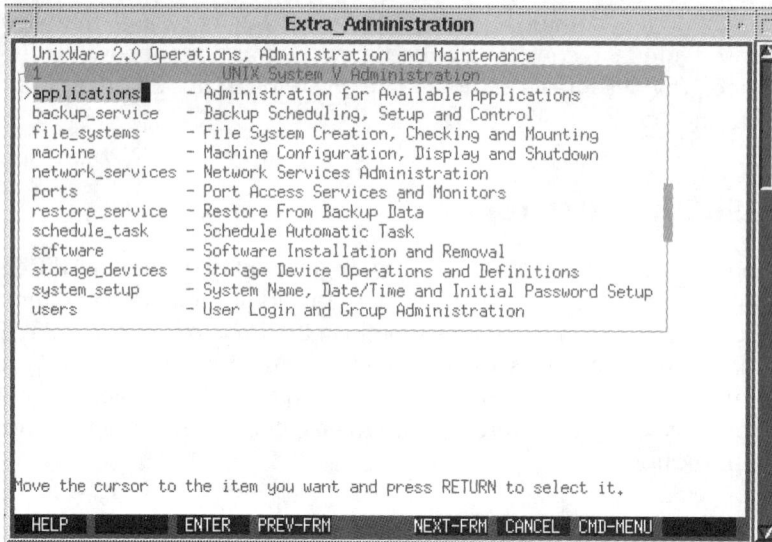

FIGURE 5-1. *A typical sysadm menu*

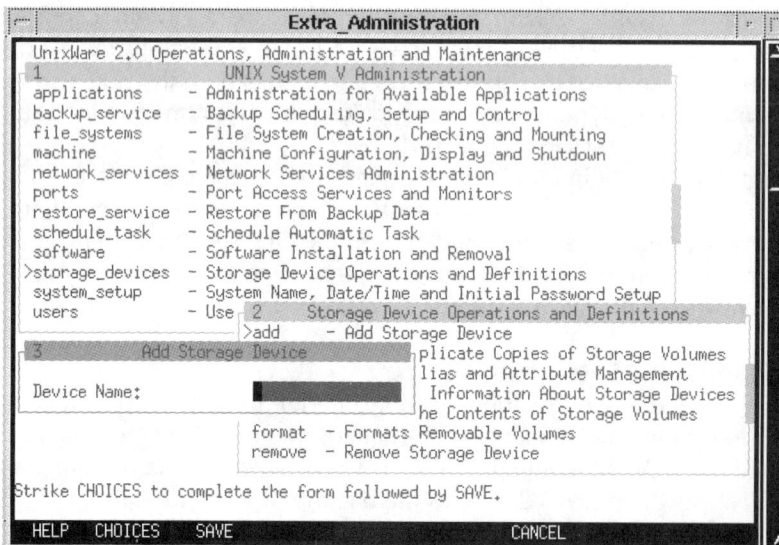

```
┌─────────────────────────────────────────────────────────────────┐
│ ░░░              Extra_Administration                          ░ │
├─────────────────────────────────────────────────────────────────┤
│ UnixWare 2.0 Operations, Administration and Maintenance        ▲ │
│ ▓▓1▓▓▓▓▓▓▓▓▓▓▓▓▓▓UNIX System V Administration▓▓▓▓▓▓▓▓▓▓▓▓▓▓▓▓▓▓ │ │
│  applications    - Administration for Available Applications   │ │
│  backup_service  - Backup Scheduling, Setup and Control        │ │
│  file_systems    - File System Creation, Checking and Mounting │ │
│  machine         - Machine Configuration, Display and Shutdown │ │
│  network_services - Network Services Administration            │ │
│  ports           - Port Access Services and Monitors           │ │
│  restore_service - Restore From Backup Data                    │ │
│  schedule_task   - Schedule Automatic Task                     │ │
│  software        - Software Installation and Removal           │ │
│ >storage_devices - Storage Device Operations and Definitions   │ │
│  system_setup    - System Name, Date/Time and Initial Password Setup │
│  users           - Use ▓2▓▓▓Storage Device Operations and Definitions │
│                       >add     - Add Storage Device            │ │
│ ▓3▓▓▓▓▓Add Storage Device▓▓▓     plicate Copies of Storage Volumes │
│                                  lias and Attribute Management  │ │
│ Device Name:        ████████      Information About Storage Devices │
│                                  he Contents of Storage Volumes │ │
│                    format  - Formats Removable Volumes         │ │
│                    remove  - Remove Storage Device             │ │
│ Strike CHOICES to complete the form followed by SAVE.          │ │
├─────────────────────────────────────────────────────────────────┤
│ HELP  CHOICES   SAVE                          CANCEL             │
└─────────────────────────────────────────────────────────────────┘
```

FIGURE 5-2. *A typical sysadm form*

usage for all file systems, tracking files based on age or size, listing all currently mounted file systems, creating a new file system, and mounting and unmounting file systems. Chapter 10 covers file system creation and processing.

Machine Configuration, Display, and Shutdown

The machine menu allows administrators to check the current system configuration, shut down the system in an orderly fashion, reboot the computer once all executing programs have stopped, and print information about all current users. Chapter 7 discusses machine configuration and shutdown in greater detail.

Network Services Administration

The network_services menu includes network management functions such as setting up administrative files, and defining machine addresses and service port information. Chapter 13 covers network management.

Port Access Services and Monitors

The ports menu provides functions for managing service access to system ports. For example, it provides functions for adding a terminal to a port, removing a terminal from a port, and setting terminal lines. Chapter 4 discusses port access in greater detail.

Restore from Backup Data

The restore_service menu lists the available levels of administrative support for restore services. These services include restoring directories, files, file systems, and data partitions from archive volumes and displaying pending restore request status. Chapter 10 covers file restoration.

Schedule Automatic Task

The schedule_task menu provides functions for scheduling tasks to run automatically via entries to the UnixWare cron table.

Software Installation and Removal

The software menu displays functions for software package installation, removal, and management of information about software packages. Functions include setting installation defaults and listing installed packages. Other functions check installed software packages for consistency, correct inconsistencies, check for hidden files, and check the contents of files that are likely to have changed. Software installation is discussed in greater detail in Chapter 6 and Appendix A.

Storage Device Operations and Definitions

The storage_devices menu provides access to processing storage devices, storage volumes, and device descriptions. For example, you would use this menu to add or remove storage devices, and copy, erase, or format storage volumes. Device operation and definition are discussed in greater detail in Chapter 10.

System Name, Date/Time, and Initial Password Setup

The system_setup menu helps set up a given computer. With this menu you can set the system date and time (including daylight savings time), set the system node name (used by communications networks for system identification), and do initial system setup. Appendix A covers system setup.

User Login and Group Administration

The users menu helps manage user IDs and groups on a given computer system. Tasks include adding, changing, and deleting users or groups on the machine, setting system defaults, and defining user password information. User login and group administration are discussed in greater detail in Chapter 8.

The Command Line Interface

The command line interface will be familiar to administrators coming from a traditional Unix background. Although the command line gives authorized personnel complete access to the UnixWare system, it is not as easy to use as the other interfaces. The default prompt for the root user, the administrator with full access privileges, is the number sign (#). The default prompt for other users, such as a trusted assistant, is the dollar sign ($). The command line is often used for writing custom programs or scripts, similar to MS-DOS batch files.

CAUTION
A user account created at the command line or via the OA&M interface will not be able to access the Desktop.

CHAPTER 6

Installing Applications on UnixWare

UnixWare can run literally thousands of third-party applications. Armed with owner permission, you can easily install applications from the Desktop with the Application Installer described in this chapter. Anyone with owner or root permission can install or remove packages from the command line and obtain information about the installed packages using the commands discussed in the concluding section of this chapter.

Using the Desktop's Application Installer

Use the Application Installer to install and remove UnixWare applications and application sets (several integrated applications) and view their properties.

NOTE
Use of the Application Installer for installing or removing applications requires permission accorded from the User Setup window described in Chapter 8.

Double-click on the App Installer icon in the Admin Tools folder to launch the Application Installer. You'll see the Application Installer window shown in Figure 6-1.

The Application Installer catalogs all your installed applications and displays them in the lower portion of the Application Installer window. It catalogs applications on removable media such as floppy disk, cartridge tape, and CD-ROM and displays them in the upper portion of the window. After cataloging all applications, the Application Installer window closes and the cataloged applications appear in the Application Installer window. An icon composed of two books and a floppy disk represents an application set, whereas an icon composed of one book and a floppy disk represents a single application package.

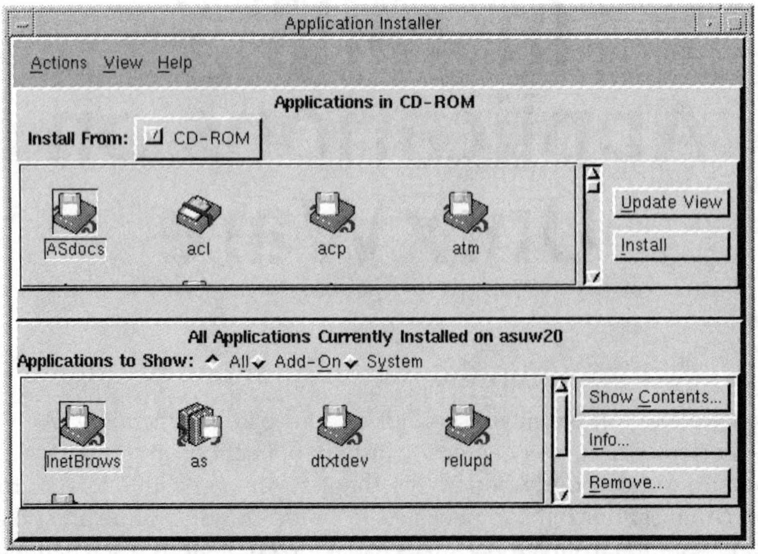

FIGURE 6-1. *Application Installer window*

You can use the Application Installer window to install UnixWare system applications and application sets from floppy diskette, cartridge tape, CD-ROM, or a remote system. You also can use this window to remove installed applications or application sets, view application properties, and copy application icons into folders.

The radio buttons near the middle of the window let you change the types of applications that are displayed:

- **Add-On**   Displays applications that are not part of the Application Server or Personal Edition operating system.

- **System**   Displays only UnixWare-provided software.

- **All**   Displays both Add-On and System software.

Installing Applications and Application Sets

Starting from the Application Installer window, use the following procedure to install UnixWare system applications or application sets:

NOTE
If you are installing an application designed to run under SCO (Santa Cruz Operation) UNIX, see the next section, "Setting Application Options."

1. Insert the disk, tape, or CD containing the new application(s).

2. Click on the Install From: option and choose the appropriate medium (Disk A, Disk B, CD-ROM, folder, etc.). When installing from cartridge tape, be sure to choose the Rewind option.

3. Select the uninstalled application or application set icon(s).

4. Choose Install to generate the Add Application: as window shown in Figure 6-2. Change any options as needed.

When installation is complete, you may need to choose the Update option to view your installed packages or sets.

NOTE
UnixWare sends a mail message to your mailbox when an application is installed. You can read this message from the Mail window or by using the **mailx** command.

```
┌                          Add Application: sdk                          ┐
├───────────────────────────────────────────────────────────────────────┤
│ Software Development Set Installation              Package Selection    │
│                                                                         │
│ The following packages are included in this set for this release. Select│
│ "Yes" in the install column for the packages you wish to install.       │
│                                                                         │
│                         Package Name   Install?                         │
│                 ──────────────────────  ────────                        │
│            Software Packaging Tools:   Yes                              │
│               Enhanced Debugger:   Yes                                  │
│                Motif Development:   Yes                                 │
│      Desktop Manager Development:   Yes                                 │
│         C++ Compilation System:   Yes                                   │
│         C++ Standard Components:   Yes                                  │
│               Kernel Debugger:   Yes                                    │
│            Graphics Development:   Yes                                  │
│                        ┌─────┐      ┌─────┐                            │
│                        │Apply│      │Reset│                            │
│                        └─────┘      └─────┘                            │
│                                                                         │
│ Press 'TAB' to move the cursor between fields.  When finished, move the  │
│ cursor to "Apply" and then press 'ENTER' to continue.                   │
├───────────────────────────────────────────────────────────────────────┤
│ Right/Left arrow keys for new choice (2 choices)      Del=Cancel  F1=Help│
└                                                                         ┘
```

FIGURE 6-2.   *The Add Application: as window*

Setting Application Options

It may be necessary to set special options before installing some third-party applications from the Application Installer. For example, installing some Santa Cruz Operation (SCO) UNIX applications may require that you set the SCOMPAT Environment Variable.

To set options like this one, use the Options command from the Actions menu.

For the SCOMPAT variable, you need to set the number associated with the operating system as required by the SCO application, such as 3.2 for SCO UNIX release 3.2.

Copying Application Icons to Folders

Once you have installed an application or application set, copy the icon(s) to the folder where you expect to run the application, such as Admin Tools or Networking. Then you need only double-click the icon to start that application.

To copy an application, find its icon in the lower part of the Application Installer window and select it. Then choose the Copy to Folder command, and select one of the following options:

- ■ **Self**   Copies the program to your own Applications folder only.

- ■ **Current Desktop Users**   Copies the program to the Applications folder for each current Desktop user.

■ **Current and Future Desktop Users**   Copies the program to the Applications folder for each current Desktop user, and assures that it is copied to the Applications folder of any subsequent Desktop users.

■ **Specific Users**   Copies programs to the Applications folder of each designated user.

Of course, if you select a different folder, these options apply to that one as well.

Removing Installed Applications or Application Sets

Anyone who uses computers soon discovers the unwritten law that says no matter how large the disk drive, it will fill up almost immediately. When your hard drive reaches capacity, you may have to weed out applications that you no longer use. Extra care must be taken not to delete an application that is used by someone else.

   To remove an application, select its icon in the lower portion of the Application Installer window, and choose the Remove button. You will be asked to confirm the deletion, and then it will be removed.

Viewing Installed Applications

The bottom portion of the Application Installer window lets you view the contents of an application or application set that is already installed on your system. Locate the application you are interested in, select it, and choose the Show Contents button.

   If the icon represents a single application, the ensuing window displays its executable programs. If the icon represents an application set, the ensuing window displays icons representing the individual applications in the set. Click on an icon, and then on Show Programs to display the executable programs in the given application.

NOTE
Not all applications are packaged as sets. To view the contents of an application that is not packaged as a set, click on Show Contents in the Application Installer window to display a window listing the associated program icons.

   You also can use the Info button to view the properties of installed applications or application sets. Table 6-1 describes the various properties.

PROPERTY	DESCRIPTION
Application Name	Gives the abbreviated application name
Description	Gives the full application name
Category	Notes whether the application is a single application or an application set
Vendor	Gives the name of the company that produced the application
Version	Shows the application version number
Architecture	Gives the computer type for which the application was written
Date Installed	Tells the application installation date and time
Size (blocks)	Tells the number of blocks of disk space the application consumes

TABLE 6-1. *Application Properties*

Using the Command Line

The command line gives you a little more flexibility when installing and removing applications than you have when you use the Desktop. This section describes the commands associated with installing software, but before looking at them, let's define the entities the commands will affect.

A *package* is a collection of related files and executables that can be independently installed. A *set* is made up of a special-purpose package, referred to as a Set Installation Package (SIP), and a collection of one or more packages that are members of the set.

The **pkgadd** command transfers a software package or set to the system. The **pkgchk** command checks the accuracy of installation. The **pkginfo** command displays software package and/or set information. The **pkgparam** command displays package parameter values. The **pkgrm** command removes a package or set from the system. The **pkgmk** command produces an installable package.

The pkgadd Command

The **pkgadd** command transfers the contents of a software package or set from the distribution medium or directory to install it on the system. It has the following syntax:

```
pkgadd [-d device] [-r response] [-n] [-q] [-l] [-a admin]
       [-p] [pkginst1 [pkginst2[ ... ]]]
pkgadd -s spool [-d device] [-q] [-l] [-p]
       [pkginst1 [pkginst2[ ... ]]]
```

When you run **pkgadd**, the command will evaluate the name and determine whether it is a single package or a set of packages known as a SIP (Set Installation Package). If it is a SIP, you will be given the option to choose which packages from the set will be installed.

When you use the **-d** option you must supply an *alias* for the device. A device alias is the unique name by which a device is known. For example, the alias for a cartridge tape drive might be **ctape1**. The name must be limited in length to 64 characters and can contain only alphanumeric characters and/or any of the following special characters: underscore (_), dollar sign ($), hyphen (-), and period (.).

> **NOTE**
> Used without the **-d** option, **pkgadd** looks in the default spool directory for the package (**/var/spool/pkg**). Used with the **-s** option, it writes the package to a spool directory instead of installing it.

Finally, when **pkgadd** terminates, it will send mail (to root by default) with all the error messages and a summary of which packages installed completely, partially, or not at all. Table 6-2 summarizes each of the command options and parameters for the **pkgadd** command.

The pkgchk Command

If you suspect that there were problems with an installation, or if someone reports a problem with an application, use the **pkgchk** command to verify that the installation was successful (and that no one has corrupted anything since). The **pkgchk** command has the following syntax:

```
pkgchk [-l|-acfqv] [-nx] [-p path1[,path2 ...] [-i file] [pkginst ... ]
pkgchk -d device [-l|v] [-p path1[,path2 ...] [-i file] [pkginst ... ]
pkgchk -m pkgmap [-e envfile] [-l|-acfqv] [-nx] [-i file] [-p path1[,path2 ... ]]
```

As you can see, the **pkgchk** command has three formats. The first checks the integrity of directory structures and the files. Discrepancies are reported on stderr along with a detailed problem explanation. If package names are not listed on the command line, the entire contents of a machine will be checked.

The second form of the command lists or checks the contents of an uninstalled package spooled on the specified device. Attributes cannot be checked for spooled

OPTION	DESCRIPTION
-d *device*	Installs or copies a package/set from a specified device.
-n	Installs package/set in non-interactive mode (the default).
-q	Performs installation in quiet mode. The screen displays only prompts requesting user input and error messages.
-l	Error message suppresses output; they are only logged to **/var/sadm/install/logs/pkginst.log**.
-a *admin*	Defines an installation administration file, **admin**, to be used in place of the default administration file to specify whether installation checks (such as the check on the amount of space, the system state, and so on) are done.
pkginst	Defines the name of the package/set. It is composed of one or two parts: **pkg** (an abbreviation for the package/set name) plus an optional instance identifier (if the set has more than one instance).
-s *spool*	Reads the package into the directory spool instead of installing it.

TABLE 6-2. *pkgadd* Options

packages. The third form lists or checks the contents and/or attributes of objects described in the indicated package map.

The major options available are described in Table 6-3 (see the manual for a complete discussion of all options).

TIP
Use the **-n** option for most post-installation checking.

OPTION	DESCRIPTION
-l	Lists information on the selected files that make up a package.
-f	Corrects file attributes if possible.
-q	Quiet mode: Does not give messages about missing files.
-v	Verbose mode: Lists files as they are processed.
-n	Does not check volatile files.

TABLE 6-3. *pkgchk* Options

The pkginfo Command

The **pkginfo** command displays software package and/or set information. It has the following syntax:

```
pkginfo [-d device] [-q] [x |l] [-a arch] [-v version]
        [-c category1,[category2[, ... ]]]
        [pkginst[,pkginst[, ... ]]]
```

pkginfo displays information about software packages or sets that are installed in a particular location (if **-d** is used) or with particular names (if *pkginst* is specified) or in the entire system. When run, **pkginfo** displays a single line of information describing every completely or partially installed package whose category is not the value "set." The display includes the primary category, package instance, and package name.

The *device* parameter can be any of the following:

- The full pathname to a directory such as **/var/tmp**

- The full pathname to a device such as **/dev/rmt/*** or **/dev/dsk/***

- A device alias

NOTE
For Unix software packages predating System V Release 4, **pkginfo** displays only the package name and abbreviation, and the word "yes" in place of the package instance, to indicate that the package is installed.

Table 6-4 summarizes the options for the **pkginfo** command.

The pkgparam Command

The **pkgparam** command displays package parameter values. It has the following syntax:

```
pkgparam [-v] [-d device] pkginst [param[ ...]]
pkgparam {-d device ¦ -f file} [-v] [param[ ...]]
```

pkgparam displays the value or values specified by the command line parameter or parameters. When a device is given, but a *pkginst* is not, parameter information appears for all packages residing on the device. One parameter value is shown per line. If no specific parameter names are included in the command,

OPTION	DESCRIPTION
-q	Prohibits display of any information. This option overrides the **-x**, **-l**, **-p**, and **-i** options.
-x	Extracts and displays the following information about the specified package abbreviation: name, and, if available, architecture and version.
-l	Displays a "long format" report that includes all available information about the specified package(s).
-p	Displays information only for partially installed packages.
-i	Displays information only for fully installed packages.
-v *version*	Specifies the package version.
pkginst	Denotes a short string that designates a package/set.
-d *device*	Display information from packages/sets that reside on a device.

TABLE 6-4. *pkginfo Options*

values for all parameters associated with the package are shown. The two other options for this command are **-v**, which specifies the verbose mode (displaying the parameter name and value) and **-f**, which directs the command to read the designated file for parameter values. This file should be in the same format as a **pkginfo** file.

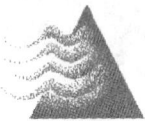

TIP
The file might be created during package development and used during software testing.

The pkgrm Command

If you no longer need an application (and have double-checked that no one else needs it), use the **pkgrm** command to remove it. This command has the following syntax:

```
pkgrm [-n] [-a admin] [pkginst1 [pkginst2[ ... ]]]
pkgrm -s spool [pkginst]
```

The command first checks to see if any other packages depend on the application to be removed (the *pkginst* parameter). The admin file defines the action taken if a dependency exists (see the **-a** option, discussed below).

The default state for the command is interactive mode, meaning that prompt messages are given during processing to allow the administrator to confirm the actions being taken. If you want the command to run on its own, you must specify the **-n** option.

This command has two other options:

- **-a** *admin*   Defines an installation administration file, *admin*, to be used in place of the default administration file.

> **NOTE**
> Unless a full pathname is given, **pkgrm** looks in the **/var/sadm/install/admin** directory for the file. The file defaults to the default for the given directory.

- **-s** *spool*   Removes the specified package(s) from the directory spool.

The pkgmk Command

The **pkgmk** command produces an installable package. It has the following syntax:

```
pkgmk [-o] [-c] [-d device] [-r rootpath] [-b basedir]
      [-l limit] [-a arch] [-v version] [-p pstamp]
      [-f prototype] [variable=value ... ] [pkginst]
```

pkgmk produces an installable package, a collection of related files and executables that can be independently installed, to be used as input to the **pkgadd** command. The package contents will be in directory structure format.

The **pkgmk** command uses the package prototype file as input and creates a **pkgmap** file. The contents for each entry in the prototype file are copied to the appropriate output location. Information concerning the contents (checksum, file size, modification date) is computed and stored in the **pkgmap** file, with attribute information specified in the prototype file. Table 6-5 describes the options and parameters for this command.

OPTION	DESCRIPTION
-o	Overwrites the same package instance.
-c	Compresses non-information files.
-d *device*	Creates the package on the specified device, which can be a full pathname to a directory or the identifier for a removable block device (for example, diskette1). The default device is the installation spool directory.
-r *rootpath*	Uses the indicated rootpath with the source pathname in the prototype file appended to locate objects on the source machine.
-b *basedir*	Prepends the indicated basedir to locate relocatable objects on the source machine.
-l *limit*	Specifies the maximum size in 512-byte blocks of the output device. By default, **pkgmk** employs the **df** command to dynamically calculate the available space on the output device, if it is a directory or mountable device.
-v *version*	Overrides version information provided in the **pkginfo** file with version you provide.
variable=value	Places the indicated variable in the packaging environment.
pkginst	Specifies the package by its instance. **pkgmk** will automatically create a new instance if the version and/or architecture is different. You should specify only a package abbreviation; a particular instance should not be specified unless the user is overwriting it.

TABLE 6-5. *pkgmk Options*

CHAPTER 7

System Configuration

Either during or after installing UnixWare, you may have to install and configure your hardware as well. To simplify the configuration process, the UnixWare Desktop includes the Device Configuration Utility (DCU). You can use the DCU to perform activities such as verifying present settings and modifying memory addresses, and you can do it with a few clicks of the mouse. Once you have completed the configuration changes, you may need to rebuild the kernel. The last section of this chapter tells you how to do this.

After briefly defining basic terminology, this chapter takes you through the process of adding and removing hardware on your machine. Then it explains the DCU procedures available to the system owner (or a trusted assistant) for configuring UnixWare to recognize new hardware and software drivers.

Hardware Terminology

The following list defines several hardware components that are discussed throughout this chapter:

- A *controller* is a hardware device directly attached to the system I/O bus.

- A *peripheral* is a hardware device attached to a controller.

- A *device driver* is a software program that allows UnixWare to access controllers and attached peripherals.

- A *Host Bus Adapter (HBA)* is a device that allows a processor and multiple peripherals to communicate.

For example, an external CD-ROM drive must be attached to a CD-ROM controller. The controller can be a dedicated CD-ROM controller interface board or a multipurpose SCSI Host Bus Adapter. A properly configured device driver is needed to access the controller.

Adding and Removing Hardware

The following sections describe the physical installation and removal of hardware controllers, peripherals, and their associated software drivers.

Installing New Controllers and Peripherals

Before you add a new hardware controller or peripheral, complete any required manual configuration such as setting DIP switches.

> ***CAUTION***
> Pay particular attention to IRQ, memory address range, I/O address range, and Direct Memory Access (DMA) channel settings to avoid conflicts with existing settings. Verify that the controllers support shared IRQ values. Use the DCU to view existing hardware settings—a procedure described in "Displaying and Changing Hardware Device Configurations" later in this chapter.

When you attach a peripheral to a SCSI host bus adapter, manually set the SCSI target ID. To view this data, log in as root and type the following:

```
/etc/scsi/pdiconfig -l
```

To add new hardware controllers and peripherals, follow this procedure:

1. Shut down the system with the command **shutdown -y -1o** and turn off the power.

2. Connect the new equipment. If adding both controllers and peripherals, connect the new controllers first. When you connect the new peripherals, be sure to follow the installation instructions carefully.

3. Turn on the power.

4. If required, run the software associated with the hardware devices you just connected. For example, many boards come with hardware initialization programs that must be executed before you boot UnixWare. Extended Industry Standard Architecture (EISA), Micro Channel Architecture (MCA), and Peripheral Component Interface (PCI) are examples of such boards.

NOTE
If these programs require DOS, first boot DOS from the UnixWare DOS diskette and then run the initialization program.

When you have completed these steps you may need to reboot the machine or cycle power one more time.

Configuring New Controllers and Peripherals

Once the hardware is physically installed, you may have more work to do to give UnixWare the ability to access that hardware. Sometimes the operating system can recognize the new hardware automatically, and your job is done. If that's not the case, use the following techniques to make the peripherals or controllers you added visible to UnixWare.

First, the hardware you installed may include some initialization software. In this case you would find a floppy disk with the hardware package. Follow the steps listed in your hardware documentation. Once the hardware is initialized, remove the diskette from the boot drive.

Also, you may need to install a device driver. Device drivers can be obtained in several ways. UnixWare offers many device drivers. Many hardware vendors provide HBA (Host Bus Adapter) diskettes. Insert the HBA diskette into the system disk drive and install it using the Application Installer.

> **NOTE**
> Device drivers for networking boards may be provided in the network interface card support (nics) package. If so, install (or reinstall) the nics package.

Once the device driver is installed, activate the DCU and verify that appropriate device driver and hardware parameter settings are specified. This process is described in "Displaying and Changing Hardware Device Configurations" later in this chapter.

Any additional configuration will depend on the type of hardware you are installing: for printers, see Chapter 9; for file systems, see Chapter 10; for modems, see Appendix D.

Removing Controllers and Peripherals

Before you remove a controller, determine whether its device driver parameter settings should be removed from the system resource database. UnixWare can tell automatically whether some controllers are installed on the system. For example, it can detect EISA, MCA, and PCI hardware controllers. When these controllers are removed, UnixWare removes the associated device drive parameter settings from the system resource database.

When UnixWare cannot detect a given controller on your system, the controller's device driver parameter settings are not automatically removed from the system resource database. Unless you plan to reinstall the controller, remove its device driver settings from the system resource database using the DCU (see "Displaying and Changing Hardware Device Configurations" later in this chapter). Once that is done, follow these steps to physically remove the hardware:

1. Enter **shutdown -y -1o** to shut down the system.

2. When prompted, turn off the power switch.

3. Turn off hardware peripherals as required.

4. Remove the hardware controllers or peripherals.

5. Execute the platform configuration utility, if one is included. EISA, MCA, and PCI systems are likely to include a platform configuration utility that

may have to be executed under DOS. Your original UnixWare medium contains a limited version of DOS.

6. Reboot the system.

Using the Device Configuration Utility

The system owner can configure the hardware from the Desktop via the DCU. The DCU lists the hardware controllers and device drivers configured on a given system. It allows the system owner to assign hardware parameter values—such as IRQs and memory address ranges—to the device drivers. UnixWare automatically determines the hardware settings for many but not all hardware controllers. In cases where UnixWare *cannot* determine hardware settings, the system owner must use the DCU to specify the hardware settings.

Invoking the DCU

The DCU can be invoked in any of three ways:

- From the Desktop, double-click on Admin Tools and then on Hardware Setup. When prompted to do so, type the root password.

- From the command line, log in at the root and enter **/sbin/dcu**.

- When booting your system, wait for the "Booting UnixWare..." prompt and the subsequent beep. Press the SPACEBAR to begin an interactive boot session. At the [boot]: prompt, enter the following:

```
DCU=yes
go
```

During the boot process, the DCU menu is displayed so you can configure *dynamically loadable* device drivers. These are device drivers that you can configure before the system completes the boot process. Most device drivers cannot be configured this way. For example, statically loadable device drivers (such as those for accessing your hard disk) cannot be configured during the boot process.

Whichever way you invoke the DCU, the first screen you'll see is the Hardware_Setup window, shown in Figure 7-1. You are now ready to navigate through the DCU screens to view or change your device driver settings. Notice the bar at the bottom of the DCU screen: It explains the keyboard navigation choices and provides field-specific information.

```
┌─────────────────────────── Hardware_Setup ───────────────────────────┐
│                  UnixWare Device Configuration Utility                 │▲
│                                                                       │
│                                                                       │
│                                                                       │
│          ┌─── Device Configuration Utility Main Menu ───┐             │
│          │                                               │             │
│          │  Hardware Device Configuration█               │             │
│          │  Software Device Drivers                       │             │
│          │  Apply Changes & Exit DCU                      │             │
│          │  Exit DCU and Cancel Changes                   │             │
│          │  Restart DCU and Cancel Changes                │             │
│          │                                               │             │
│          └───────────────────────────────────────────────┘             │
│                                                                       │
│                                                                       │
│ Select this to view boards configured in system.                      │
│          Use up/down arrow keys and ENTER to select, F1=Help.         │▼
└───────────────────────────────────────────────────────────────────────┘
```

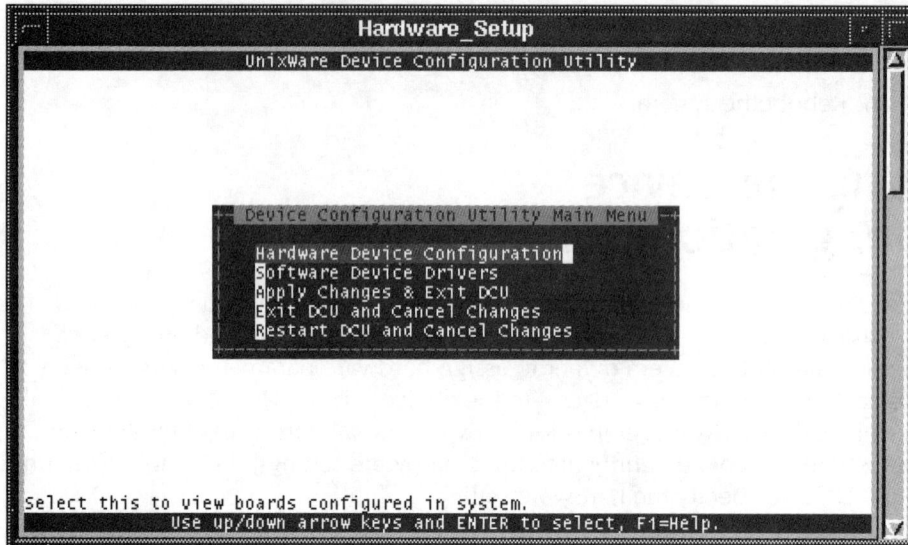

FIGURE 7-1. *The DCU Hardware_Setup window*

NOTE
Changes made through the Hardware Device Configuration and
Software Device Drivers screens take effect only when you select
Apply Configuration Changes and Exit DCU from the DCU main
menu. Press ESC to cancel your selections and exit a screen.

There are three commands that reset the configuration and/or exit the system:

■ Use Apply Changes and Exit DCU when you are satisfied with your
changes and are ready to leave the DCU.

■ Select Exit DCU and Cancel Changes to end the DCU session without
saving any configuration changes you made.

■ Choose Restart DCU and Cancel Changes to reset to the configuration that
existed when the DCU was invoked, but remain in the DCU.

When you exit the DCU you will be returned to the Desktop, command-line
interface, or boot process, based on how you invoked the DCU.

Displaying and Changing Hardware Device Configurations

To view configured hardware controllers or to change their device parameter settings, select Hardware Device Configuration from the DCU main menu. You may see a message that the DCU is loading device driver information. After a short time, the Hardware Device Configuration screen appears in the Hardware_Setup window, as shown in Figure 7-2.

Each row in this window represents a configured hardware controller and its device driver parameter settings. The screen contains eight fields or columns:

■ Field 1 indicates whether the hardware controller should be configured on your system. Possible values are Y (Yes) and N (No). When field 1 is empty, UnixWare automatically determines whether the controller is installed. If it is, UnixWare configures the controller.

■ Field 2, the Device Name field, specifies the hardware controller name.

■ Field 3, the IRQ field, lists the current interrupt vector (IRQ) value for the hardware controller.

■ Fields 4 and 5, the IOStart and IOEnd fields, list the start and end values for the hardware controller's I/O address range.

■ Fields 6 and 7, the MemStart and MemEnd fields, list the start and end values for the hardware controller's memory address range.

■ Field 8, the DMA field, lists the DMA (Direct Memory Access) channel from the controller.

To view more information about a hardware controller, move the cursor to the appropriate row and press F6. You'll see the controller's name, its board ID, its device driver, the hardware bus type, and, where applicable, the settings for the interrupt priority level (IPL), interrupt type (ITYPE), interrupt vector (IRQ), I/O address range, memory address range, DMA channels, and Bind CPU. Press ENTER to return to the Hardware Device Configuration screen.

Modifying Device Parameters

To change a device driver parameter that is listed on the Hardware Device Configuration screen, place the cursor on the parameter to be changed, and press F2 for the Choices menu (given shortly). If you want to change the Bind CPU, IPL,

```
                        Hardware_Setup
              UnixWare Device Configuration Utility
                   Hardware Device Configuration
     Device Name       IRQ  IOStart  IOEnd  MemStart  MemEnd   DMA
     ===============    ===  =======  =====  ========  =======  ===
 Y   Parallel Port      7    378      37f    -         -        -
 Y   Real Time Clock    8    -        -      -         -        -
 Y   kdvm               -    -        -      -         -        -
 Y   Keyboard & Display 1    60       62     a0000     bffff    -
 Y   Keyboard & Display -    64       64     c0000     c7fff    -
 Y   Floppy Drive       6    3f0      3f7    -         -        2
 Y   Direct Memory Access  -  0       1f     -         -        -
 Y   Direct Memory Access  -  c0      df     -         -        0
 Y   Direct Memory Access  -  80      9f     -         -        -
 Y   CMOS RAM           -    70       7f     -         -        -
 Y   cmux               -    -        -      -         -        -
 Y   AT Platform (UP)   13   -        -      -         -        -
 Y   AT Platform (UP)   -    40       5f     -         -        -
 Y   AT Platform (UP)   -    20       3f     -         -        -
 Y   AT Platform (UP)   -    a0       bf     -         -        -
 Y   Com Port           4    3f8      3ff    -         -        -
 Y   Com Port           3    2f8      2ff    -         -        -
            (Page Up/Page Down for more)

 TAB/arrow=Move, F1=Help, F2=Choices, F4=Verify, F6=Info, F7=Adv, F10=Return
```

FIGURE 7-2. *The DCU Hardware Device Configuration window*

or ITYPE parameter values, or any optional device-specific parameters, press F7. The Advanced Parameter Selection menu appears. Place the cursor on the desired parameter, and press F2 for the Choices menu (see below).

Here are rules associated with the Choices menu:

■ If the parameter was not defined (that is, if it was not represented by a dash in the field), press F2 to enter a choice. To return a parameter to the undefined state, backspace to the beginning of the field and enter a dash (-).

■ If more than two choices are valid, a menu appears displaying all your choices. Highlight your selection and press ENTER.

■ If only two choices are valid, press F2 to replace a field's current choice with the alternate choice. To restore the original value, press F2 again.

■ If no other choices are valid, the field will not change. You'll see this message at the bottom of the screen: *There are no known choices for this field, edit manually.*

Each time you make a change, press F4 to see whether there are any hardware parameter conflicts. For example, a conflict results if multiple devices have the same IRQ or DMA value, overlapping I/O address ranges, or if the system may not boot or access some hardware devices. To prevent such conflicts, *active devices* must have unique IRQ and DMA values and non-overlapping I/O and memory address ranges. Active devices are the controllers displayed on the Hardware Device Configuration screen whose first field value is different from *N* (*No*) and whose second field value is different from *unused*.

> **NOTE**
> Multiple controllers can be assigned the same IRQ value if each controller supports shareable IRQ values.

When satisfied with your work, press F5 to save your changes and F10 to return to the DCU main menu.

Deactivating a Controller

To deactivate a controller without removing its configuration data from the system resource database, use the Choices menu to set the value in its Device Name field to *unused*. Deactivate a controller this way if you think you might someday reattach the controller to your system. By keeping the configuration data intact, you will not have to reenter it later. This is also useful when temporarily disabling all peripherals attached to a given controller.

To delete a controller completely from the system resource database, set the first field of the hardware device entry to N (No).

Displaying and Changing Software Device Drivers

To view device drivers or to specify their hardware controller parameters, select Software Device Drivers from the DCU main menu. After a short wait, you'll see the Software Device Driver Selection menu. This menu classifies drivers into several categories: Network Interface Cards, Host Bus Adapters, Communication Cards, Video Cards, Sound Boards, and Miscellaneous. Select one of these categories or choose All Software Device Drivers.

> **NOTE**
> Device drivers created for systems prior to UnixWare 2.0 or device drivers without the complete UnixWare 2.0 configuration capabilities are listed in the Miscellaneous category.

You should now see the Software Device Drivers screen shown in Figure 7-3. This screen includes three fields for each driver:

■ Field 1 indicates whether the device driver is active or not. (The system accesses hardware controllers for active device drivers only.) An asterisk indicates whether the device driver is active.

■ Field 2 tells you the device driver name.

■ Field 3 lists the hardware controllers that the device driver supports.

Many device drivers support multiple controllers. The Software Device Drivers screen lists the controllers supported by each device driver.

To view more information about a device driver, move the cursor to the device driver status (active or inactive) field and press F6. You'll see the driver's device name, as well as the valid driver name for the IPL, ITYPE, IRQ, I/O address range, DMA channel, and Bind CPU. Press ENTER to return to the Software Device Drivers screen.

To change the status (active or inactive) for a device driver, move the cursor to its status field and press the SPACEBAR.

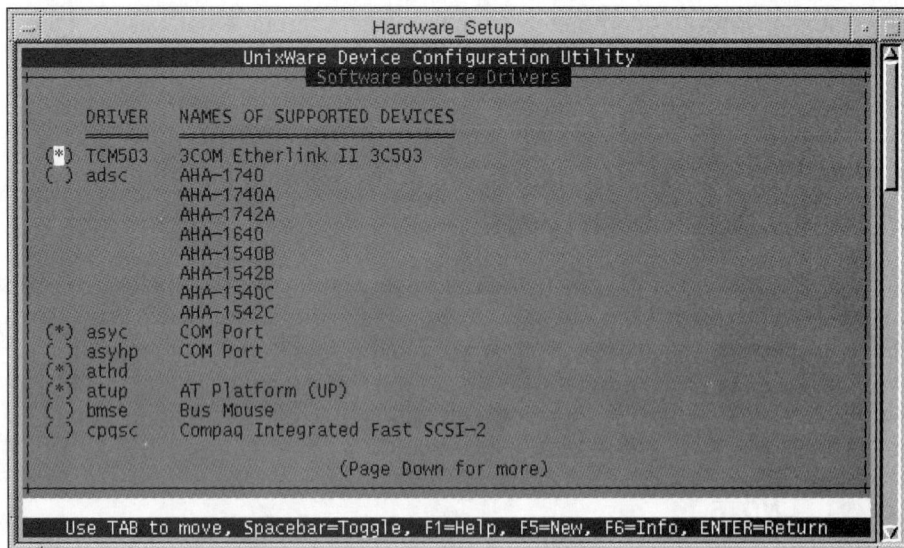

```
┌─                    Hardware_Setup                    ─┐
│          UnixWare Device Configuration Utility          │▲
│                 Software Device Drivers                 │
│                                                         │
│     DRIVER   NAMES OF SUPPORTED DEVICES                 │
│                                                         │
│   (*) TCM503  3COM Etherlink II 3C503                    │
│   ( ) adsc    AHA-1740                                  │
│               AHA-1740A                                 │
│               AHA-1742A                                 │
│               AHA-1640                                  │
│               AHA-1540B                                 │
│               AHA-1542B                                 │
│               AHA-1540C                                 │
│               AHA-1542C                                 │
│   (*) asyc    COM Port                                  │
│   ( ) asyhp   COM Port                                  │
│   (*) athd                                              │
│   (*) atup    AT Platform (UP)                          │
│   ( ) bmse    Bus Mouse                                 │
│   ( ) cpqsc   Compaq Integrated Fast SCSI-2             │
│                                                         │
│                  (Page Down for more)                   │
│                                                         │
│  Use TAB to move, Spacebar=Toggle, F1=Help, F5=New, F6=Info, ENTER=Return │▼
└─                                                       ─┘
```

FIGURE 7-3. *Software Device Drivers screen*

NOTE

Before you can add a controller, the device driver that supports it must be active.

CAUTION

Do not deactivate a device driver if any of your controllers are configured to use it. Removing the asterisk next to a device driver deactivates all controllers that it supports. Deactivating a device driver you need may prevent the system from booting or operating correctly.

TIP

If you are sure that you won't need certain device drivers on your HBA diskettes, you can instruct the installation software to skip these device drivers. Do this by removing the asterisk next to them.

The following steps specify a new controller for a device driver:

1. Place the cursor on the field containing the device driver status.

2. Press F5 to display the New Hardware Configuration screen. The screen contains fields for the device name, IPL, ITYPE, IRQ, I/O address range start address, I/O address range end address, memory address range start address, memory range end address, DMA channel, and Bind CPU. It may contain default values. To display device-specific parameters, return to the Hardware Device Configuration screen and press F7 to generate the Advanced Parameter Selection screen.

3. Enter the device name. Use the F2 key to display and change the values for all other fields. Press the TAB key to navigate between the fields.

4. Press F5 to enter the configuration data. In case of error, repeat step 3 to update the parameter settings. (Up to this point you can press the ESC key at any time to cancel this operation.)

5. Press F4 to verify whether there are any hardware parameter conflicts. In case of error, repeat the previous steps until verify succeeds. It is possible to get the message "Driver does not support the verify function," so you will not know whether there are conflicts until you discover them by accident.

When satisfied with your changes, press F10 to return to the Software Driver Selections screen, then select Return to DCU Main Menu.

NOTE
If you defined any new controllers, examine the Hardware Device Configuration screen and verify that the new hardware parameters do not conflict with the existing hardware controllers. See the previous section, "Displaying and Changing Hardware Device Configurations."

Rebuilding the Kernel

Adding hardware or software, including device drivers, may require you to rebuild the kernel, which you do with the **idbuild** command. This command generates informative error messages in the event of a failure. To use **idbuild**, log in at the root and type **/etc/conf/idbuild -B**. The **-B** option tells UnixWare to rebuild the kernel immediately.

In case of a failure, look for the following errors:

■ For a recently added hardware controller, use the DCU to check if its device driver is installed and if its device driver parameters match its hardware parameter values.

■ For a recently removed hardware controller, use the DCU to check if it is no longer listed as active in the DCU Hardware Device Configuration screen.

See "Displaying and Changing Hardware Device Configurations" earlier in this chapter for more information on using the DCU.

If you changed any kernel configuration parameters, verify that these parameters are valid and do not conflict with each other. See Chapter 11 for more information.

NOTE
The file **/stand/unix** contains the new kernel, while the previous version is saved in **/stand/unix.old**. If you have a problem rebooting with the new kernel, you can always reboot with the old one. To do so, press the SPACEBAR at the Booting UnixWare message display. At the boot prompt (#), enter the following:

```
KERNEL=unix.old
go
```

CHAPTER 8

Managing Users

UnixWare is a multiuser operating system. Under normal circumstances users may access UnixWare without fearing interference from other users. In other words, one user needn't worry about errors in another user's programs because UnixWare traps errors in the original program before they can damage the files or programs of other users. UnixWare is designed so that, in a worst-case scenario, one user's programs will crash without affecting any other users. (Of course, things don't always work as they are supposed to, especially if a user is intent on wreaking mischief or doing damage. Chapter 10 discusses commands that enhance system security.)

The system administrator is not bound by the constraints affecting most users. The administrator has the right and, in fact, the obligation to intervene when a user is abusing the system. For example, many installations have a clear policy denying user privileges to individuals running programs that generate racist or sexist output. The system administrator must be able to kill a runaway process. He or she is also responsible for creating user accounts. To accomplish such tasks requires privileged system access, which is available via the owner, root, or sysadm account, depending on the job to be done and the installation account configuration. These three privileged accounts are discussed in detail in Chapter 5.

This chapter discusses how a system administrator can regulate and monitor normal use of UnixWare. The login ID is a system administrator's most basic tool in regulating which users have access to specific commands and data. You determine which privileges a user acquires when you create a new user account. It pays in the long run to put some thought into which users have more than the basic user abilities, and to carefully consider how you will assign passwords to best protect the users in your system. More about passwords later in this chapter. First, let's look at the three types of user accounts—user, group, and reserved—and the methods available for managing these accounts.

The Three Types of Accounts

When most people think of accounts they consider only those that refer to users who log on to the system. UnixWare, however, defines three distinct types of accounts: user accounts, group accounts, and reserved accounts.

User Accounts
User accounts let you log on to a UnixWare system and get work done. All accounts that you can log in as are user accounts. By default, people logged in to user accounts (other than root or sysadm) cannot perform system administration activities. The system owner may authorize certain users to perform certain tasks; see the section "Assigning User Permissions" later in this chapter.

Group Accounts
A *group account*, or simply *group*, defines a set of users who have common access to various files and folders. For instance, file permissions are often set so that only the owner of the file or a member of a particular group can write over the file. If you are not the owner or a member of that group, you may have only read permission. Groups are covered later in this chapter.

Reserved Accounts
UnixWare automatically creates certain accounts, known as *reserved accounts*. Two examples of reserved accounts are cron and UUCP. You cannot create a user account with the same name as a reserved account. The System Administration guide included with the Application Server provides more detailed information about each reserved account.

Account Processing

System administrators can manage accounts in several ways. The owner account can use only the Desktop. The sysadm account can use the OA&M interface. The root account can use the OA&M interface or the command line.

Using the Desktop to process accounts involves a tradeoff—it's easier but takes a bit more time. Most system administrators process multiple accounts via the command line (perhaps executing a shell script) because the command line provides the most complete account processing facilities.

Using the Desktop

The system owner can use the Desktop to create, modify, and delete users and groups. The User Setup window allows the system owner to add, delete, and change properties and permissions for UnixWare accounts. It also lets you add and remove users from group accounts.

Double-click on User Setup in the Admin Tools folder to generate the User Setup window shown in Figure 8-1. It displays an icon for each regular user account on the system. This window is the starting point for adding or deleting users and viewing or changing permissions or properties.

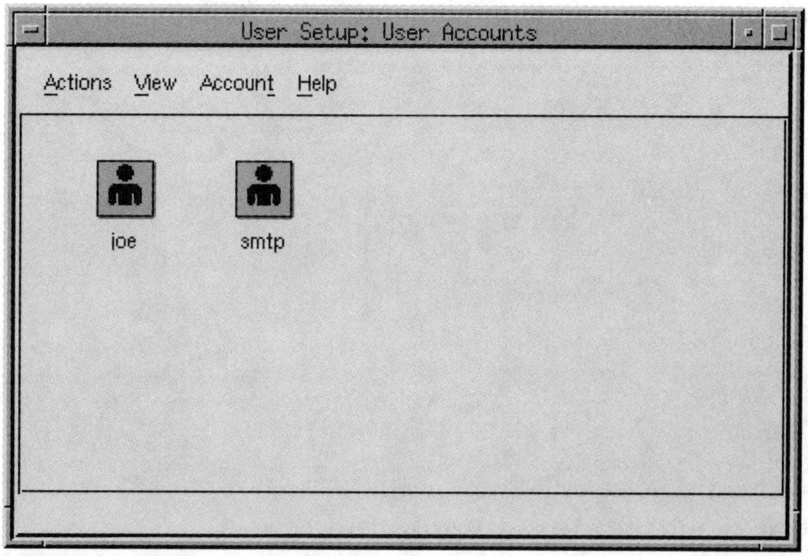

FIGURE 8-1.   *The User Setup window*

Adding a New User

To add a new user to the system, choose the New command from the Account menu. This will generate the Add New User Account window shown in Figure 8-2. Fill in the desired options based on the descriptions given in Table 8-1. Then click on Add to add the new user, and confirm. When prompted, type the new user's password. Assign account permissions as discussed in "Assigning User Permissions" later in this chapter.

TIP
Save time by creating an account with default values. To do so, type the new user name in the Login ID option and press ENTER. A Confirmation window appears. Click on Yes and type a password.

Deleting a User

Access the User Setup window and use the following procedure to delete a user from the Desktop:

1. Click on the user account to be deleted.

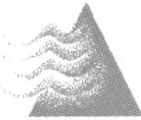

FIGURE 8-2. *The Add New User Account window*

2. Click on Account in the menu bar and select Delete. A confirmation window appears.

3. Choose Remove User's Files or Backup User's Files (or neither) depending on your requirements.

4. Click on Yes to delete the user's login, and click on Yes again in the ensuing confirmation window.

Deleting a user account removes that user's icon from the User Setup window.

OPTION	DESCRIPTION
Login ID	Specify here the unique name that the user enters at system login. Use lowercase letters. You will also need to enter a password.
Type	Click on Desktop to enable the user to access the Desktop, or click on Nondesktop to define the user as a command-line only user.
Comment	Enter additional user information, such as the user's full name.
Home Folder	Indicates the storage location of the user's files. By default, the home folder is **/home/*login_ID***, where **login_ID** is the username.
X-terminal Name	Specifies the name of another workstation or X terminal on the network available for user login, without typing the X terminal name at each login. The workstation or X terminal must be configured for TCP/IP networking as discussed in Chapter 13.
Shell	Specifies the command interpreter to be used (for example, **/usr/bin/sh**, **/usr/bin/ksh**, and **/usr/bin/csh**).
User ID	Indicates the ID assigned to the new user. If the new user has a user ID on another system, enter the same number.
Groups	Specifies the new user's group. When a group is selected, the group name appears in the Selection option.

TABLE 8-1. *Add New User Account Options*

CAUTION

Do not delete reserved accounts or preexisting groups. Deleting preexisting groups causes permission problems when users try to read or access certain files and could disable certain tasks on your system. Deleting reserved accounts or groups could severely disable your system.

Changing User Account Properties

Once you have created a user account, you can change the values of most options, or properties. Access the User Setup window and use the following procedure to change user account properties:

1. Click on the icon for the given user.

2. Choose the Properties command from the Account menu.

3. Set the desired properties, as shown in Table 8-1 earlier in this chapter.

4. Click on OK to save the changed properties and close the window, and click Yes on the ensuing confirmation window.

Assigning User Permissions

You can offload system tasks, such as administering printers to other users. Select the icon for the lucky user in the User Setup window. Then choose the Permissions command from the Account menu. In the User Permissions window, use the description in Table 8-2 to help you set the permissions for each account. You also can use this window to remove permissions for a user.

PERMISSION	DESCRIPTION
Account <username> has Owner Privileges	Assigns the user the full set of system owner permissions.
Shutdown System	Allows the user to shut down your system using the Shutdown icon.
Access Disks, Tapes, etc.	Allows the user to use a floppy diskette or cartridge tape device on the system via the Backup-Restore window or the media icons in the Disks-etc folder.
Access Remote Systems	Allows the user to access a remote UnixWare system or the Remote Access icon.

TABLE 8-2. *Permissions Listed in the User Permissions Window*

PERMISSION	DESCRIPTION
Change Dialup Setup	Allows the user to use the Dialup Setup window to add, configure, or remove modem or direct connections to the system.
Change Internet Setup	Allows the user to configure TCP/IP and network connections to remote systems on the system via the Internet Setup window.
Administer Printers	Allows the user to add, configure, and remove printers on the system via the Printer Setup window.
Administer UNIX Mail	Allows the user to perform administrative mail tasks in the Mail Setup window.
Add/Remove Fonts	Allows the user to install and remove fonts on the system via the Fonts window.
Add/Remove Applications	Allows the user to install, manage, and remove applications on the system via the Application Installer window.
Advertise Local Folders/Files	Allows the user to share local files and folders with remote systems via the File Sharing window. This option requires the NFS add-on software.
Connect to Remote Folders/Files	Allows the user to connect to remote files and folders via the File Sharing window. This option requires the NFS add-on software.
Access System Monitor	Allows the user to perform system monitor tasks, such as setting resource limits via the System Monitor window.
Change System Tunables	Allows the user to change the kernel tunable parameters in the System Tuner window.
Start and Stop Processor	Allows the user to use Processor Setup to start a licensed processor. This command is available only for multiprocessor systems.
Change Video Display Setup	Allows the user to change the colors and resolution displayed on the system via the Video Display Setup window.

TABLE 8-2. *Permissions Listed in the User Permissions Window* (continued)

PERMISSION	DESCRIPTION
Setup Network Installation	Allows the user to configure how Personal Edition or Application Server applications are installed from the Install Server on the network.
Detect Video Board Type	Allows the user to check the installed video board type in the Display Setup window.
Test Video Display Driver	Allows the user to test the video driver in the Display Setup window.
Administer MHS Mail	Allows the user to set up the MHS mail gateway on the system via the MHS Setup window.
Access NetWare Setup	Allows the user to set up NetWare access on the system via the NetWare Setup window.
Access Install Server	Allows the user to configure the system as an Install Server via the Install Server icon in the NetWare Server window. This option is limited to the Application Server.
Share Applications	Allows the user to advertise applications on the system via the Applications Sharing window.
Hardware Setup	Allows the user to change hardware settings via the Hardware Setup window.

TABLE 8-2. *Permissions Listed in the User Permissions Window* (continued)

NOTE
Additional permissions may appear if you are running add-on software packages.

By default, a new user has permission for Access Disk, Tapes, etc., and Access Remote Systems.

Using the sysadm Interface

Using the sysadm interface to process user accounts is as simple as clicking a few buttons. See Chapter 5 for an overview of the sysadm interface. To access the User Login and Group Administration menu, type **sysadm users** from a terminal window. To create a new account, choose the Add Users or Groups option, shown in Figure 8-3. Figure 8-4 shows the completed user account for joe.

```
┌─┐                        Terminal                       ┌┬┐┌┐
│_│                                                       └┴┘└┘
  UNIX System V/386 Operations, Administration and Maintenance
  1        User Login and Group Administration        2 List Users or Groups
 >add      - Add Users or Groups
  defaults - Define Defaults for Adding Users         User or group: user
  list     - List Users or Groups
  modify   - Modify Attributes of Users or Groups     3 Add Users or Groups
  password - (Re-)define User Password Information
  remove   - Remove Users or Groups                   User or group: user

  4                           Add a User

    Comments:
    Login:
    User ID: 102
    Primary group: other
    Supplementary group(s):
    Create home directory? no

    Shell: /usr/bin/sh
    Number of days of login inactivity after which user cannot log in:
    Login expiration date:

 Fill in the form and then press SAVE.

   HELP   CHOICES   SAVE   PREV-FRM        NEXT-FRM  CANCEL  CMD-MENU  RESET
```

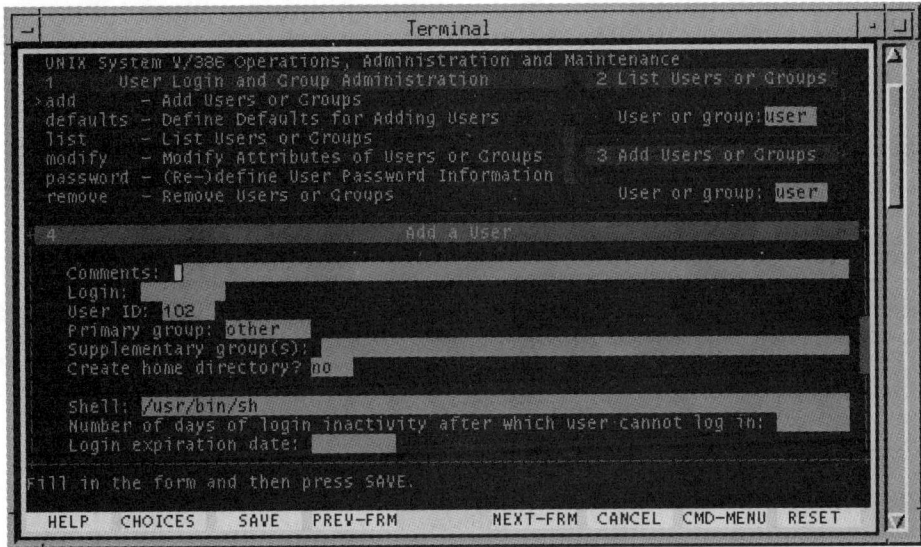

FIGURE 8-3.   *The Add User sysadm window*

```
┌─┐                        Terminal                       ┌┬┐┌┐
│_│                                                       └┴┘└┘
  UNIX System V/386 Operations, Administration and Maintenance
  1        User Login and Group Administration        2 Remove Users or Groups
  add      - Add Users or Groups
  defaults - Define Defaults for Adding Users          User or group: user
  5                  User Definition for Login: joe

     Login:  joe                        User ID:
     Primary group:  other         Primary group ID:
     Comment:   Joseph Radin
     Password status:  password    Last changed on:   06/12/94
     Home Directory:  /home/joe
     Shell:  /usr/bin/sh
     Minimum number of days allowed between password changes:   0
     Maximum number of days the password  is valid:   168
     Number of days for password warning message:   7
     Number of days of login inactivity allowed:   undefined
     Login expiration date:   Never

 Press CANCEL to return to previous frame.

   HELP   PREVPAGE NEXTPAGE PREV-FRM        NEXT-FRM  CANCEL  CMD-MENU
```

FIGURE 8-4.   *The Add User window for "joe"*

Using the Command Line

You can use a set of commands to create a login for a new user, change the status of a user's account, and implement other tasks from the command line. User account processing commands include **useradd**, **usermod**, and **userdel**, each of which is described in the following sections.

The useradd Command

You use the **useradd** command to create a login for a new user. It defines and creates a default directory for the new user's home directory, and creates default values for the new user's environment. Information associated with the new user is placed in the **/etc/passwd** and **/etc/shadow** files.

> **NOTE**
> If you want the newly created user to access the Desktop, run the command **/usr/X/adm/dtadduser** *user_name*. This command sets up the Desktop environment and automatically initiates the Desktop at the user's first login.

The usermod Command

If you need to change one of the attributes of an account you have already created, use the **usermod** command. For example, the following command,

```
usermod -d /home/joe2/ joe
```

changes the home world of user joe to **/home/joe2**.

The userdel Command

The **userdel** command deletes a user's login and prevents the system from reusing that user's UID for a specified time period (in months using the **-n** option). The **userdel -r** command removes a user's login and all associated files and directories.

> **CAUTION**
> The **userdel** command without an option does not remove the user's files, directories, or privileges. The **rm** command removes files and directories, and the **rmdir** command removes directories. The **adminuser** command (which you'll learn more about shortly) removes privileges.

User Information Commands

No system administrator should ever try to remember all account and group information. Luckily, a set of UnixWare commands helps you list most groupings that you might want to see. Here are a few of the commands at your disposal:

- **listusers**   Lists all users and groups.

- **listusers -g *group_name_list***   Lists all users belonging to the specified groups.

- **logins -d**   Lists logins with duplicate names.

- **logins -p**   Lists logins with unassigned passwords.

- **logins -x**   Lists extended information for logins.

The Trusted Facility Management Tools

Besides the Desktop, another way to control user privileges is to use the TFM (Trusted Facility Management) tools. The TFM tools let you maintain a database of administrators and see which commands each may execute (or which privileges each has). An administrator who is in the TFM database must execute the **tfadmin** command before running these commands (and users not in the TFM database cannot execute these commands at all).

To simplify the process, UnixWare defines four roles that contain the set of commands applicable to that role. The roles are AUD (Auditor), OP (Operator), SOP (Security Operator), and SSO (Site Security Officer).

The roles and the users are contained in the directories **/etc/security/tfm/roles** and **/etc/security/tfm/users**.

- **adminrole**   Displays, adds, changes, or deletes roles in the TFM.

- **adminuser**   Associates roles with various administrators or an administrator with individual privileged commands (such as **chown**).

- **tfadmin**   Executes privileged commands. Only administrators can use this command.

Passwords

A *password* is a secret code by which a user identifies him- or herself to the system. While there is no strategy for selecting unbreakable passwords, following the password selection guidelines in this chapter makes it just that much harder for individuals to obtain unauthorized access to the system. When creating an account, the system administrator enters information into the file containing the passwords. Passwords only maintain their security value if their owners change them from time to time. This chapter discusses options available for changing passwords.

Password Selection

Passwords form the first line of defense for system security. Unfortunately, users tend to view passwords as an annoyance rather than as a means of protecting their work. The system administrator is responsible for installing initial passwords, monitoring password usage, and instituting a climate in which users view passwords as an essential component of system security. Once a user changes the initial password, only that user knows it—the system administrator has no tool to determine another user's password. Of course, the system administrator can bypass some password protections by using the root account.

Password Rules
The following rules apply to UnixWare passwords:

- A password must contain at least six characters. Only the first eight characters are significant; for example, the passwords AbCdEfG5 and AbCdEfG5i are identical.

- A password is case-sensitive; for example, the passwords AbCdEfG5 and aBcDeFg5 are not identical.

- A password must contain at least two letters and at least one number or special character, such as a comma (,).

- A password cannot be the username or be obtained from the username by shifting or reversing the characters in the user name. In this case no distinction is made between uppercase and lowercase letters; that is, neither TomSteel nor tomsteel will work as a password for Tom Steel.

- A new password must differ from the old password by at least three characters. In this case, no distinction is made between uppercase and lowercase letters.

TIP
A user's password must differ from the login name. The password is meant to be secret whereas the login name is meant to be public.

Password Guidelines

The whole idea of a password is to block system access to unauthorized individuals. These days, when worldwide computer networks can be accessed with a single telephone call, users must realize that protecting their own password goes far beyond personal considerations.

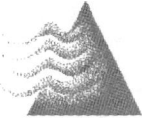

TIP
Carefully chosen passwords will discourage some amateurs and make it harder for professionals to break the system.

There is no magic formula for selecting a password that cannot be broken. Criminals and pranksters have written programs that generate thousands of potential passwords. Users should avoid the following devices when selecting passwords:

- A user's name, or the name of anyone in their family or entourage. Anyone who so desires can find out your pet's name without arousing suspicion.

- All names associated with your company and its products.

- Birthdays, anniversaries, social security numbers for you, family, friends, or associates.

- The names of famous people or places. The best policy is to avoid names altogether.

- English-language words. Many people feel that no words belonging to any human language should be used although exceptions may be made for extinct languages. Some programs attempting unauthorized access use a dictionary file to generate potential passwords.

- Easily guessed numbers such as 9999 or 9876. The number on your license plate is easy for a program to guess.

- Simple modifications of any excluded password, such as a user's name followed by a digit (TomSteel2, for example).

What is an acceptable password? Consider the password 69FDjtPo. This password clearly does not belong to any of the excluded categories mentioned above. It does, however, have several drawbacks. It is hard to remember and hard to type. Users might feel the need to write it down, which might destroy its worth as a password. They are likely to type such passwords slowly, allowing interested parties to follow their keystrokes from afar. And finally, once a password is published it is useless. In conclusion, a password should be hard to guess but easy to remember and type.

A password example that follows these guidelines is i4getY.

CAUTION
Now that this password is published, you shouldn't use it.

The passwd File and Shadow Password Files

The **passwd** file, located in the **/etc** directory, contains the list of users recognized by the system. Each line in this file is associated with a single user.

TIP
It is standard practice to copy the **passwd** file before modification to ensure easy recovery in case of errors.

NOTE
In very critical situations, the root account may edit the **/etc/passwd** file with the **vi** editor—after backing it up—by issuing the **cp /etc/passwd /etc/passwd.sav** command from the shell prompt. If corruption occurs, restore the original file by issuing the **mv /etc/passwd.sav /etc/passwd** command from the shell prompt.

For extra security, UnixWare provides *shadow password files*—files that store encrypted passwords and aging information. Shadow password files (**/etc/shadow**) are accessible only by the superuser.

The **/etc/passwd** file entries contain seven fields separated by colons, as shown in Figure 8-5.

Each entry contains the following fields:

- Login ID
- Encrypted password
- UID number
- Default GID number
- GCOS field
- Home directory
- Login shell

```
                              Terminal
root:x:0:3:0000-Admin(0000):/:/sbin/sh
daemon:x:1:12:0000-Admin(0000):/:
bin:x:2:2:0000-Admin(0000):/usr/bin:
sys:x:3:3:0000-Admin(0000):/:
adm:x:4:4:0000-Admin(0000):/var/adm:
uucp:x:5:5:0000-uucp(0000):/usr/lib/uucp:
nuucp:x:10:10:0000-uucp(0000):/var/spool/uucppublic:/usr/lib/uucp/uucico
nobody:x:60001:60001:uid no body:/:
noaccess:x:60002:60002:uid no access:/:
lp:x:7:9:0000-LP(0000):/var/spool/lp:/sbin/sh
listen:x:37:4:Network Admin:/usr/net/nls:/usr/bin/sh
sysadm:x:0:0:general system administration:/usr/sadm:/usr/sbin/sysadm
mhsmail:x:61:6:MHS Admin Processes:/var/spool/smf:/usr/bin/sh
joe:x:101:1:Joseph Radin:/home/joe:/usr/bin/sh
smtp:x:100:6:SMTP Processes:/var/spool/smtpq:/usr/bin/sh
~
~
~
~
~
~
~
~
"passwd" [Read only] 15 lines, 704 characters
```

FIGURE 8-5.   *Sample /etc/passwd file*

These entries are described in the following sections.

The Login ID

Also known as the username, the login ID is the name by which a user identifies her- or himself to the system. Login IDs must be unique and not exceed eight characters. Login IDs are often composed of uppercase letters and numbers. Because the login ID is used for interuser communication, it should be chosen for convenience, not for security.

TIP

Employ the user's first initial and last name as the login ID. Of course, the system administrator or her agent must devise a policy to handle the inevitable complications, including long names and potential duplicate names.

CAUTION

Different users should not have the same login ID on different systems or the likelihood of a security breach is increased.

The Encrypted Password

The encrypted password is set using the **passwd** program. For manual user account creation only, the encrypted password field is initially set to x. This value prevents everyone, including the intended user, from accessing the new account before the account creation process is completed.

> ### CAUTION
> Do not leave this field blank. Before terminating the manual account creation process, the system administrator should remove the "x" and set the initial password using the **passwd** program.

If the password field is set to the value "," (manually or by shell script), UnixWare forces the new user to enter a password at the initial login.

All entries in the sample **passwd** file show an "x" in the encrypted password field. In UnixWare the encrypted password appears on the shadow file for additional security.

The UID Number

The UID number, also called userID number, is a unique integer between 0 and 32,767. It identifies a login ID throughout a network. UIDs less than 100 are commonly reserved for system usage. Entries in the **/etc/passwd** file are usually maintained in order of the UID number. When an individual leaves the organization, the associated UID number should be retired to avoid problems when restoring files.

The Default GID Number

The default GID number, also called the default group ID number, is a unique integer between 0 and 32,767. It indicates the collection of users or the group to which the login user belongs, in the absence of an alternative specification. Groups are covered in more detail later in this chapter.

The GCOS Field

The GCOS field is not used by UnixWare itself, but normally contains personal information for each user. The system administrator defines this field according to system needs, and communicates this information to the user. Here are some lines from a sample **/etc/passwd** file:

```
root:x:0:3:superuser:/:/sbin/sh
sysadm:x:0:0:general system administration:/usr/sadm:/usr/sbin/sysadm
joe:x:101:1:Joseph Radin:/home/joe:/usr/bin/sh
```

In the first line of the example the GCOS field is Superuser. This can be interpreted as follows: the full username is Superuser; the system administrator did not supply additional information. In the last line, the GCOS field is Joseph Radin.

Other information, such as a phone number, is usually not included since the file can be read by anyone and thus is a security risk.

The Home Directory

The home directory is the directory in which users are placed when they log into the system. In the first account the home directory will be **/**; the home directory of the superuser is the root. In the last account, the home directory will be **/home/joe**.

The Login Shell

The login shell is the shell initially available to the user. The most common shells are the Korn shell (**/bin/ksh**) and the Bourne shell (**/bin/sh**).

Changing Passwords

Sooner or later, individual passwords tend to lose their effectiveness. Perhaps a user has let a colleague access her account, just once. Perhaps a malicious program has finally discovered a user's password by sheer determination. Many organizations require users to change their passwords on a predetermined basis.

Using the Desktop

To change your password from the Desktop, start in the Preference folder. Once there, double-click on the Password icon. The system will prompt you for your old password, then ask you to enter your new password twice.

The passwd Command

The **passwd** command gives you a little more power than using the Desktop because it provides an option to set the minimum and maximum password life in days for individual users. For example, the command

```
passwd -n7 -x91 lreiss
```

specifies that user **lreiss** must change his or her password within 91 days. Once the password has been changed, the new password must remain in effect for a minimum of 7 days. This helps the user resist the temptation to change passwords, then quickly change back to the original password.

> *TIP*
> Send warning messages to users at least several days before they are actually required to change their password.

The **passwd** command assigns or modifies a user password on a temporary or semipermanent basis. The following procedure assigns or changes a user password:

1. Execute the password command for the designated user **passwd** *login_name*.

2. In response to the "New password" prompt, enter a temporary password.

3. In response to the "Re-enter new password" prompt, retype the temporary password.

Groups

In UnixWare a group is a named collection of users who share files or other system resources. Groups are an important tool for improving system security because they allow you to limit access to a file or folder to the members of a certain group. Group membership is defined via two mechanisms: the **passwd** file (the fourth parameter) previously discussed, and the **group** file, discussed below.

To give you a better idea of how groups are used, consider a company where all computers are networked together. You want to give the four payroll employees—and no one else—access to the payroll database. Using the techniques described in the next sections, you can create a group called "payroll," and add each payroll employee's username to that group.

The group File

The **/etc/group** file lists the system's groups. Each entry has the following form (no spaces allowed):

```
group-name:*:GID:additional-users
```

Here, ***group-name*** is a unique name that identifies the group, ***** is coded to maintain compatibility with older Unix systems, ***GID*** is the group identification number discussed in the **passwd** file section, and ***additional-users*** gives usernames and group names that also belong to this group. It is not necessary to specify users whose group membership has already been coded in the **/etc/passwd** file. Sample entries appear below:

```
root::0:root
other::1:root
dos::100:
```

Managing Groups from the Desktop

As usual, UnixWare attempts to be as flexible as possible by letting you manage groups from both the Desktop and the command line. Which one you choose will depend on your personal preferences. This section describes how to modify groups using the Desktop.

Adding a New Group

To add a new group first access the User Setup window. Click on View in the menu bar and select Groups. Click on Group in the menu bar and select New. The Add New Group window appears; set the desired options, as follows:

■ **Group Name**   Enter the name of the group account to be created.

■ **Manage User Info via NIS**   Click here to indicate that the user's account information is managed on an NIS server. This inactivates the Group ID Number options. More information appears in the System Administration guide.

■ **Group ID Number**   This option is filled in by the system. Enter a new number to overwrite the existing one if desired. For example, if the group is defined on another system, you can use the same number here.

> **CAUTION**
> Numbers 0-99 are reserved and may not be used.

Deleting a New Group

Access the User Setup window and use the following procedure to delete a new group:

> **CAUTION**
> Do not delete system process group accounts.

1. Click on View in the menu bar and select Groups.

2. Click on the group you want to delete.

3. Click on Group in the menu bar and select Delete. Click on Yes in the ensuing confirmation window.

Changing Group Account Properties

Access the User Setup window and use the following procedure to change group account properties:

1. Choose Groups from the View menu.

2. Select the group you want to change.

3. Choose the Properties command from the Group menu. The Group Account Properties window is displayed.

4. Change the desired settings as described in the "Adding a New Group" section earlier in the chapter.

5. Click on OK to save the changed properties. Click on Yes in the ensuing confirmation window.

Using the Command Line

If you are more comfortable with the command line, UnixWare provides commands that let you create a new group, remove a group, or modify a group in some way: **groupadd**, **groupdel**, and **groupmod**.

The groupadd Command

The **groupadd** command creates a new group. To create a new group whose GID is assigned automatically, enter the following:

```
groupadd group_name
```

To create a new group with a designated GID enter the following:

```
groupadd -g GID group_name
```

Add users to the group with a command such as this:

```
adduser -g GID login_name
```

The groupdel Command

The **groupdel** command removes a group definition from the system by deleting an entry from the **/etc/group** file. It does not remove a user from a group.

The groupmod Command

The **groupmod** command modifies the appropriate entry in the **/etc/group** file. It can be used to change specifications such as the group ID and the group name.

CHAPTER 9

Printing and Printers

A major responsibility of the system administrator is installing and maintaining printers. You can gauge the importance of printers by noting what happens when a printer is unavailable—users get extremely frustrated. UnixWare offers excellent point-and-click interfaces in the Desktop for printing and for adding and configuring printers. You also can use the command line; this chapter describes both interfaces.

Printing

Most printing is done either from the Desktop or directly from an application such as a word processor. However, authorized users can print from either the sysadm interface or the command line.

> **NOTE**
> When you print to a NetWare printer for the first time, an authentication window appears with the server name and your UnixWare username. Reenter your NetWare username if it's different from your UnixWare username. Type your password, if you have one, for the NetWare server and click on Apply.

Printing from the Desktop

The UnixWare Desktop window includes a toolbar located below the menu bar. Giving commands by clicking on the toolbar can be easier than clicking on menu selections.

The Printer Setup window includes a toolbar with icons for common activities such as adding a local printer and adding a remote Unix printer. For example, a fast way to print is to click on the file you want to print and select the printer icon from the toolbar. This method and several others are described in this section.

Printing a File

One of the easiest ways to print a file is to drag and drop the file onto a printer icon. Or, you can select the file, and choose Print from the Print menu. In either case, the Request Properties window appears. You can set any of these options:

- **Banner Page Title**   Enter the title to appear on the banner (first) page. Banner pages give the requester name and other information. The default title is the filename.

- **Copies**   Enter the number of copies you wish to print.

- **Send Mail When Done?**   Click on Yes if you want UnixWare to inform you by mail when the file is done printing. Click on No if you don't care to be informed.

- **Print Banner Page**   Click on Yes to print a banner page. Click on No if you don't want to print one.

NOTE

The Print Banner Page option can be changed only if the Allow Banner Page Override is set to Yes in the Printer Properties window.

■ **File to be Printed Is** Specifies the file type. Text is the default. Click on the arrow box if you'd like to make other choices—PostScript, HP PCL, Troff Output, or Other. If you select Other, the Specify Type field appears so you can enter the file type.

NOTE

If you choose Other, the file filtering mechanism for the selected file type must be loaded on your system. UnixWare includes filters for simple text, PCL (HP LaserJet, DeskJet, etc.), Troff, and PostScript.

When you are satisfied with the options, click on Print to send the request to the printer. You'll see a window informing you that the print job was accepted. This window also displays the job request ID, which you can use when working with the print queue (discussed in the next section).

Controlling the Print Queue

As you probably know, your print request does not go directly to the printer; rather, it is placed in a queue. A print queue is an area where print jobs wait to be processed. If you have a single-user system and a single printer, your jobs won't stay long in the queue. If you are part of a multiuser system, however, you can use the commands described in this section to monitor and change the order of jobs in the print queue.

To locate the print queue, find the folder that contains the icon for the printer whose queued requests you want to see. When you double-click on the printer icon, you'll see a window with an icon for each queued print request.

To view or change the properties of a queued print request, follow these steps:

1. Click on the print request you want to change.

2. Click on Print Request in the menu bar and select Properties. A window appears with the properties you set previously (in the "Printing a File" section).

3. Apply the options as desired and click on OK to confirm any changes and close the window.

To delete a print request, use the Delete command from the Print Request menu. A pop-up window appears to let you confirm that you really want to delete the print request.

Copying a Printer Icon to a Folder

If you find yourself consistently printing files that reside in a particular folder, you may find it frustrating to keep both the working folder and the Printer Setup folder onscreen at the same time. To give you a simpler drag-and-drop, you can make a copy of your printer icon in that folder.

Use the following procedure to copy a printer icon to a folder starting from the Printer Setup window:

1. Click on the printer icon you want to copy.

2. Choose the Copy to Folder command from the File menu.

3. In the Selection field, enter the absolute pathname of the folder to receive the printer icon. Selecting the default (home folder) displays the printer icon on your UnixWare Desktop window.

4. Click on OK to confirm and close the window.

Alternatively, you can have both the Printer Setup window and the destination folder window on the screen at the same time; then drag and drop the printer icon into the folder.

Printing from the Command Line

While it is easier to use the Desktop for most printing tasks, you may print from the command line if you are already working from it.

TIP
Set the $PATH variable to search for the **/usr/sbin** and **/usr/lib** directories so that you can use the **lp** commands without specifying the full pathname.

Starting Print Requests

To initiate a print job, open a Terminal window and type **lp *filename***, where ***filename*** is the name of the file to be printed.

CAUTION
The command **lp** prints an unformatted text page only. To customize your printing, see the Desktop User Handbook that comes with UnixWare.

NOTE
The **lp** command is also available from the Desktop.

Sending Print Jobs to Remote Systems
The procedure described here establishes a connection to a remote system and then prints on that system. Before trying to use a remote UNIX System V or BSD system printer, make sure its printer is available to your system.

For remote UnixWare systems, follow the directions in "Sharing Your Local Printer with Remote Systems" later in this chapter. Again, be sure that the remote system supports printing by your local system.

For remote UNIX System V machines that do not support the UnixWare desktop, use the **lpsystem** command line utility on the remote system so that it can print from the local system. To do so first log in to the remote system as root. Then open a Terminal window and type the following at the command line where **timeout** is the number of minutes that the print service allows a network connection to be idle and **system** is the local system's name:

```
lpsystem -T timeout s5 system
```

Use the System Status icon in Admin Tools to view your system (Chapter 11 gives more information) or type **uname -n** in a Terminal window.

You can print on a remote System V or BSD system (such as the one on Sun computers) as long as the remote system can both locate your system and accept print jobs from it. Your system must exist in a DNS server database and also in the **/etc/hosts** file on the system where the printer resides. (If you have an Application Server, see the information on **lpadmin** in Print Services Administration in the System Administration guide.) An entry in **/etc/lp/Systems** must exist on both your system and the remote system where the printer exists. An **lpsystem** entry must exist on the local system.

NOTE
If either system is running UnixWare 2.0 or later, the correct **lpsystem** default entries may already exist in **/etc/lp/Systems**.

Canceling Print Requests
To cancel a print job, first open a Terminal window, then type **lpstat -o** to list all active print requests on your system. When you see the name of the job you need to cancel, take note of the number you see next to it; this is the *request-id*. To cancel the print job, type **cancel *request-id***.

NOTE
The **cancel** command is also available from the Desktop.

Checking the Status of a Print Job

To find out the status of a print job in the LP Print Service, open a Terminal window and type **lpstat**. This command displays information about which printers are available, which are active, and lists any current print requests.

You also can use several different options to display more information. For instance, the **-o** option shows print requests for all users; **-t** shows more detail about the status of each printer.

Adding and Configuring Printers

As stated previously, most of the time the system administrator or a trusted assistant will use the Desktop to add and configure printers. They may also use the LP Print Service, from the command line.

Using the Desktop Printer Setup

Use Printer Setup to add, delete, change, manage, or control printer properties for serial printers, parallel printers, remote Unix systems, or remote NetWare printers.

NOTE
If your system is not configured for Domain Name Server (DNS) access, then your **/etc/hosts** file must contain an entry for the remote Unix computer system that connects to your local printer. Your system must be configured for TCP/IP networking.

Start Printer Setup by double-clicking on the Printer Setup icon in the Admin Tools folder. The Printer Setup window appears. This window is initially empty.

NOTE
Administering printers (adding, deleting, sharing, and controlling printers, or changing their properties) requires the appropriate permission as discussed in Chapter 8.

This section discusses how to add or reconfigure the following: a parallel printer, a serial printer, a remote Unix system printer, a remote NetWare printer, or a local Unix printer servicing a remote NetWare print queue (NPrinter). You can use the menu bar or the toolbar to perform these tasks.

CAUTION
When reconfiguring a printer, you cannot change its name. You must add the printer as a new printer.

Your system displays a brief message about what the icon represents when you position the mouse pointer over an icon.

NOTE
Only the system owner can define a default printer on a given account.

Adding a Parallel Printer

To add a parallel printer to UnixWare from the Printer Setup window, click on Printer in the menu bar and select Add Local Printer. You'll see the Add Local Printer window shown in Figure 9-1. Set the options to suit your needs, using Table 9-1 for guidance.

FIGURE 9-1. *The Add Local Printer window*

OPTION	DESCRIPTION
Printer Name	The name that identifies the printer. Use **doslp** if you want to access it from DOS.
Printer	The printer type (make, model, or PostScript).
Connection Type	Parallel or serial.
Port	Either the active parallel port (synchronous port, defined for UnixWare or DOS), usually LPT1 or LPT2, or the active serial port, usually COM1 or COM2. You also can select Other and type the port device pathname or the name of a file to receive printer output.
Send Mail if Printer Fails	If Yes (the default), UnixWare will send mail if the printer fails. Mail is sent to the system owner or to the last user who modified the printer's properties.
Print Banner Page by Default	Determines whether a banner page is printed by default. A *banner page* is a page that identifies the print job.
Allow Banner Page Override	Gives users the option of printing banner pages. Click on No to force banner pages.
Page Length (in Show Other Options)	The page length in inches, centimeters, or characters.
Page Width	The page width in inches, centimeters, or characters.
Char Pitch	The character pitch in inches, centimeters, or characters.
Line Pitch	The line pitch in inches, centimeters, or characters.

TABLE 9-1. *Add Local Printer Options*

For the printer type, select DOS Printer for normal DOS filtering (with this selection, all output is passed to the printer unchanged). A DOS application recognizes the type of the printer it is using and formats data accordingly. Choose DOS Printer to correspond with **doslp** in the Printer Name option. If your printer is not on the list, look in the manual for a printer emulation mode that your printer supports. If you can't find one, click on Other for generic printing.

When finished, click on OK to save the settings and close the window or click on Add to save the settings, add the printer, and close the window.

NOTE
After you've added a local printer, you can enable remote access by following the procedures in "Sharing Your Local Printer with Remote Systems" later in this chapter. To enable access from a NetWare system, see "Connecting a Local Printer to a NetWare Queue," also later in this chapter.

After you've added a parallel printer, you can print using its factory-set configuration settings. To change these settings, use the Properties command from the Print menu.

Adding a Serial Printer

Most of the steps for adding a serial printer are the same as those for adding a parallel printer, which was covered in the previous section. The major difference is the Serial Configuration window, which appears when you click the Serial Configuration button. This window has the following options:

- **Baud Rate**   Choose a value that matches the line-switching speed on your printer.

- **Parity**   Click to set the parity to Even, Odd, or None (the default).

- **Stop Bits**   Click 1 (the default) or 2. Stop bits are transmitted after each character to tell the printer that a character has been sent.

- **Character Size**   Click on 7 or 8 (the default). To print accented characters and other non-English characters, select 8. Make sure that your printer is set to 8 as well.

To make sure the printer is available for printing, see the "Controlling a Printer" section later in this chapter.

TIP
If your printer does not work, check the serial cable. UnixWare requires all hardware handshaking signals to be handled, but not all serial cables support handshaking. You may need a null modem on the end of the cable.

Adding a Remote Unix System Printer

Before adding a remote system printer, identify the printer closest to you so that you can route print jobs to it. Determine whether it is attached to System V or BSD UNIX, and get the system name of the remote printer as well. (You may have to ask your system administrator or the remote system owner for this information.)

Once you have the information you need, access the Printer Setup window and add a remote Unix system printer. Here's how to do it:

1. Choose the Add UNIX Printer command from the Printer menu. You'll see the window shown in Figure 9-2.

2. Enter a name that identifies the printer in the Printer Name field, and choose its type from the Type field.

TIP
Name the printer **doslp** if you want to access the printer from DOS.

3. For the Remote Operating System Type field click on System V or BSD, depending on the operating system of the remote machine.

4. Click on either Domain Name Server, Network Information Server, or System Files (**/etc/hosts**) on the left side of the window, whichever is the name of the system to which the printer is connected. After you click on the name, locate and select the system on the right side of the window.

5. Type the printer name as it is known by the remote system in the Remote Printer Name field.

6. Click on Add to save the settings, add the printer, and close the window.

NOTE
Domain Name Servers are discussed in Chapter 13.

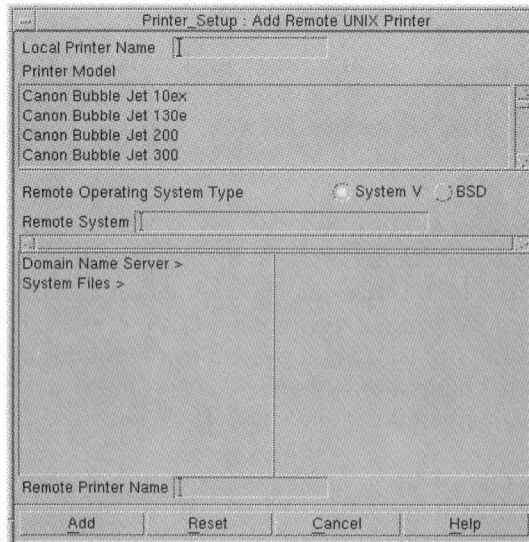

FIGURE 9-2. *The Add Remote UNIX Printer window*

Once you add a remote Unix system printer, you can print using the factory-set configuration settings. To change these settings, use the Properties command from the Printer menu.

Adding a Remote NetWare Printer

Before you add a remote system printer, find out which printer is physically closest to you and use that one for routing print jobs. Make sure that NetWare is set up and you have access to NetWare servers. You must know the NetWare system to which the printer is attached.

To configure access to a remote NetWare printer from the Printer Setup window, follow these steps:

1. Choose the Add NetWare Printer command from the Printer menu. You'll see the window shown in Figure 9-3.

2. Enter a name that identifies the printer in the Printer Name field, and choose its type from the Type field.

TIP
Name the printer **doslp** if you want to access the printer from DOS.

FIGURE 9-3. *The Add NetWare Printer window*

3. On the left side of the window, click on the name of the NetWare server to which the printer is connected. If requested, type your NetWare login and password to the server. The file server is highlighted and a list of printers appears in the Printers box. Select the printer you want to access.

4. Set the other print options as needed.

5. Click on Add to save the settings, add the printer, and close the window.

After you've added a remote NetWare system printer, you can use the factory-set configuration settings or configure the settings on your own. To change the settings, use the Properties command from the Printer menu.

Connecting a Local Printer to a NetWare Queue

To enable a local printer to service print jobs sent to the NetWare printer queue, follow these steps:

1. Configure your printer as a local Unix printer (see "Adding a Serial Printer" and "Adding a Parallel Printer" earlier in this chapter).

2. Select the printer icon.

3. Choose the NPrinter command from the Printer menu. In the confirmation window, choose Yes to connect to a NetWare Print Server. The NPrinter window appears, as shown in Figure 9-4.

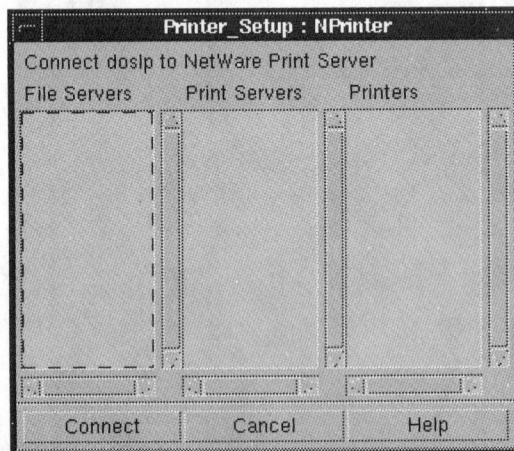

FIGURE 9-4. *The NPrinter Setup window*

4. Select the correct NetWare server from the list in the File Servers field. If requested, enter your NetWare login and password for the server.

5. Select the correct print server from the resulting list in the Print Servers field.

6. Select the correct NetWare queue from the resulting list in the Printers field. The printer you select must have been configured on the NetWare system as a NetWare print queue. See your NetWare documentation for details.

7. Click on Connect to connect your local printer to the file server and print server you selected.

Sharing Your Local Printer with Remote Systems

To allow a remote Unix system to print to a local printer using the Printer Setup utility, you must first define the remote system in Internet Setup (see Chapter 13 for instructions). Doing so requires either an entry in the **/etc/hosts** file on your system or a DNS server that can obtain the system's address.

To share a local printer with users on an accessible remote system from the Printer Setup window, choose the Set Remote Access command from the Printer menu. This command displays the window shown in Figure 9-5. Choose either Allow All Systems Except or Deny All Systems Except, depending on how tight your security is.

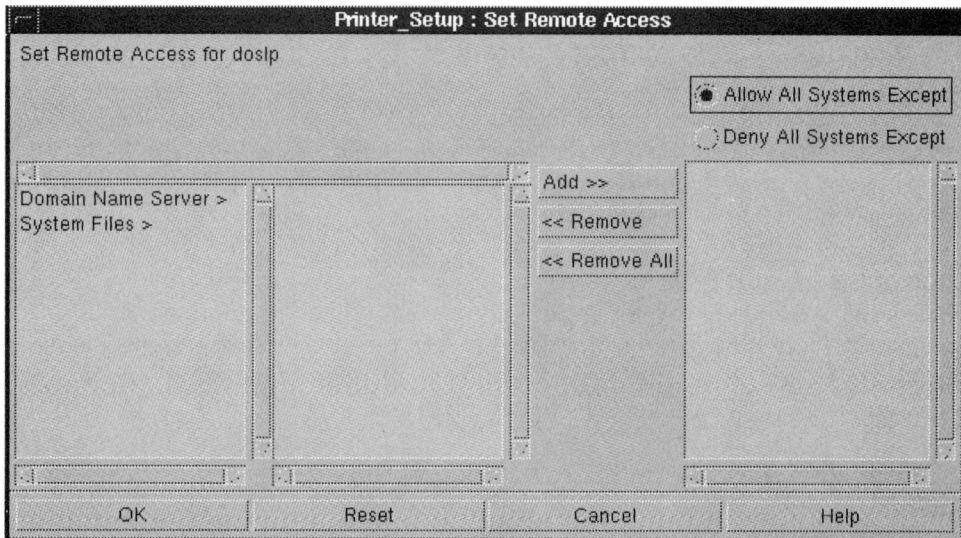

FIGURE 9-5. *The Set Remote Access window*

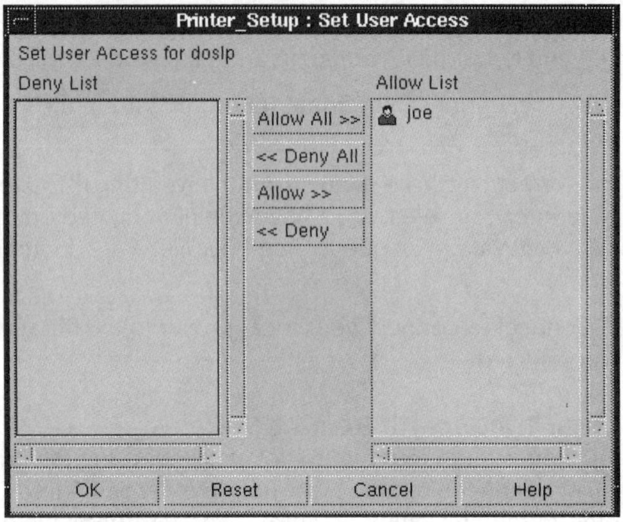

FIGURE 9-6. *The Set User Access window*

From there, locate the remote systems on the left side of the window, and use the Add button to add the remote system to the Allow or Deny exception list. If you need to make a change, use Remove or Remove All.

Allowing Users Access to Your Printers

By default, all users have access to set up printers. To restrict other users from accessing one of your printers, use the Set User Access command from the Printer menu. You'll see the Set User Access window shown in Figure 9-6. Use the buttons Allow, Deny, Allow All, and Deny All, to place only the privileged users in the Allow List on the right side of the window.

Choosing a Default Printer

Once you have added a printer, make it the default printer for future print commands. From the Printer Setup window, select the icon that represents the new default printer and choose the Make Default command from the Printer menu. An arrow appears over the printer selected as the default.

Disconnecting a Local Printer from a NetWare Queue

Follow these steps to disconnect a local Unix printer from a remote NetWare print queue:

1. Select the printer that is currently connected to a NetWare print queue.

2. Choose the NPrinter command from the Printer menu.

3. Click on Yes in the NetWare Print Server Connection Status window. The following message is displayed: "Printer is connected to print server *n* as a remote printer. Do you want to disconnect?"

4. Click on Yes to disconnect the local printer from the remote NetWare print queue.

Controlling a Printer

Printers are automatically enabled when you add them, but if the automatic enabling fails or a printer is disabled, the printer must be enabled manually. (Printers are disabled, for example, when paper jams or runs out.) A disabled printer can queue print requests, but it must be enabled to print them.

The Control command in the Printer menu lets you enable or disable a printer, or set it to accept or reject print requests. The command displays this window:

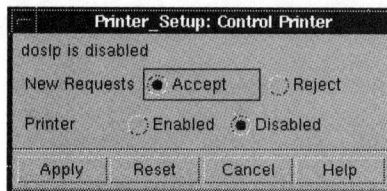

Click on Accept or Reject to allow or prevent additional print jobs from entering the queue. Click on Enabled or Disabled to allow or prevent the printing of jobs in the print queue.

An error message appears if your printer will not enable. If that happens, follow these steps:

1. Make sure your printer has paper in it and that no paper is stuck within the machine.

2. Make sure the print scheduler is running. To do so, type **ps -eaf | grep lpsched** at the Terminal window command line.

3. If you configured a DOS printer, try to print from a DOS window.

4. If you configured a Unix printer, try to print from a Terminal window.

5. If the printer still does not work, examine the address of your parallel port. UnixWare expects the beginning and ending parallel port addresses to be 378 and 37F.

Using the Command Line

This section describes how to control printers from the command line. As a first step, double-click on Terminal icon in the Applications folder of the UnixWare Desktop to open a Terminal window.

Controlling Printers

The LP Print Service is a set of software utilities for printing and checking the status of print jobs while performing other tasks from the Desktop. To enable a local printer, follow these steps:

1. Open a Terminal window.

2. Enter the command **accept *printername*** to order the LP Print Service to accept print requests for the new printer.

3. Enable the printer with the command **enable *printername***. You can enable several printers with a single command. To do so, simply separate each printer name with a space, like this: **enable *printerA printerB***.

The **reject** command disconnects a printer. The **disable** command stops a print request. See the Command Reference Manual that comes with UnixWare for more information on the above commands. The system administrator (the root user) can change access permissions to **/usr/bin/enable** for other users. For example, the command **chmod 755 /usr/bin/enable** allows all users to enable and disable printers.

> *NOTE*
> The **accept**, **enable**, **reject**, and **disable** commands are also available from the Desktop.

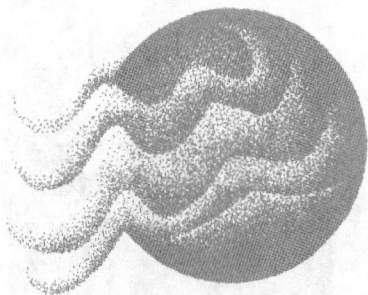

CHAPTER 10

Maintaining File Systems

One of the system administrator's key tasks is file system management. Before effectively managing a file system, an administrator must first understand it. The first section of this chapter explains the basics of UnixWare file systems. The chapter then discusses the commands, sysadm menu options, and Desktop operations required to initialize, manipulate, backup, and restore file systems. Along the way you will gather valuable tips about file system processing.

UnixWare File Systems Basics

UnixWare supports multiple file system types. These include vxfs (Veritas File System), which is the default, s5, ufs (Unix File System), sfs (Secure File System), and bfs (Boot File System). This chapter focuses generically on UnixWare file systems. After you've finished reading the chapter, see the manual for specific differences among these file systems.

This section introduces basic vocabulary associated with the file system. It then examines a UnixWare file system's basic components and their interrelationships. You must be familiar with this material before you can profitably examine your file systems, much less repair them.

Two Important Terms

You will need to understand these two terms in order to work with file systems. Other basic terms are discussed in greater detail in the following section.

- **Logical disk** A *logical disk* is the view of a hard drive that is presented by the disk controller. Underneath there is a physical disk, but the physical details are hidden (fortunately). The system administrator may need to know about the logical disk.

- **Partition** A *partition* is a segment of the logical disk. Dividing a logical disk into partitions improves its use, such as limiting the maximum disk space a greedy user can reserve. The **/dev/dsk** logical disk may be divided into several partitions, such as **/dev/dsk/0s0** and **/dev/dsk/0s1**. Partitions vary widely in size and may overlap. They are described in a partition table.

File System Components

The file system includes several major components: data blocks containing programs and data; the superblock containing system control information; inodes describing files and directories; and device drivers, programs that control hardware devices. These components and their interaction are described next.

Blocks and Superblocks

The *superblock* contains valuable information, including the file system name and size, the address of the first data block, the count and list of inodes, the count and list of free data blocks, and the time of last (superblock) update. A copy of the superblock is maintained in memory for increased efficiency. However, because the disk-resident copy of the superblock does not necessarily change whenever the memory-resident copy changes, you should not simply turn off the system. Doing so may cause system inconsistencies, requiring you to repair the file system with the **fsck** command. How to do this is discussed later in this chapter.

The **sync** command writes the superblock and other system information to disk, in effect synchronizing the disk image and memory image of the system. The **cron** daemon automatically issues **sync** commands on a regular basis.

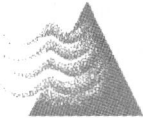

> ### TIP
> In case of emergency, issue several **sync** commands. Why several? Because the **sync** command does not necessarily take effect immediately when issued, so it is a good idea to issue several **sync** commands to limit the likelihood of lost information.

Inodes

A major component of UnixWare file systems is an *inode* (short for index node). The inode on disk does not change during file processing. It contains the following fields: File Owner Identifier, file type, file access permissions, file access information (including the time when the file was last modified, when it was last accessed, and when the associated inode was last modified), the number of names that the file has in the directory hierarchy, the list of data addresses for the file, and the file size in bytes. The inode in memory contains all this information and more, such as whether the file is locked (protected against simultaneous access by another process). Furthermore, the in-memory inode changes whenever the file system changes—for example, when a user creates a new file, reducing the number of free blocks in the file system. As was the case with the superblock, disk resident inodes are not necessarily immediately updated.

Inode 0 and inode 1 are reserved for system use. Inode 2 describes the file system's root directory. An inode may contain a directory name. In this case it is said that the directory name is *linked* (with a hard link) to the inode number. More than one directory name may be linked to a given inode number. Thus you can refer to the same file (inode) by more than one name. Sometimes a given file must be executed from a specified directory. Instead of copying the file into that directory, simply link the file using the **ln** command. This generates a *symbolic link* (a soft link). The use of symbolic links saves time and disk space.

Device Drivers and Other Components

Device drivers are programs that control a specific device such as a laser printer. They are defined in the **/dev** directory. They also contain inodes describing special file types, as discussed next.

Block special files, also known as *block files*, move data a block at a time between the file system and a block device such as a disk drive. *Character special files*, also known as *character files*, move data a character at a time between the file system and a character device such as a terminal. Appendix A discusses in detail device creation and management, both of which are major responsibilities for system administrators.

General UnixWare File System Command Syntax

Although each individual UnixWare file system command has its own specific syntax, many commands share the characteristics and options shown below. When the listed options are not generic, they refer to the s5 file system. Other file system types do not necessarily support these options. The following options are often available:

- **-F** Specifies the file system type (FSType) on which to operate. The FSType should either be specified here or be determinable from **/etc/vfstab** by matching the **inputfs** (input file system) with an entry in the table.

- **-V** Echoes the complete command line, but does not execute the command. The command line is generated from user-supplied options, arguments, and information derived from **/etc/vfstab**. This option should be used to verify and validate the command line.

- **-o** Specifies FSType-specific options. The **/etc/vfstab** table lists default parameters for each file system. See the manual for a detailed explanation of its contents.

Initializing File Systems

Creating a file system consists of two basic steps. After planning your file system, issue the **mkfs** command to make the physical file system. Then issue the **mount** command to link the new file system to the previously existing file system. Issue the **umount** command to unlink the new file system. After examining these commands and the related **mountall** and **umountall** commands, this section briefly describes how to use the sysadm interface to perform these operations.

Making File Systems

You have to make a file system prior to mounting a disk. This is done via the **mkfs** command. The basic process is fairly easy. However, when system efficiency is a major issue, you may have to experiment a bit. For example, the partition size can affect system performance substantially.

The **mkfs** command constructs a file system by writing on the special device file for the disk drive associated with this file system; the device file must be the first argument. The following command makes a ufs file system with a size of 35,340 512-byte sectors (17,670 KB) on a special device file c0t0d0s2 located in the raw disk device directory **/dev/rdsk**:

```
mkfs -F ufs /dev/rdsk/c0t0d0s2 35340
```

During construction, you can abort the command by pressing the DELETE key. See the section "General UnixWare File System Command Syntax" earlier in this chapter for the major options.

Whenever you use the **mkfs** command, be sure to create a new **lost+found** directory. This directory is required to repair file systems, as discussed in the chapter's concluding section.

Mounting and Unmounting File Systems

Mounting a disk (or a diskette) links its file system with one of the installation's existing file systems. A file system must be mounted before it can be accessed. Unmounting a disk reverses the mount operation; it breaks the link between the unmounted disk and the original larger file system. Generally, file systems are unmounted as part of the system shutdown process.

The mount Command
The **mount** command mounts a file structure. It has the following syntax:

```
mount options special_device mount_point
```

The **mount** command attaches a ufs file system, referenced by **special_device**, to the file system hierarchy at the pathname location **mount_point**, which must already exist. If **mount_point** was not empty prior to the mount operation, its contents remain hidden until the file system is again unmounted.

These are the major options:

- **-F ufs**   Specifies the ufs-FSType.
- **-r**   Mounts the file system in a read-only mode.

TIP
The **mount** command does not check for file-system integrity. Issue an **fsck** command before issuing a **mount** command to do this.

The umount Command

The **umount** command dismounts a file structure. It has the following syntax:

```
umount special_device
```

umount announces to the system that the previously mounted removable file structure on **special_device** is to be removed. Pending file system I/O is completed, and the file structure is flagged clean. File structures containing an open file or a user's working directory cannot be dismounted with **umount**.

> **NOTE**
> The **umount** command issues a **sync** command to copy modified parts of the file system to disk before unmounting the file system.

The mountall and umountall Commands

The **mountall** and **umountall** commands mount and unmount multiple file systems. They may be executed only by a privileged user. They have the following syntax:

```
mountall options
```

and

```
umountall options
```

The **mountall** command mounts file systems according to a file system table (by default **/etc/vfstab**). The special filename "-" reads from the standard input, which must be in the same format as **/etc/vfstab**. With no arguments, **mountall** mounts all systems in the file system table whose automnt field is set to yes.

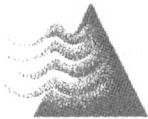

> **TIP**
> Before each file system is mounted, use **fsck** to see if it appears mountable. If necessary, fix the file system using **fsck** before attempting the mount.

The **umountall** command unmounts all mounted file systems except **root**, **/proc**, **/stand**, and **/dev/fd**. These are the major options:

- **-F** Specifies the file system type to be mounted or unmounted.
- **-l** Limits the action to local file systems.
- **-r** Limits the action to remote file system types.

Using the sysadm Interface

Many file system administration tasks such as making, mounting, and unmounting file systems may be handled via the sysadm interface. Generate the appropriate file system menu by entering the command **sysadm file_system** from the command line, and then click on the appropriate menu item.

Manipulating File Systems

This section deals with file systems that do not need repair. It describes the Desktop features and command-line commands that change file ownership and that may access files. It concludes with commands for monitoring and reorganizing file systems.

Ownership and Permissions

UnixWare provides several commands that enable the system administrator to change user and group ownership of files, directories, and devices, and to accord access permissions for owners, group owners, and other users. The **chown** command assigns user ownership, the **chgrp** command assigns group ownership, and the **chmod** command assigns access permissions. The correct use of these commands tends to increase system security and efficiency.

The chown Command   The **chown** command is used to change ownership of a file or a directory. It employs the following syntax:

```
chown logname filename
```

Here, *logname* is the login name identifying the user gaining ownership, and *filename* is the name of the file or directory whose ownership is changed.

The chgrp Command   The **chgrp** command changes the group ownership of files, directories, and devices. It employs the following syntax:

```
chgrp groupid filename
```

Here, *groupid* is the group identification number designating the group gaining ownership, and *filename* is the name of the file, directory, or device whose group ownership is changed.

The chmod Command   The **chmod** command and the corresponding **chmod** systems call use bits to provide three distinct file permissions. The permission code 4 (binary 100) accords read permission, the permission code 2 (binary 10) accords write permission, and the permission code 1 (binary 1) accords execute permission. These permissions may be granted separately or together. For example, a permission code of 7 (binary 111) accords read, write, and execute permission (7 equals 4 + 2 + 1). A permission code of 3 (binary 11) accords write and execute permission (3 equals 2 + 1). And a permission code of 0 accords no permission for the designated file.

The **chmod** command sets file protection for three categories of users: Owner set by the **chown** command, group owner set by the **chgrp** command, and others.

The following command sets permissions on the file **abc**. It accords the user full (read, write, and execute) permission; accords the group write and read permission; and accords other users no permission.

```
chmod 730 abc
```

The superuser has full permission on all files when using the root password. It is easier to accord permissions with symbolic modes than by setting the bits. The exact syntax may differ from one system to another. The following abbreviations are often used: **r** for read, **w** for write, and **x** for execute; **u** for user or owner, **g** for group, and **o** for other. The + adds permission and the - removes permission. Consider a few examples:

```
chmod g+r abc
```

accords the group read permission on the **abc** file.

The command **chmod u-w abc** removes write permission from the owner (user) of the **abc** file.

While the meaning of file read, write, and execute permissions should be clear, the associated directory permissions may require explanation.

- Directory read permission accords the right to see the filenames in the specified directory. It does not accord the right to issue a **cd** command to access the directory.

- Directory write permission accords the right to modify directory contents, even if no write permission is accorded for the individual files in this directory. Grant directory write permission with care.

■ Directory execute permission accords the right to access the directory with the **cd** command and to use the directory name within the pathname.

Monitoring File Systems

Carefully monitoring the file system will reduce the inevitable malfunctions, such as running out of disk space. The system administrator should be familiar with the monitoring commands, such as **du** and **df**, that are described in Chapter 11. Another command, the **find** command, locates files that meet specified selection criteria. Use **find** to search for a specific file or set of files in a directory tree. It has the following syntax:

```
find pathname-list expression
```

where **pathname-list** is the set of directories to recursively search. Here are several valid expressions:

■ **-name *pattern***   True if ***pattern*** matches the current filename.

■ **-size *n*[*c*]**   True if the file is ***n*** blocks (512 bytes per block) long. If ***n*** is followed by a ***c***, the size is ***n*** bytes.

■ **-mtime *n***   True if the file's data was modified within ***n*** days.

■ **-atime *n***   True if the file was accessed within ***n*** days.

■ **-exec *cmd***   True if the executed ***cmd*** returns a zero value as exit status; a command argument {} is replaced by the current pathname.

■ **-print**   Always true; causes the current pathname to be printed.

One use of the **find** command is to locate files that may be deleted. For example, core files are generated when a program aborts. These large files may be useful for program debugging but should be deleted if not actually used. The following command deletes all core files that have not been accessed in the last seven days:

```
find / -name core -atime +7 -exec rm {} \;
```

TIP
To avoid problems, inform users in writing that you plan to delete files at least a few days before you actually delete them.

Reorganizing File Systems

Over a period of time, the file system, especially the user file system, becomes fragmented. As users create, enlarge, and remove files and directories, the system's free blocks are scattered. Accessing a file may require moving the physical access mechanism several times. The **dcopy** command reorganizes disks to reduce fragmentation. Depending on system activity, you may issue a **dcopy** every few days. Do this when there are no users on the system, perhaps at night or on the weekend.

The **dcopy** command copies file systems for optimal access time. It has the following syntax:

```
dcopy options inputfs outputfs
```

where **inputfs** is the file system you are copying from, and **outputfs** is the file system you are copying to. These are the valid **options**:

- **-F *FSType*** Specifies the file system type, for example ufs.

- **-d** Leaves order of directory entries as is.

- **-v** Reports how many files were processed.

File Backup

Never underestimate the importance of file system backup and restoration. If you have ever lost a file, especially an important one, then you already realize the value of correctly designed and executed backup procedures. Users will hold you, the system administrator, responsible whenever they cannot restore lost files.

System administrators have a wide variety of types of backups and storage media at their disposal. For maximum efficiency and minimum likelihood of lost files, choose the appropriate backup media for your installation. This section concludes with advice on backups and restorations. If applying this advice means one less file lost, your efforts will be worthwhile.

The Backup-Restore application in the UnixWare Admin Tools folder is employed to back up hard disk files to a NetWare or Unix file server, to diskettes, or to cartridge tapes, and to restore these files to the hard disk.

When backing up files, UnixWare packs the data into a single file. The Restore utility unpacks the data into the component files.

Create an Emergency Recovery Tape to back up your entire system as protection against disaster such as a hard disk failure.

> ### *CAUTION*
> You must have read permission on a file to back it up. You must have write permission on a file to restore it.

Types of Backups

The system administrator needs to know how to make backups, and, just as important, when to make them. Backups require time, energy, and file storage media. They are disruptive because users should not access the file system during a file backup; although most users understand the importance of a backup, many are grumpy at relinquishing their computers.

There are three types of backups:

- A *full backup* copies the entire file system.

- A *partial backup* is a complete copy of any file system or directory tree.

- An *incremental backup* is a copy of new files and files that have changed since the last backup.

How often you perform each type of backup depends in large part on the system you manage, but as a rule of thumb make a full backup when you first install the system and immediately after important system modifications, such as installing a new central hard disk. Be sure to make partial backups for frequently changing file systems and directories on a regular basis. Making an incremental backup at least once during each working day will almost always prove worth the effort.

Storage Media

The system administrator has a wide variety of choices when it comes to backup storage media. Choosing the appropriate storage medium (or media) for your installation makes the backup process more convenient, and consequently increases the possibility that the backups will actually be done and done correctly. Popular choices include floppy disk, cartridge tape, and DAT tapes.

Floppy Disk   Floppy disks are a convenient medium for incremental backups, particularly for single-user UnixWare systems. They are inexpensive, offer a familiar technology, and are extremely portable. (Their portability can be a disadvantage from the security point of view.) However, because of their relatively tiny storage capacity (usually a maximum of 1.44MB, but 2.88 MB diskettes are gaining in popularity), floppy disks are not a serious option for complete system backups, even for single-user UnixWare systems. When their storage capacity increases substantially, floppy disks will become a more important storage option for all types of backups.

Cartridge Tape   Most workstations and many microcomputer-based Unix systems rely on cartridge tape as a backup media. Although more expensive than floppy disk drives, cartridge tape units are not costly, especially when you consider the time they save, and the cost of missed backups. Use cartridge tape for incremental backups of any system and for full backups of single-user UnixWare systems.

DAT Tapes   DAT (digital audio) tapes were originally developed for recording music. Given their high data-transfer rates and extensive storage capacity, they have become an important data storage medium. Present models store up to 2 gigabytes (GB) of uncompressed data, and up to 8GB of compressed data. They read and write data sequentially, but work is progressing on similar media able to access data randomly.

Using the Desktop

When backing up data from the Desktop, configure the Backup application and then select an immediate or a scheduled backup. Decision tables follow to help in planning. Once your selections are made, step-by-step procedures will lead you through the application. Each function description follows.

Before you configure the backup to a file, you may need to consider file size. If error messages appear concerning size limitations, refer to the *System Owner Handbook* for instructions on changing your system's limit size.

Launching a backup is easy: Either double-click on the Backup-Restore icon in the Admin Tools folder or double-click on the Disk-etc icon in the UnixWare Desktop. This generates the window shown in Figure 10-1.

Configuring the Backup

Besides the storage media, there are two other decisions you must make before starting a backup: class and type. Although these two words are practically synonyms, in UnixWare they mean different things. *Class* determines whose files

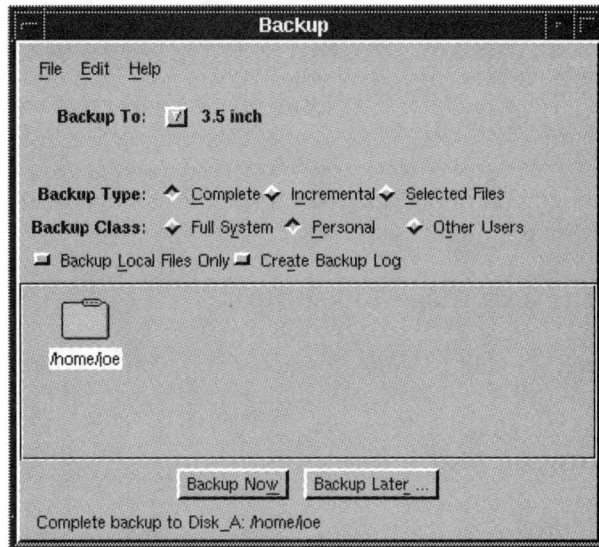

FIGURE 10-1. *The Backup window*

systems will be backed up; type determines what files on those file systems will be backed up.

The following Backup Type options are available:

- ■ **Complete**   Backs up all files.

- ■ **Incremental**   Backs up only files that have changed since the last backup.

- ■ **Selected Files**   Backs up specific files and folders. After selecting this option, open the folder containing the specified files or folders. Drag and drop the file and folder icons into the box at the bottom of the Backup window. Users with system owner permission can employ the Backup Class option to specify multiple files and folders for backup instead of specifying them individually.

> **NOTE**
> Select Exclude from the Edit menu to remove a file from the selected file set.

- ■ **Full System**   Backs up all the files from the root folder. This option is not recommended. Instead, back up the entire system using the Emergency Recovery procedures described later in this chapter.

- ■ **Personal** Backs up files in your home folder.
- ■ **Other Users** Backs up files in another user's home folder. Selecting this option displays a Backup: User List with the name of configured users on your system.

One final configuration option, Backup Local Files Only prevents you from backing up files located on a remote system.

Backing Up Files to a Cartridge Tape or to Diskettes

Once you have selected your backup media, backup type, and backup class as described previously, all you need to do is insert the media and choose Backup Now. You can also schedule the backup for a later time, as described in "Scheduling a Backup" later in this chapter.

CAUTION
Label and number your media when backing up to multiple diskettes or tapes.

Backing Up Files to a NetWare File Server

Many people like to back up their files to the network file server. If you do so, use the Task Scheduler to schedule backups during periods of reduced network activity. Make sure that you don't conflict with the file server's maintenance schedule.

If you schedule backups, you must be authenticated to the server. Authenticate to a server by double-clicking on the NetWare icon on the desktop and then double-clicking on that server. An authentication window appears. Enter your login ID and password.

To backup files on a NetWare file server, you follow the same procedures as you do for disk or tape, except you must select File on the Backup To option. The Target File field will appear. In it you enter the location on the file server where the backup will reside, such as:

```
/.NetWare/myfileserv.nws/docs/systemA.backup
```

The **.NetWare** indicates that it is a NetWare file server; **myfileserv.nws** is the file server name; **docs** is the directory name, and **systemA.backup** is the name of the file to receive the backup. This file is created by Backup/Restore.

Scheduling a Backup

Often it makes more sense to run a backup in the middle of the night, when you are not there to monitor it. UnixWare lets you schedule a backup for a later time. Follow these steps:

1. Click on Backup Later (instead of Backup Now) at the bottom of the Backup window. You'll see the Task Scheduler: Add Task window shown in Figure 10-2.

2. Insert your media (tape or diskette).

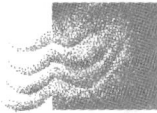

CAUTION
The system will notify you if the inserted media contains any files. You can change media or overwrite existing data.

3. Enter the exact time (in 24-hour format) for the backup to begin or click in the Time box and use the arrows to change the time.

4. Select Specific Day or Specific Date(s) on the On setting. Both have pop-up menus. For example, to back up every Friday at 4:30 p.m., enter **16:30** in the Time field. Choose Specific Day and select Friday from the pop-up menu.

5. Use the setting Perform Task for frequent backups. Click on Every Hour to run the backup at hour increments, or schedule the backup time using At Specific Times above.

6. Click on Add Task at the bottom of the menu to create the backup task.

7. Click on File in the menu bar and select Save to save the task and close the window.

If you want to change a backup after it has been modified, select the task and use the Properties option from the Edit menu.

If you need to cancel a scheduled backup, select the task and use the Delete command from the Edit menu.

Using Backup Scripts

If you regularly back up the same files, create a *backup script* with the list of files you want to back up and the selected backup options.

Starting from a configured Backup window, choose the Save As command from the File menu. Then enter the name of the file that will contain the list of backed

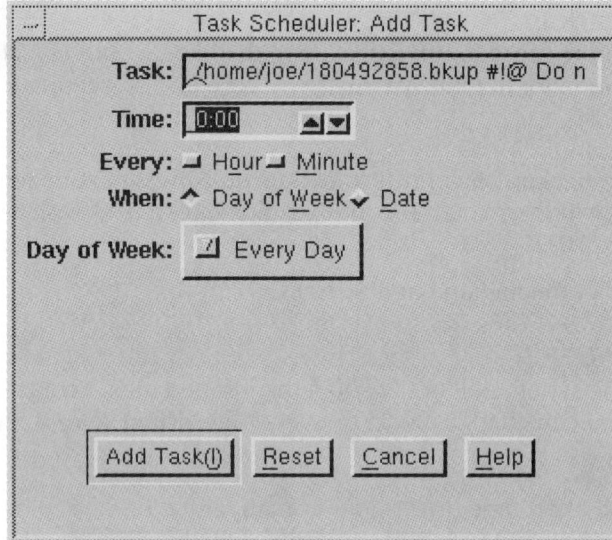

FIGURE 10-2. *The Task Scheduler: Add Task window*

up files, and choose Save. This script includes options selected in the Backup window and has the extension **.bkup**.

To run a backup script that has been saved, use the Open command in the File menu. Select the name of the script you want, and choose Open.

Command Line Backups

UnixWare provides several commands for file backups. These include the **backup** command, available in a basic and extended version, and the **cpio** and **tar** commands, which are used for both backups, restores, and even copies.

The backup Command
UnixWare comes with two backup facilities: the basic version and the extended version. Basic backup commands are adequate for most small machines and machines running a minimal amount of software. The basic backup command is delivered in the Personal Edition. The extended backup command is delivered in the Application Server version.

NOTE
Some basic backup commands may be executed by all users. Only a privileged user may execute the extended **backup** command.

The **backup** command initiates or controls a system backup session. It has the following syntax (see the manual to determine which options may coexist):

```
backup options
```

The valid options are summarized here:

- **-d** Device specifies the device to be used.
- **-f** File backups files specified by the files argument; the files argument must be in quotes.
- **-h** Produces a history of backups.
- **-p** Performs a partial (known as incremental) backup.
- **-u** Performs a backup of a user's home directory.
- **-w** Performs a complete backup.

The extended version has all the options just listed and these additional options as well:

- **-s** During a backup operation, displays a "**.**" for each 100 (512 byte) blocks transferred to the destination device.
- **-m *user*** Sends mail to the named ***user*** when all backup operations are completed.
- **-C** Cancels backup jobs.
- **-R** Resumes suspended backup jobs.
- **-A** Controls backup jobs for all users.
- **-S** Suspends backup jobs.

Without options, the **backup** command performs all backup operations specified for the current day and week of the backup rotation in the backup register. This set of backup operations is considered a single job and is assigned a backup job ID, which is useful for controlling the backup's progress. As backup operations are completed, they are recorded in the history log. A backup job can be canceled, suspended, or resumed.

NOTE
Backup operations may require operator intervention for such tasks as inserting volumes into devices or confirming proper volume labels.

NOTE
The **backup** command with no options assumes that an operator is present, at a terminal other than where the **backup** command was issued.

backup -i establishes interactive mode, which assumes that an operator is present at the terminal where the **backup** command was issued.

The cpio Command
The **cpio** command (when used for file backup) has the following syntax:

```
cpio -o backup_options
cpio -o (copy out)
```

(The **cpio** command is also used for file restoration, as discussed in the "File Restoration" section.) Above, the **cpio** command reads standard input to obtain a list of pathnames and copies those files onto standard output together with pathname and status information. The major backup options are listed here:

- **-B** Blocks input/output 5,120 bytes to the record.
- **-c** Writes header information in ASCII character form for portability.

TIP
Always use the **-c** option when origin and destination machines are different types.

- **-C bufsize** Blocks input/output with **bufsize** number of bytes per record. The default buffer size is 512 bytes when this and **-B** option are not used.
- **-d** Creates directories as needed.
- **-m** Retains previous file modification time. This option is ineffective on directories that are being copied.
- **-v** Causes a list of filenames to be printed. When used with the **-t** option (table of contents), it looks like the output of an **ls -l** command.

The following example illustrates a **cpio** command for file backup:

```
find . -print | cpio - ocvB > ctape1
```

This example finds all files in the current directory, and pipes these filenames to **cpio**, which backs them up to a tape device.

The tar Command

The **tar** command archives files. It has the following syntax:

```
tar [ key ] [ files ]
```

tar backs up and restores files to and from an archive medium, typically a floppy disk or tape. Its actions are controlled by the **key** argument, a set of options that can be prefaced with a hyphen. Other command arguments are files or directory names that specify the files to be backed up or restored. A directory name refers to the files and all subdirectories for that directory.

A single letter specifies the **key** function portion. These are the most commonly used letters for file backup:

- **t**   Lists names of specified files whenever they occur on the archive. If no **files** argument is given, all names on the archive are listed.

- **c**   Creates a new archive; it writes from the archive's beginning, not after the last file.

- **v**   Displays the name of each file treated, preceded by the function letter and additional information.

- **b**   Defines the next argument as the blocking factor for archive records.

See the "File Restoration" section later in this chapter for information on using **tar** as a restore command.

> **CAUTION**
> A critical consideration when creating a **tar** volume is the use of absolute or relative pathnames. Absolute pathnames specify the file location relative to the root directory (/); relative pathnames are relative to the current directory. Take pathnames into account when making a **tar** tape or disk. Backup volumes use absolute pathnames so that they can be restored to the proper directory. Use relative pathnames when creating a **tar** volume where absolute pathnames are unnecessary.

Consider the following **tar** command examples:

```
tar cv /home/arrow_tar
tar cv ./arrow
```

The first command creates a **tar** volume with the absolute pathname: **/home/arrow**. The second yields a **tar** volume with a relative pathname: **./arrow**. (The **./** is implicit and shown here as an example. **./** should not be specified when retrieving the file from the archive.) When restored, the first example writes the file **arrow** to the directory **/home** (if it exists and you have write permission), no matter what your working directory. The second example writes the file **arrow** to your present working directory.

File Restoration

Needless to say, file backup without file restoration is of no value. UnixWare provides file restore services for authorized users at three levels: from the Desktop, from the sysadm interface, and from the command line.

Using the Desktop

To restore files, first configure the Restore utility and then choose the backup files you wish to restore. Each function is described in the next section.

Configuring Restore

Starting from the Admin Tools window, follow these steps to start the Restore application:

1. If the backup file is on diskette or cartridge tape, insert the backup media.

2. Right-click on the Backup-Restore icon and select Restore. You'll see a window similar to that shown in Figure 10-3.

3. Select your backup media from the Restore From Setting. If your backup file is on hard disk or on a NetWare file server, enter the filename in the Target File field.

4. Click on Overwrite files if they exist to replace current Desktop files with files from your Restore medium.

CAUTION
If the Desktop files have changed since the last backup, this option must not be enabled or you will lose your changes.

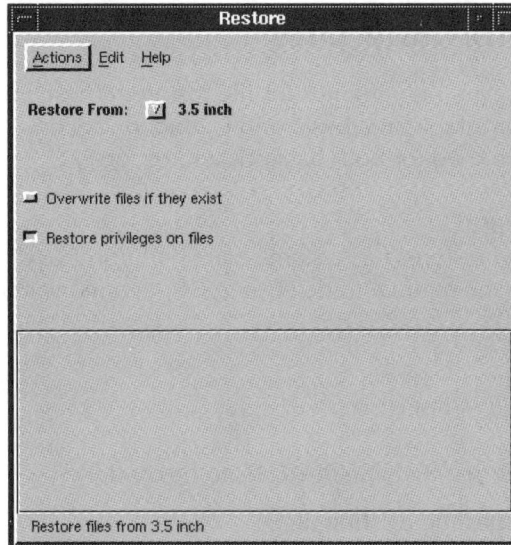

FIGURE 10-3. *Restore window*

Selecting Files

Starting from the Restore window, follow these steps to select and restore files from a diskette or tape:

1. Choose the Show Files command from the Actions menu. The window displays the files to be restored.

2. Click once on the name of each file you want to restore. The file is highlighted. If you want to restore all files, use the Select All command from the Edit menu.

3. Select Restore from the Actions menu.

UnixWare displays a progress window as the files are restored.

> **NOTE**
> The system alerts you if multiple tapes or diskettes are required. Insert them in the order in which they were created.

Using the Command Line

UnixWare provides several commands for file restores. These include the **restore** command, which is available in a basic and extended version, and the **cpio** and **tar** commands, which are used for both backups and restores.

The restore Command

The **restore** command restores file systems, data partitions, or disks. It has the following syntax (see the manual to determine which options may coexist):

```
restore options
```

These are the valid options:

- **-T** Indicates that the tape device is to be used.
- **-O** Overwrites the existing file.
- **-W** *device* *device* is the device special pathname to be used; defaults to **/dev/rdsk/f0**.
- **-i** Retrieves the index file.
- **-w** Performs a complete restore.

The extended version has all the options just listed and these additional options:

- **-d** *date* Restores the partition as of *date*.
- **-m** *user* Sends mail to the named *user* when all restore operations are completed.
- **-s** During a restore operation, displays a "**.**" for each 100 (512 byte) blocks transferred from the destination device.
- **-A** Initiates restore of the entire disk.
- **-P** Initiates restore of the data partition.
- **-S** Initiates restore of the file system partition.
- **-O** Overwrites existing files.

UnixWare comes with two restore facilities, the basic version and the extended version. Basic **restore** commands are adequate for most small machines and machines running a minimal amount of software.

> **NOTE**
> Some basic **restore** commands may be executed by all users.
> The extended **restore** command may be executed only by a
> privileged user.

The Extended Restore Facility posts requests to restore a data partition, a file-system partition, or a disk from most system-maintained archives. If the appropriate archive containing the required partition is online, the partition is restored immediately. If not, a restore request is posted to a restore status table, **/etc/bkup/rsstatus.tab**.

The following examples show how the extended **restore** command is applied:

```
restore -S -m /usr
```

This command posts a request to restore the most current archived version of **/usr**. If the restore cannot be done immediately, the invoking user is notified when the request has been completed.

```
restore -P -o /dev/rdsk/* /dev/rdsk/y
```

This command posts a request that the archived data partition **/dev/rdsk/y** be restored to the target device partition **/dev/rdsk/***, where the value of * and *y* are machine specific.

```
restore -A -d "july 15, 1994" /dev/rdsk/*
```

This command posts a request for the restoration of the entire disk **/dev/rdsk/***, where the value of * is machine-specific. The restore will be made as of July 15, 1994.

The cpio Command

When used for file restorations, the **cpio** command has the following syntax:

```
cpio -o restore_options
cpio -i (copy in)
```

This command extracts files from the standard input, which is assumed to have been created by a previous backup (**cpio -o**) as discussed in the "File Backup" section earlier in this chapter.

NOTE
If **cpio -i** tries to create a file that already exists and the existing file is the same age or newer, **cpio** issues a warning message and does not replace the file.

These are the major options:

■ **-B**   Blocks input/output to the tune of 5,120 bytes to the record.

■ **-c**   Writes header information in ASCII character form for portability.

TIP
Always use the **-c** option when origin and destination machines are different types.

■ **-C bufsize**   Blocks input/output with a positive integer number of bytes per record. The default buffer size is 512 bytes when this and the **-B** option are not used.

■ **-d**   Creates directories as needed.

■ **-m**   Retains the previous file modification time. This option is ineffective on directories that are being copied.

■ **-v**   Prints a list of filenames. When used with the **-t** option (table of contents), produces output like that of an **ls -l** command.

The following example illustrates a **cpio** command for file restoration:

```
cpio - icdmB /usr/target/arrow < ctape1
```

This example extracts the **arrow** file from the backup tape.

The tar Command
The **tar** command archives files. It has the following syntax:

```
tar [ key ] [ files ]
```

tar saves and restores files to and from an archive medium, typically a floppy disk or tape. Its actions are controlled by the **key** argument, a set of options that can be prefaced with a hyphen. Other command arguments are **files** or directory names specifying the files to be backed up or restored. A directory name refers to the files and all subdirectories for that directory.

A single letter specifies the key function portion. The most commonly used letters are described below:

- **x**   Extracts (restores) named files from the archive.

- **t**   Lists names of specified files whenever they occur on the archive. If no file argument is given, all names on the archive are listed.

- **c**   Creates a new archive; it writes from the archive's beginning, not after the last file.

- **v**   Displays the name of each file treated, preceded by the function letter and additional information.

- **b**   Defines the next argument as the blocking factor for archive records.

See the "File Backup" section earlier in this chapter for information on the use of **tar** as a backup command.

CAUTION
A critical consideration when creating a **tar** volume is the use of absolute or relative pathnames. Absolute pathnames specify the file location relative to the root directory (/); relative pathnames are relative to the current directory. Take pathnames into account when making a **tar** tape or disk. Backup volumes use absolute pathnames so that they can be restored to the proper directory. Use relative pathnames when creating a **tar** volume where absolute pathnames are unnecessary.

TIP
tar can move files on the directory tree. It allows you to replace archived files with a different version and to append new files to the end of the archive.

TIP
cpio has several advantages. It can back up files describing devices as well as data files. **cpio** tends to be faster than **tar** and also stores data more efficiently.

Emergency Recovery

Back up your system regularly. Depending on how much traffic you have on your system and how much work you and others do on it, back up daily or weekly. In case of disk failure or power interruption, data created after the most recent backup may be lost.

For emergency recovery, the Unix System partitions and—if it exists—the system partition are backed up. (Or, depending on the options chosen when the emergency recovery tape was created, your entire primary hard disk is backed up.) If you restore data using the emergency diskettes and tape, the Unix partition or entire hard disk is overwritten. The backup and restore method allows you to select what is backed up and restored but limits backups and restores to the user data files in your Unix partition.

NOTE
The emergency recovery feature also backs up the following file systems if they are mounted on the secondary disk: **/usr**, **/home**, and **/home2**. However, the emergency recovery feature does not back up any other file systems or partitions on the secondary disk. Use the **backup** or **restore** command to back up any additional file systems on the secondary disk.

To maintain maximum flexibility with minimal administrative overhead, create emergency recovery diskettes and tapes after your system software is installed. (If you later install additional software, create new emergency recovery diskettes and tapes.) Then, on a regular basis, back up user data as explained earlier in this chapter.

Emergency recovery diskettes contain different information than the emergency recovery tape; you will need both for disaster recovery.

Creating Emergency Recovery Diskettes

To create emergency recovery diskettes from the command line, follow these steps:

1. Enter **su** to become the root.

2. Insert a diskette in floppy disk drive 1 or floppy disk drive 2.

3. Select a working directory in a file system with at least 22MB of free space.

4. Enter **/sbin/emergency_disk -d** *pathname diskette*, where *pathname* is the working directory name and *diskette* is the floppy disk drive.

5. When prompted (after fifteen minutes or so), remove the first emergency recovery diskette, and insert the second diskette.

When finished, attach labels to both emergency recovery diskettes so that their function is clearly understood. Include the name of the system for which the diskettes were created and number the diskettes sequentially. Writing the system name on the labels is critical because a recovery diskette is customized for a particular system and works only on that system.

Creating Emergency Recovery Tapes

Before creating an emergency recovery tape, notify users on the system that you need to shut it down to perform a backup and that they should log off. Then follow these steps from the command line:

1. Enter **su** to become root.

2. Enter the command

   ```
   cd /
   /sbin/shutdown -I1 -y -g0
   ```

   to change the system state to single-user mode.

3. Insert a tape into cartridge drive 1 or cartridge drive 2.

4. Decide whether to back up the Unix and system partitions or to back up the entire primary hard disk. By default, the **emergency_rec** command backs up the UnixWare partition and system partition, if there is one, from the primary hard disk.

   If one or more of the **/home**, **/home2**, and **/usr** file systems are on a secondary hard disk, and if they are mounted file systems, **emergency_rec** also backs up these file systems. If more than one tape is needed to back up the data, you will be prompted to insert additional tapes.

   Optionally, you can have **emergency_rec** back up your entire primary hard disk. In this case, you must supply a single cartridge tape that is large enough to hold all the data to be backed up.

5. Create the emergency recovery tape(s). To back up the Unix and system partition, if they exist, enter **/sbin/emergency_rec *tape***, where *tape* is the tape drive location of the tape (**ctape1** or **ctape2**). If more than one tape is needed to back up your system, you will be prompted to insert more tapes. Wait for this command to finish processing.

6. To back up the entire primary hard disk, enter **/sbin/emergency_rec -e** *tape*, where *tape* is the tape drive location (**ctape1** or **ctape2**). Wait for this command to finish processing.

When finished, attach labels to each tape that clearly indicate their function. Include the name of the system and date, and number them sequentially. Writing the system name on the labels is critical because a recovery tape is customized for a particular system and works only on that system.

Restoring from Emergency Recovery Diskettes and Tapes

If your system will not boot, your system software is corrupted beyond repair, or your hard disk has been reformatted or replaced, you will need to use your emergency disks and tapes to recover.

1. Place the first emergency recovery diskette for the system in the boot disk drive and reboot your system.

2. If prompted, type the UnixWare serial number. Emergency diskettes are designed to reinstall software and data on a system and not to transfer data between systems. If the serial number prompt appears, the copy of UnixWare installed on your system is different from the copy used to create the emergency recovery diskettes.

If you mistakenly inserted the wrong diskette, replace the current diskette with the correct emergency diskette and repeat this procedure.

If you want to use this diskette, enter the ten-digit serial number for the version of UnixWare installed on your system. The UnixWare serial number is provided with the original UnixWare software. Entering the serial number confirms that you did not enter the wrong media.

3. Correct the system damage or restore data from the emergency recovery tape(s). The emergency recovery main menu provides options to start a limited UnixWare operating system command-line shell, to restore data from emergency recovery tapes, to mount or unmount all file systems (if UnixWare data is accessible on the hard disk), and to reboot the system.

4. If you invoke an emergency shell, a shell prompt is displayed and the following commands become available: **cat**, **chroot**, **cpio**, **date**, **dd**, **disksetup**, **echo**, **edvtoc**, **fdisk**, **find**, **fsck**, **ksh**, **labelit**, **ln**, **ls**, **mkdir**, **mkfs**, **mount**, **prtvtoc**, **rm**, **stty**, and **vi**. Use these commands to investigate and fix the problem. Then press the ESC key to return to the main menu.

CAUTION
The emergency recovery shell is designed for advanced users only.

5. If you choose to reinstall your system, insert the emergency recovery tape(s) when prompted to do so. Wait for the last tape to finish processing before going to step 4. If you choose to mount file systems, the UnixWare file systems are mounted. If you then invoke the emergency shell, you can access all the UnixWare commands on your system.

NOTE
Depending on the amount of damage to your hard disk, this option may not be available.

6. If you select to unmount file systems, the UnixWare file systems are unmounted. Depending on the amount of damage to your hard disk, this option may not be available.

7. If you select to reboot your system, the system reboots. If you used the emergency recovery shell to repair your system, remove the second emergency recovery diskette from the disk drive and then select this option to reboot your system.

If you created full or incremental backups of your system after creating the emergency recovery tape(s), restore those backups using the standard backup and restore facilities presented earlier in this chapter.

Fixing File Systems with fsck

File systems sometimes go bad. UnixWare offers several tools for checking and repairing them but the primary tool is the **fsck** program. Mastering the **fsck** command is necessary to keep the file system (and consequently the computer system) in working order.

The **fsck** (file system check) program uncovers and repairs file system inconsistencies. System administrators should use it on a regular basis. Unlike many other commands, **fsck** is interactive. Whenever it runs into a potential problem, it asks you to choose from alternatives that it provides.

CAUTION
The wrong choice can cause substantial damage to your file system.

When **fsck** detects a problem with a given inode, run the **ncheck** command to determine the associated filename.

The fsck Phases

Before examining this command in detail, let's examine the command's phases. The **fsck** program executes in eight well-defined phases. Each phase carries out specific tasks and may generate error messages. You must respond to these error messages before proceeding to the next phase. Appendix B lists these error messages and tells you what actions your response to each will generate.

- **Initialization Phase**   This phase invokes the command-line options and opens the special device file. It compares the total file system size to the sizes in the inode list. If the total file system size is less than the sizes in the inode list, the superblock is corrupted.

- **Phase 1 - Check Blocks and Sizes**   This phase checks the inodes for valid size, file type, and block addresses, and for a nonzero link count.

- **Phase 2 - Check Pathnames**   This phase checks all directory entries, starting with the root, for a valid inode as determined in phase 1. It completes the link counts for each inode.

- **Phase 3 - Check Connectivity**   This phase may create a directory entry for a directory type inode that presently is not connected to any directory.

- **Phase 4 - Check Reference Counts**   This phase may create directory entries for inodes whose type is not directory.

- **Phase 5 - Check Free List**   This phase checks the validity of the free list, making sure that no block addresses appear in the inodes. Except for bad blocks, all blocks in the file system must be in the free block list or be allocated to an inode.

- **Phase 6 - Salvage Free Block List**   This phase reconstructs the free block list.

- **Cleanup Phase**   After checking a file system, **fsck** performs a few cleanup functions.

The fsck Syntax and Options

fsck audits and interactively repairs inconsistent conditions for all supported file systems. If the file system is consistent, it reports the number of files, number of blocks used, and number of free blocks. If the file system is inconsistent, the operator is prompted for permission to attempt each correction.

> **CAUTION**
> Most corrective actions result in some loss of data. The amount and severity of the data loss may be determined from the diagnostic output. The file system should be unmounted when **fsck** is used. If this is impossible, be sure that the system is quiescent and reboot it immediately afterward, in the case of a critical file system such as root.

The s5 specific version of **fsck** has the following syntax:

```
fsck [-F s5] [generic_options] [special_device ...]
fsck [-F FSType] [-V] [generic_options] [-y] [-n] [-sX] [-SX]
     [-tfile] \ [-l] [-q] [-D] [-f] [special_device ...]
```

These are the major options:

- **-F**   Specifies the FSType to be constructed.

- **-V**   Echoes the complete command line, but does not execute the command.

- **-m**   Checks whether the file system is suitable for mounting, but doesn't make repairs.

- **-o**   Specifies FSType-specific options.

> **CAUTION**
> When **fsck** removes bad blocks, it does so silently, so you won't know which blocks to restore.

Important Points about Using fsck

Consider the following points with respect to **fsck**:

■ Run this program on a regular basis when there are no active UnixWare users, such as nights and weekends.

■ Run this program only on unmounted file systems.

■ Do not use the **-q** or **-y** option.

■ Let **fsck** do it. Answer **y** to most questions except as they relate to (1) the **lost+found** directory and (2) DUP TABLE overflow. In the first case, fix the **lost+found** directory manually and then rerun **fsck**. In the second case, **fsck** terminates when you answer **n**. Regenerate **fsck** with a larger table size (see your system manual for details). Rerun **fsck**.

■ Keep a record of files deleted in Phase 2 (Check Pathnames). You may have to restore these files from backups.

■ If **fsck** finds and corrects any errors, run it again to be sure that the file system is clean.

Errors Running fsck

fsck generates different error messages at each phase of its operation. Unless you run it with the **-y** option (which is not recommended), it waits for your response before continuing its operation. See Appendix B for a description of these errors.

Associated Commands

When checking and repairing file systems, system administrators make extensive use of the **fsck** command. However, they should also be familiar with the **ncheck** and **fsdb** commands. The **ncheck** command generates names from inode numbers. The **fsdb** command is a file-system debugger used for the manual repair of a file system after a crash. It is intended for experienced users only. Consult the manual for detailed command descriptions.

CHAPTER 11

Monitoring and Tuning the System

As system administrator, you are responsible for running the UnixWare system. You must make sure that the system doesn't crawl, stumble, or sputter. Above all, you must see that it serves all users effectively, efficiently, and equitably. Perhaps the best news is that system administrators usually don't have to do much system tuning. However, they must be familiar with the process. The system tuning process consists of two basic steps. First you determine the specific performance flaw or inequity, and then you change the appropriate system parameters.

Monitoring System Performance

The two major Desktop interfaces that let you see exactly what your system is doing are the System Status utility and the System Monitor window. These interfaces are available to all users. In addition, the system owner or root can monitor the system from the command line. System statistics can be displayed graphically or saved to a log file for further analysis. You can set thresholds so that an alarm sounds when a resource is nearing a specific limit.

The System Status Utility

Precise information about your UnixWare system is available from the System Status utility in the Admin Tools folder. You'll use this utility primarily to view read-only system information, but you also can use it to set the system clock, change the time zone, and change disk monitoring frequency.

To use the System Status utility, double-click on the System Status icon in the Admin Tools folder. The System Status window appears, as shown in Figure 11-1. The window displays the following information:

- The UnixWare version number
- Your network node name (the name by which other machines recognize your machine)
- Your UnixWare login ID (user account)
- The current date and time
- The time zone
- The amount of memory installed in your system
- The type of math coprocessor chip installed, if any
- The size of each floppy disk drive and cartridge tape drive
- The total space in megabytes of each file system
- The amount of disk space used in each file system, represented by the slider bar and the number above the bar

If the system clock is incorrect, choose the Properties command from the Actions menu. Change the year, month, date, hour, minute, and time zone either by entering new values or clicking the up/down arrows. Use the Update Clock

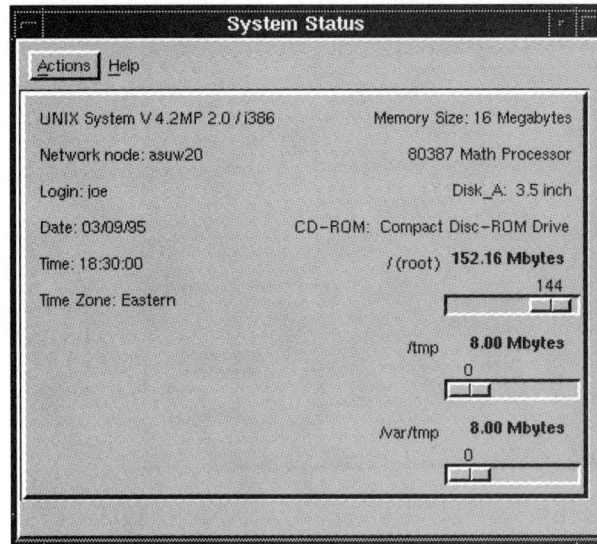

FIGURE 11-1. *The System Status window*

Every field to determine how often time displayed in the System Status window is updated.

　To change how often the disk space is monitored (and the resulting information updated), modify the value in the Check Disks Every field. Obviously you don't want to set this value too small or the system will spend more time evaluating disk space than accessing it.

The System Monitor Window

The System Monitor window displays graphs that describe system activity, including how heavily the CPU is being used, how much RAM is available, how much disk space is available, and how often the system uses disk swap space for virtual memory. To display the System Monitor window, shown in Figure 11-2, double-click on the System Monitor icon in the Admin Tools window.

　The graph at the top of the System Monitor window contains colored lines that each represent a selected system monitor option. The initial window will have all options disabled. The chart is updated to reflect changes in monitored values. By default, the monitored values are updated every five seconds. If you

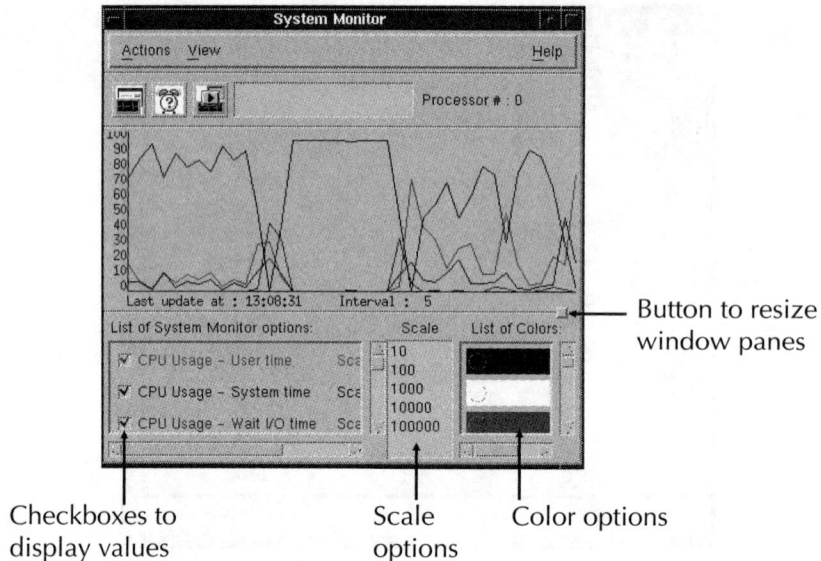

FIGURE 11-2. *The System Monitor window*

want to start monitoring system CPU usage, for example, you would check the appropriate option.

> **NOTE**
> Descriptions of System Monitor options are contained in the **sar** manual page of the Command Reference.

You can change the graph parameters as follows:

■ **Resize within the window**   Click on the small square toward the right side of the line dividing the top and bottom sections of the window. Hold the mouse button and move up or down to increase the top or bottom area.

■ **Turn display on or off**   In the List of System Monitor options area, click the check button next to each option to display or not display different types of information on the chart.

■ **Change colors**   Click on an option and then click on the color you want to apply to it from the List of Colors box at the right side of the window.

■ **Change scale**   Click on any number from the Scale box in the middle of the window to change the scale for the selected option.

CAUTION
The scale for the four CPU Usage options cannot be changed. They are presented only as percentages.

Other options are available from the Options command in the Actions menu:

■ **Interval**   Changes the frequency (in seconds) with which the System Monitor checks system resource usage.

■ **Vertical Grid**   Toggles the display of vertical lines in the graph pane of the window.

■ **Horizontal Grid**   Toggles the display of horizontal lines in the graph pane of the window.

■ **Processor #**   Lets you change processors for multiprocessor systems.

TIP
When you have changed the windows to suit your preferences, you may want to use the Save Settings command in the Actions menu.

From within the System Monitor window, you can run commands to log monitoring data or set monitoring alarms using either the menu bar or the toolbar.

Logging Monitored Data

If you have been a system administrator for any period of time, you already know that the most common complaint from users is, "The system is SLOW today." Part of your job is to determine whether it is unusually slow. If it is, find what's causing the slowness. The ability to log monitored data is the key to accessing information that will tell you why the system is slow. Think of logging data as similar to using a videotape recorder. First you record what you see on the screen, then you play it back.

To start recording, run the Log data to file... command from the Actions menu. When prompted, enter the name of the file that will contain the recording. By default, the log file is **sys_mon.log.0** in your home directory.

NOTE
If the file exists, specify whether to overwrite it or add the log data to it.

When you have gathered enough data, use the Stop logging data command from the Actions menu. To play back logged data, select the Playback log data... command from the Actions menu. Select the name of the file to play it, and watch as the graphs are updated in playback mode. Suppose you're trying to determine whether you need to purchase an additional Applications server—to go from, say, two servers to three. You could monitor the CPU usage of the two existing machines for several days, logging the data to a file. Then you can playback the data to confirm for yourself (or prove to your boss) that the existing servers are 100 percent utilized most of the day.

Setting System Monitor Alarms

Wouldn't it be great to know when there's less than a megabyte of free space on disk? You could actually do something about it before there's *no* free space and everyone is in a panic. Monitor alarms give you this ability; they inform you when system values cross predefined limits for selected resources.

To set (or change) an alarm, select the Alarms command from the View menu. This will generate the Alarm Setup window, shown in Figure 11-3. Enter specific values in either the Alarm Above or Alarm Below box. If the resource becomes greater than the specified maximum or less than the specified minimum, an alarm icon appears next to the options list in the main window. Be sure to select values that give you enough time to react to the alarm. For example, you might want to create an alarm for swap space. Without the alarm, you might not be aware of a problem until you are completely out of space. If the alarm is set for 4000 free blocks, you'll probably ignore it. Set the alarm to 1000 free blocks, however, and you probably won't ignore it, plus you'll still have time to pinpoint the problem and/or increase the size of the swap space.

There are two possible machine reactions to an alarm:

- **Beep**   Causes the System Monitor to beep if the selected resource becomes greater than the specified maximum or less than the specified minimum.

- **Flash Header**   Causes the selected option to flash on the main window if the resource becomes greater than the specified maximum or less than the specified minimum.

Monitoring from the Command Line

UnixWare 2.0 offers excellent facilities for monitoring the system from the Desktop. However, if you prefer you can enter commands from the Terminal window to find out exactly what the system is doing. This section briefly discusses major system

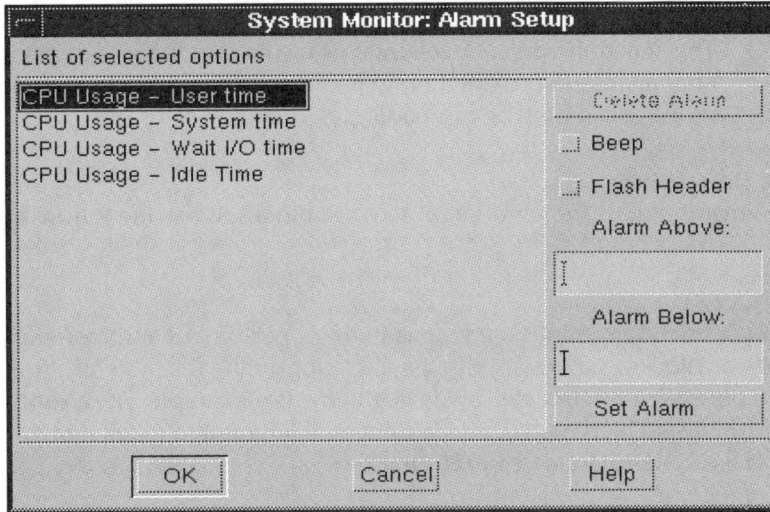

FIGURE 11-3.   *The Alarm Setup window*

reporting commands. See the **man** pages to get the details on these and other commands.

Displaying Process Status

The **ps** command reports process status. It has the following syntax:

```
ps [ options ]
```

ps prints selected information about active processes. **ps** without options describes processes associated with the current terminal. The default is a short listing of the process ID, terminal (tty) identifier, cumulative execution time, and the command name. The following major options may be used:

- **-e**   Prints information about all processes.

- **-f**   Generates a full listing. **ps** tries to determine and print the process's original command name and arguments. If it cannot, it prints the short listing version of the command name within square brackets. A full listing contains more than a dozen column headings.

- **-l**   Generates a long listing, including status, priority, location, and memory-usage information for each process.

NOTE
The situation can change while **ps** is running; the picture it gives is only a close approximation to reality. Ignore data printed for defunct processes; it may be misleading.

Checking Disk Space

The **df** command reports the number of free disk blocks. It has the following syntax:

```
df [ -t ] [ -f ] [ -v -i ] [ file systems ]
```

The **df** command examines the counts in the super-blocks and then prints the number of free blocks and free inodes available for online file systems. You can specify the **file systems** parameter by device name (for example, **/dev/root**). If this parameter is not specified, you'll get statistics for all mounted file systems. The list of mounted file systems appears in **/etc/mnttab**.

Options include:

- **-t**   Prints total allocated blocks as well as total free blocks.
- **-f**   Prints only the actual count of blocks in the free list and not free inodes. With this option, **df** reports on raw devices.
- **-v**   Prints the percent of blocks used, the number of blocks used, and the number of free 512-byte blocks.
- **-i**   Prints the percent of inodes used, the number of inodes used, and the number of free inodes. The **-v** and **-i** options may be used together but may not be used with other **df** options.

There is an anomaly you should be aware of: UnixWare divides file systems into 1024-byte groups, or blocks, whereas the **df** utility reports sizes in 512-byte blocks. If you create a file with only one character in it, **df** will report two blocks less free space, rather than one block less, since the file uses one system block of 1024 bytes.

Monitoring Disk Usage

The **du** command summarizes disk usage by directory. It is especially useful in determining which users are consuming the largest amount of disk space, possibly indicating that they need to clean up their home directories. It has the following syntax:

```
du [ -afrsu ] [ names ]
```

The **du** command gives the number of blocks in all files and directories recursively within each directory and file specified by the ***names*** argument. The block count includes indirect file blocks. If ***names*** is missing, the current directory is used. **du** is normally silent about directories that cannot be read, files that cannot be opened, etc. The options are defined as follows:

- **-s**   Generates only the grand total (for each specified name).

- **-a**   Generates an entry for each file. If neither **-s** nor **-a** is coded, **du** generates an entry for each directory only.

- **-f**   Displays file usage in the current file system only. It ignores directories containing mounted file systems.

- **-u**   Ignores files with more than one link.

- **-r**   Generates messages for directories that cannot be read and files that cannot be opened. A file with two or more links is only counted once.

NOTE
Unless the **-a** option is used, files included in names are ignored. If there are too many distinct linked files, **du** will count the excess files more than once. Files with holes will cause an incorrect block count. This utility reports sizes in 512-byte blocks. **du** interprets one block from a 1024-byte block system as two of its own 512-byte blocks. Thus a 500-byte file is interpreted as two blocks rather than one.

Monitoring Swap Space

Real memory is usually in short supply. If it is filled with system processes, UnixWare must swap (or move) idle processes to disk so that memory can be used for active processes.

Swap space is located in a separate disk area on your UnixWare partition. The swap space required depends on system use. A typical UnixWare Desktop session uses about 8MB of swap space. When running DOS on the desktop, for example, each DOS session requires 4.5MB of swap space per user. Windows uses 7.5MB of swap space per session. Users running many processes, in particular graphical processes, usually require additional swap space.

TIP
If an application such as Windows does not start when double-clicked, the problem may be insufficient swap space. Check the Message Monitor for messages about running out of memory.

To determine swap space usage, enter the **/usr/sbin/swap -s** command. The output may be similar to the following:

```
total: 21504 allocated + 3320d reserved = 28424d blocks used, 24912d blocks
       available
```

To determine the number of megabytes of swap space available, divide the number of blocks available (24912 in the example) by 2048 (equal to 12MB of free swap space in this example).

To determine the total amount of swap space in blocks, add the number of blocks used to the number of blocks available (28424 + 24912 = 53336, in this example). Divide this number by 2048 (for 2K blocks) to determine the total number of megabytes of swap space (about 26MB in this example).

Tuning System Performance

Upscale products such as high-performance cars must be tuned from time to time to obtain maximum performance. UnixWare does too. However, because system administrators have so many duties, and because the system-tuning process takes the system out of use for a period of time, system administrators do not tune the system often. Although it is a bit of an exaggeration, the familiar phrase "If it ain't broke, don't fix it" applies. Consider tuning the system under the following circumstances:

- **When setting up the system** As it comes out of the box, UnixWare is configured to meet general needs. Sites with special needs should change parameters to increase system efficiency. For example, sites with very large databases may increase the default number of file locks. On the other hand, sites that definitely do not require facilities such as UUCP might increase performance slightly by disabling them.

- **When adding system resources** When you add a disk drive or a line printer, you must reconfigure the system to recognize the new unit. When you add memory, reconfigure the system to optimize its use.

- **When the system "always" runs slowly** Be careful before making changes. According to most users, the system always runs too slowly.

- **When the system generates errors** Error messages often indicate failing hardware, insufficient network resources, or incorrectly configured software. Correcting these problems will obviously improve system performance.

Everything your system does (running processes, reading files, saving data) uses part of your system's limited CPU, RAM, and disk-space resources. To prevent users or processes from consuming excessive resources, UnixWare uses *tunable parameters.*

Each tunable parameter is set to a specific value for the given system. For example, the MAXUP parameter defines the number of processes any system user (besides root) can execute simultaneously. Its default value is 60, but individual users may be assigned a maximum value between 15 and 60.

CAUTION
You can also change these parameters by using a text editor; however, this method is discouraged because the text editor will not stop you from entering erroneous or undesirable values.

Tuning from the Desktop

The UnixWare Desktop includes a System Tuner window for displaying or changing tunable parameters, a Message Monitor window for tracking system messages, and a Processor Setup window to maintain processors in a multiprocess environment.

Using the System Tuner
You may change literally dozens of parameters from the System Tuner window. For ease of modification, these parameters are divided into categories that you display by clicking on the category button at the top of the window.

Users with system owner permission can access the System Tuner window by double-clicking on the System Tuner window in the Admin Tools folder. This window is shown in Figure 11-4.

To change a tunable parameter, find its name by looking in the appropriate category. When you click on a parameter, its description and current value are displayed in the associated text boxes. To change a value, either enter the new value or move the slider bar near the bottom of the window until the value you want is displayed. Alternatively, click on auto (if it is available) to direct the system to select the value automatically.

When you choose OK to save the settings, the system asks if you want to rebuild the kernel now, a process that incorporates the changes into UnixWare. Click on Yes to rebuild it now or on No to rebuild it when you next boot the system.

TIP
Errors generated when rebuilding the system are stored in the **/tmp/kernel_status** file.

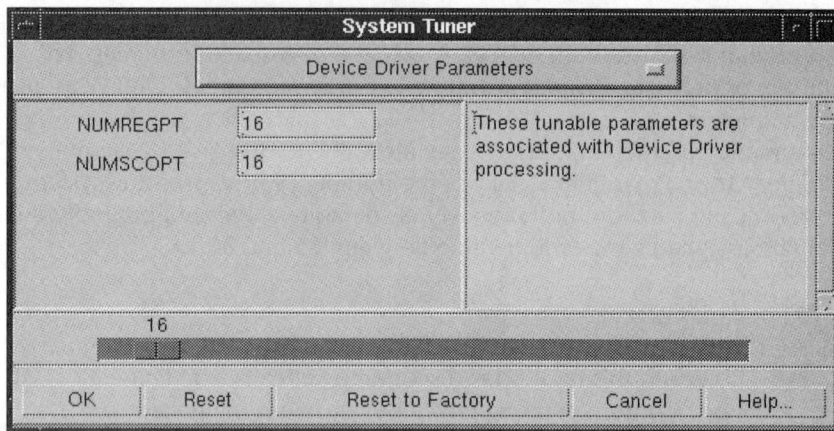

FIGURE 11-4.   *The System Tuner window*

Using the Message Monitor

UnixWare sends error messages, warnings, and kernel login information to the kernel messaging system and the system console. You can see these messages in the Message Monitor window.

TIP
Get in the habit of accessing the Message Monitor window. Not only is it useful for debugging programs, it also informs you of potential security breaches. For example, if an unauthorized person attempts to access the system, you can have the Message Monitor window alert you in one of several ways (described shortly).

Access the Message Monitor by double-clicking on the Message Monitor icon in the Applications folder. The Msg Monitor (Message Monitor) window, shown in Figure 11-5, displays the system name for the console log and any current messages.

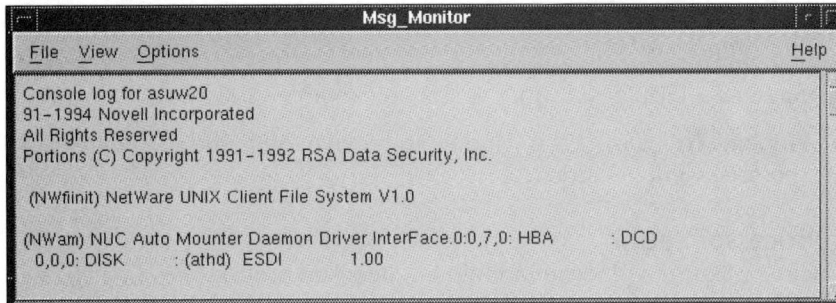

FIGURE 11-5.   *The Message Monitor window*

To save space or desktop clutter, you can minimize the Message Monitor window. To be alerted of new Message Monitor messages, select the Notification command from the Options menu. Then select one of the following:

■ **Deiconify**   The minimized Message Monitor window reappears when the next message arrives. This is the default method.

■ **Flash**   Small balloons on the iconized Message Monitor window blink when a new message arrives.

■ **Color Change**   Small balloons on the iconized Message Monitor window change to a solid color when the next message comes in and remain that way until a user views the messages.

■ **Off**   Ignore the arrival of a new message. The message appears the next time you open the window, but the icon neither changes nor opens on its own.

The arrival of a new message, after you minimize the window, launches the action you selected above. To clear messages from the Message Monitor window, use the Clear command from the View menu. To either save messages to a new file or add messages to an existing file, use one of the following commands from the File menu:

- **Save**   Saves the current messages to the last specified file. By default, the file **/tmp/osm/Log** is used.

- **Save As**   Displays a window so you can enter a different filename.

- **Append To**   Displays a window to receive the name of the file to which messages will be added.

Using Processor Setup

Use Processor Setup to place an additional, licensed processor online. To start Processor Setup, double-click on the Processor Setup icon in the Admin Tools folder. This window shows the number of processors attached, how many processors are licensed, and which processors are online.

> *CAUTION*
> The Change Processor Setup Permissions must be set to use all of the tasks in Processor Setup, as described in Chapter 7. The system owner automatically has permission to do this.

Use the Properties command from the Actions menu to view information for a selected processor. The following options are available:

- **Processor ID**   Displays the processor number.

- **State**   Displays whether the processor is online or offline.

- **Clock Speed**   Displays the processor clock speed.

- **Processor Type**   Displays the processor type, such as 486.

- **Floating Point Type**   Displays the name of the floating point processor.

To take a processor online or offline, click on the processor icon, and then click either the Online or Offline button.

Tuning from the Command Line

You can also modify several system parameters from the command line. This section describes the **ulimit** and **nice** commands.

Changing the Maximum Allowed File Size

The **ulimit** command sets the maximum size of a file that can be created or copied. This size restriction prevents processes from taking up too much disk space.

NOTE
The default file-system limit size also applies to the NUCFS.
See Chapter 14.

Use the following procedure to change your file size limit (for the current session only):

1. Log in as root or type **su** to become root.

2. Type **ulimit** to view your current limit in blocks.

3. Type **ulimit** *new_size* to set your limit to the new file size limit (in bytes).

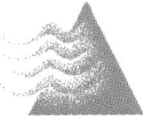

TIP
You can also set a limit in the **/etc/profile** or **/etc/default/login** file to make the setting permanent.

CAUTION
Set the **ulimit** to 8000000 or less. While a logged-in user may temporarily change this value to 99999999, setting this limit in your **/etc/profile** or **/etc/default/login** file may prevent you from logging in. The **ulimit** cannot exceed the values of the SFSZLIM and HFSZLIM tunable parameters.

Tuning Scheduling Priorities

When you want to run a job in the "background," or run a high-priority job, use the **nice** command to change the scheduling priority for the specified command.
It has the following syntax:

```
nice [ -increment ] command [ arguments ]
```

The **nice** command makes a specified ***command*** (with its ***arguments***) execute at a different scheduling priority than usual. Each process has a **nice** value used in calculating its priority. **nice** values range from 0 to 39; the higher the number, the lower the priority. The default **nice** value is 20. **nice** sets the **nice** value to 20 plus the ***increment***. If you have a set of files to delete, you can delete them at a lower priority (30) with the following command:

```
nice -10 rm *
```

The superuser may increase command priority by using a double negative increment. For example, an argument of **--8** decrements the default value and generates a **nice** value of 12. Users cannot give their jobs a higher priority.

The **nice** command returns the command exit status. A calculated nice value greater than 39 is set to 39. A calculated nice value less than 0 is set to 0.

NOTE
This description of **nice** applies only to programs run under the Bourne Shell. The C Shell has its own **nice** command, which is documented in the online help for **csh**.

PART 3

Networking

CHAPTER 12

Introduction to Networking

A few decades ago computer users relied solely on big mainframes—you had to be near the computer to use it, and when it failed, no one could get any work done. Networking and operating systems like Unix have let the industry *downsize*; now, instead of one big mainframe, a typical system can consist of several smaller machines linked together. This gives users the ability to spread themselves across the globe, and if one server is down people on other servers can still get work done. This chapter presents the basics of networking, including terminology and an introduction to network protocols and services. It concludes with a brief discussion of the major UnixWare networking commands.

CAUTION

Getting a network to run successfully requires a working knowledge of cables, telephone lines, and various types of connectors. As you might imagine, networks need not be isolated from each other. This rapidly evolving subject is discussed in many books, and of course in vendor manuals as well. Appendix C shows you how to connect UnixWare to a variety of computer systems and describes the network components of the small LAN used in developing this text.

Networking Fundamentals

The first step in dealing with networking is learning the basic terminology. This section introduces both new terms and communication protocols that will be explored in detail in later chapters.

Basic Terminology

If there is one area of computing in which newcomers are easily overwhelmed by the terminology, it's networking. Novices and pros alike complain about drowning in alphabet soup. For the sake of convenience, this chapter introduces only the networking terminology that you will need for the purposes of this book. As you become more proficient with networks, you'll find your vocabulary increases exponentially.

- **Network**   A computer network is two or more linked computers. The old-fashioned (but sometimes still useful) system composed of a mainframe computer assisted by a smaller computer dedicated to communications tasks (the front-end computer) and linked to dozens or hundreds of computer terminals is an example of a computer network. So is the state-of-the-art system connecting dozens of independently functioning computer systems.

- **Host**   A host is a computer attached to the computer network. The host may be of any size or level of processing power. As discussed in the following chapters, the network administrator assigns the host a name, an address, and possibly one or more aliases to meet the network's naming conventions.

- **Local area network (LAN)**   A local area network (LAN) is a network whose components are directly linked either by private communications lines or the public telephone system. In general, LANs extend over a distance of a kilometer or less and do not involve hardware that modifies the signal through boosting or filtering.

■ **Wide area network (WAN)**   A wide area network (WAN) is a network whose components are linked over a large distance (perhaps across a continent or across the ocean). WANs usually use the services of common carriers such as the public telephone system.

■ **Medium**   A medium is the path through which communications flow. Common communications media are shielded or unshielded copper wire (similar to traditional telephone lines known as twisted pair), coaxial cable, fiber optics cable, and air—the medium for microwave and satellite transmission.

■ **Protocol**   A protocol is the set of formal rules and conventions used when processes or hosts communicate. Until protocol signals have been exchanged and verified, communication may not take place. The following section introduces communications and file-transfer protocols.

■ **Message**   A message is a unit of information communicated from one location to another. Typically, a message consists of three parts: a message header indicating the start of the message and including control information such as source, destination, date, and time; message text, the actual information to be transmitted; and an end-of-message indicator.

■ **Packets**   Messages are broken up into sequences known as *packets*. Networking software uses packets to ensure accurate transmission of data. If a packet is not passed completely, only that particular packet needs to be retransmitted, rather than the entire message.

■ **Packet switching**   Packet switching is a type of message transmission in which packets are transmitted independently and then reassembled at the destination.

Protocols and Network Services

Efficient network performance requires correct selection of the network protocol. The use of an appropriate protocol increases file transfer speed and accuracy, while reducing the inevitable security risk. Consider the following protocols.

TCP/IP
TCP/IP is an abbreviation for *Transmission Control Protocol/Internet Protocol*. As the name indicates, the Internet network, the network that connects hundreds of thousands of computers across the globe, relies on TCP/IP. This protocol was originally developed for the ARPA (Advanced Research Projects Agency),

associated with the U.S. Department of Defense. In spite of its age (20 years), it remains a major data transmission protocol. TCP/IP provides reliable data transmission; in fact, the system guarantees that you will be notified if every byte transmitted doesn't reach its destination in the order that it was sent, without duplication or loss.

TCP/IP provides many commands so that users can access remote hosts. These commands include logging in to remote systems and transferring files across the network. Some TCP/IP commands are discussed later in this chapter.

UDP/IP

UDP/IP is an abbreviation for *User Datagram Protocol/Internet Protocol.* It is a fast way to transmit data packets between two or more programs but does not guarantee that every byte transmitted will reach its destination in the order that it was sent. If your message did not reach its addressee, UDP/IP won't notify you as TCP/IP does.

Because it performs less verification and monitoring than TCP/IP, it can generate much greater throughput. UDP/IP is often used with NFS and NIS, described next.

Network File System

Sun Microsystems is a major manufacturer of engineering workstations that run under Unix. Sun developed the Network File System (NFS) and the associated Network Information Services (NIS) that rely on the UDP/IP protocol, with its own method for assuring reliability. The Network File System allows users to access disks transparently, independently of their physical location. The Network Information Services aids network administrators in configuring a network-based system. These two products are available on UnixWare, most Unix systems, and some non-Unix systems.

TELNET

The TELNET protocol, which is part of the TCP/IP suite, enables users to log in to a remote computer as if they were sitting at a directly attached terminal. Logging into a remote Internet computer via TELNET requires only that you know its name. The **telnet** command is discussed later in this chapter.

Internet Addresses

Each host computer in a TCP/IP network is identified by a unique 32-bit address, known as an *IP address.* The IP address is composed of four numbers separated by dots, for example, 102.74.115.96. Each of the four numbers is itself an 8-bit field, whose values range from 0 to 255, except for technical reasons the last number may be restricted to values between 1 and 254. The IP address consists of three parts: the network ID, the host ID, and the optional subnet ID, as you see in this example of a class B address:

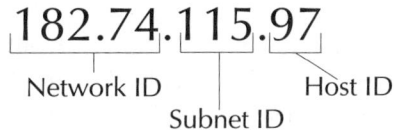

$$182.74.115.97$$

Network ID   Host ID

Subnet ID

The Network ID

The network ID is the leftmost portion of the IP address. Its value is assigned by the Network Information Center (NIC), a network clearinghouse. To accommodate the wide variety of networks, the NIC assigns three common types of Network IDs, corresponding to three common network classes designated as Class A, Class B, and Class C. The value that precedes the first decimal point identifies the network class.

- ■ **Class A Networks**   Class A network addresses start with a value of 1 to 127. This value is the complete network ID. The rest of the IP address identifies the host ID. One possible IP address for a Class A network is 107.234.211.97, in which the NIC-assigned value 107 identifies the network and the user-assigned value 234.211.97 identifies the host.

- ■ **Class B Networks**   Class B network addresses start with a value of 128 to 191. The network ID consists of the first two parts of the IP address, and the last two parts identify the host ID. One possible IP address for a Class B network is 177.234.211.97, in which the NIC-assigned value 177.234 identifies the network and the user-assigned value 211.97 identifies the host.

- ■ **Class C Networks**   Class C network addresses start with a value of 192 to 223. The network ID consists of the first three parts of the IP address, while the last part identifies the host ID. One possible IP address for a Class C network is 207.234.211.97, in which the NIC-assigned value 207.234.211 identifies the network and the user-assigned value 97 identifies the host.

The Host ID

The host ID uniquely identifies a host for a given network. The number of bits composing the host ID depends on the network class, as described above. A host ID may not be either all 0's or all 1's, so the minimum host ID for Class C networks is 1 and the maximum host ID is 254. As explained in the previous section, the host ID may be the last one, two, or three values, depending on the network class.

The Subnet ID

The subnet ID is an optional part of the IP address used to identify multiple physical networks associated with a single network ID. Subnetting is a way of dividing the addresses for a single network to accommodate the fact that the network consists of several physical networks. In the absence of subnetting, a Class B network can contain 256*254 hosts. Rather than deal with such an unwieldy number of hosts, many installations assign the third segment of the IP address to represent the subnet ID. For example, a Class B network whose IP address is 177.234.211.97 could be interpreted as follows: the NIC-assigned value 177.234 identifies the network, the user-assigned value 211 identifies the subnet, and the user-assigned value 97 identifies the host.

Network Names

Networks that form part of the Internet use two types of names. The domain name identifies your *domain,* a group of machines administered as a single entity. The system name or network node name is an internal name.

Domain Name

The domain name must conform to Internet naming conventions and be registered with the Network Information Center (NIC). The NIC domain name is HOSTMASTER@SRI-NIC.ARPA; its phone number is (415) 859-3695 or (800) 235-3155. The domain name is unique and is required when communicating with external networks.

System Name

The system name is used to set up addresses within the internal network. It is required by TCP/IP commands such as **ftp**, **rlogin**, and **telnet**. The **setuname** command sets the system name. The **uname -n** command, issued from the Terminal window or the System Status window, displays the system name.

Network Commands

UnixWare offers a wide variety of commands that enable users to access files and services on a remote machine. The network administrator and system administrator will each employ these commands from time to time. As well, the network administrator is responsible for network configuration. This section includes valuable information on configuring TCP/IP networks. It concludes by examining network information commands that tell the network administrator what's going on in the network, a prerequisite for fine-tuning the network, a never-ending task.

Network Use Commands

One advantage of networking is that it lets you access files and services on a remote machine, with the aid of a few simple yet powerful commands. This section explains how you use those commands.

TIP
The use of remote machines can lead to important savings—for example, in disk storage and personnel. Some installations choose to store all files on remote, massive hard disks instead of equipping individual hosts with their own hard disks.

The telnet Command
The **telnet** command allows users to access a remote machine on the network. The remote machine need not run UnixWare or Unix but must support the TELNET protocol, available on some DOS-based local area networks. The **telnet** command supports both character-at-a-time and line-by-line data entry. Available options include: opening and closing a connection to a host; discarding all previously typed (but not yet read) input on the remote system; and aborting the process currently running on the remote system.

The following command accesses a remote host:

```
telnet ocg2uw
```

The rlogin Command
The **rlogin** command allows users to access a remote machine running BSD Unix on the network. Users must have a valid password on the remote machine. This command is relatively user-friendly; it places users on the remote machine in their home directory, which it passes selected environment variables such as PATH. The following command logs in to the remote host called **ocg2uw** as user joe:

```
rlogin ocg2uw -l joe
```

The rcp Command
The **rcp** command copies files between hosts in a network. It copies the *srchost:srcfile* to *desthost:destfile*, where *srchost:* and *desthost:* are optional system names in the network, and *srcfile* and *destfile* are file pathnames. The current system name is the default. Coding for the *srcfile* specifies the standard input as the source. Destination directories must have write permission, and directories and files named on a remote source machine must have read permission.

These are the available options:

■ **-m** Mails and reports completion of the command, whether there is an error or not.

■ **-u** [*machine*:]*user* Any mail goes to the named **user** on **machine**. The default **machine** is the one on which the **rcp** command is completed or the one on which an error was detected.

The **rcp** command is useful for transferring a few files across the network. The network consists of daemons that periodically awaken and send files from one system to another. For example, to copy the file **/tmp/abc** from the local machine **here** to the remote machine **there**, you would execute the following command:

```
here$ rcp /tmp/abc there:
```

The rsh Command

The **rsh** (remote shell) command executes a shell command on a remote Unix machine. It copies input entered at the local computer to the remote machine before executing the command. After executing the command, it copies output and error files (if any) from the remote machine to the local computer. The remote hostname appears prior to the shell command. The following command displays the remote file **/tmp/abc** on the local machine:

```
here$ rsh there cat /tmp/abc
```

The **rsh** command may use pipes and redirection to mix local and remote hosts in a single command. The system administrator should master this command, for example, to offload programs from a busy computer to an idle one. Do not confuse the remote shell command **/usr/bin/rsh** with the restricted shell command **/usr/lib/rsh**.

The ftp Command

A major way in which documents and software are distributed on the Internet is called *anonymous ftp*. This procedure relies on the **ftp** command, the user interface to the TCP/IP standard File Transfer Protocol, and does not require a specific user password (but may require that you give your electronic mail address).

The command line may specify a remote client host. In this case, **ftp** immediately attempts to establish a connection to an FTP server on that host. Otherwise, it displays the prompt **ftp>** and waits for the user to enter additional information. The following command returns the size of the **abc** file on the remote machine:

```
ftp size abc
```

Consult your system manual for a more complete discussion of the **ftp** command options.

Network Information Commands

UnixWare includes several commands that monitor an existing network and enable authorized personnel to fine-tune it. Other commands generate the list of user names and determine whether a host is transmitting properly.

The rusers Command

The **rusers** (remote users) command lists the user names of current users on all hosts in the network. The following command generates a long listing of all users attached to the host **ocg2uw**:

```
rusers ocg2uw -l
```

The finger Command

The **finger** command displays the name of each logged-in user, the terminal port, the time in minutes since the user entered a command, the day and time of login, and the name of the remote host, if appropriate.

The ping Command

The **ping** command is a troubleshooting tool for tracking a single-point hardware or software failure in the Internet. It issues a message to the designated host and then informs you whether the message was successfully transmitted.

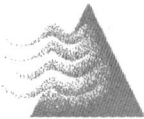

TIP
When attempting to locate a communication error, first run **ping** on the local host to verify that the local network interface is up and running. If this is unsuccessful, run **ping** again to examine remote hosts and gateways starting with those connected to the local host.

CAUTION
The **ping** command is intended for use in network testing, measurement, and management. It is often used to see if a remote host is up and responding, and for manual fault isolation. The **ping** command requires extensive system resources and should not be used in normal network operations.

The netstat Command

The **netstat** command symbolically displays the contents of various network-related data structures. The following command shows the numeric network addresses for devices using the TCP/IP protocol:

```
netstat -n -p tcp
```

With **netstat**, you can monitor the network all the way down to its lowest level, the socket.

CHAPTER 13

Networking Using TCP/IP, NFS, and SNMP

UnixWare makes it fairly easy to connect to common networking protocols such as Transmission Control Protocol/Internet Protocol (TCP/IP). This protocol allows you, among other activities, to access the Internet and the Network File System (NFS). You can make the connection in three ways: with the command line for maximum power and flexibility, with the sysadm interface, or with the Desktop. This chapter concludes with an examination of the Simple Network Management Protocol (SNMP), which is used to monitor, troubleshoot, and control TCP/IP networks. We'll leave it to you to decide whether SNMP is, in fact, simple.

For TCP/IP or any other networking protocol to work, the host machine must have an installed network adapter that is recognized by UnixWare. After the physical installation, it may be necessary to set some parameters so that UnixWare can "talk to" the network board. In many cases, UnixWare provides default settings that you may choose to modify to improve performance. Appendix C describes a typical installation in full detail. Unless you are a networking expert, consult Appendix C and the UnixWare Installation Handbook frequently.

Once UnixWare and the necessary networking hardware have been installed, the root or system owner can begin installing TCP/IP or NFS networking software. The software can be installed from the command line, the sysadm interface, or the Desktop using the Application Installer, using the steps described in Chapter 6.

Configuring TCP/IP

Armed with the appropriate permissions, you can configure TCP/IP from the command line, with the sysadm (or OA&M) interface, or from the Desktop. In most cases, you will use the Desktop.

Configuring TCP/IP from the Command Line

You can use the following commands to configure TCP/IP:

- **configure**   Maps existing networking boards and protocols.
- **ifconfig**   Configures network interface parameters.
- **netinfo**   Provides the interface to the **netdrivers** file so that packages and applications can update a file, independent of its format.
- **netstat**   Shows network status.
- **ping**   A troubleshooting tool for tracking a single-point hardware or software failure in a network.

The following sections discuss each command in more detail.

The configure Command

The **configure** command maps existing networking boards and protocols. You must run the **configure** command in any of these three situations:

- Your network is using subnets, as described in Chapter 12.
- Multiple network cards are installed in the system.

■ You did not enter the Internet Protocol (IP) address when you first installed UnixWare.

In other cases you may be able to configure the network from the sysadm interface or the Desktop, as described later in this chapter.

The ifconfig Command
The **ifconfig** command configures network interface parameters and is a part of the configure command. Only superusers can use the **ifconfig** command. It has the following syntax:

```
ifconfig {-a|interface} [[parameters] | [protocol_family]]
```

The **ifconfig** command assigns an address to a network interface and/or configures network interface parameters. The **-a** argument selects all previously initialized network boards. The **ifconfig** command must be used when the system is booted to define the network address for each interface; it may be used subsequently to redefine an interface's address or other operating parameters. The interface parameter is a string in the form *PrefixUnit#*, such as **lo0** or **wd0**.
The following option is available:

■ **-a**   Displays information for all installed network interfaces.

CAUTION
Coding **-a** followed by one or more valid parameters applies the designated change to all the initialized interfaces. This can cause unpredictable results when used with a broadcast address.

The netinfo Command
The **netinfo** command provides the interface to add, list, or remove entries in the **/etc/confnet.d/netdrivers** file. It does not configure or unconfigure a device or protocol. It has the following syntax:

```
netinfo options
```

Major options include:

■ **-l** *dev*   Lists all devices in the **netdrivers** file.

■ **-l** *proto*   Lists all protocols currently mapped to devices in **netdrivers**.

■ **-d** *device*   Lists the protocols currently configured for the specified device.

- **-p** *protocol*   Lists the devices currently configured for the specified protocol.

- **-a -d** *device*   Adds an entry for a device to the **netdrivers** file.

- **-r -d** *device*   Removes all entries for the specified device from the **netdrivers** file.

- **-r -p** *protocol*   Removes all entries for the specified protocol from the **netdrivers** file.

> **TIP**
> Use the **-r -d** *device* option if you are removing the device from the machine.

The netstat Command

The **netstat** command shows network status. It has the following syntax:

```
netstat options
```

The **netstat** command displays the contents of various network-related data structures in various formats, depending on the selected option. It may display a list of active sockets for each protocol, select a single network data structure, or display running statistics of packet traffic on configured network interfaces.

Major options include:

- **-a**   Shows the state of all sockets.

- **-A**   Shows the address of any protocol control blocks associated with sockets; used for debugging.

- **-n**   Shows network addresses as numbers, instead of as default symbolic addresses.

- **-r**   Shows the routing tables.

- **-s**   Shows per-protocol statistics.

- **-I** *interface*   Highlights information about the indicated *interface* in a separate column.

> **NOTE**
> Use **-r** and **-s** options together to show routing statistics.

The ping Command

The **ping** command helps you track a single-point hardware or software failure in a network. It has the following syntax:

```
ping host [timeout]
```

If the **host** responds, **ping** prints a message stating that the host is alive on the standard output and then exits. Otherwise, after a designated timeout (in seconds), **ping** prints a "no answer from host" message. The default timeout value is 20 seconds.

TIP

When using **ping** for fault isolation, first **ping** the local host to verify that the local network interface is running.

Setting Up TCP/IP Values

To initialize TCP/IP from the command line, open a terminal window and enter **su** to become the root. Then run **/etc/confnet.d/configure -i** to configure TCP/IP. This command steps you through setting each required parameter. It does not let you change broadcast and other **ifconfig** options.

Alternatively, you can edit the interface file directly. You can change an entry for an interface board to reflect subnetting, where available. For example, **wd:0::/dev/wd_0:netmask 255.255.255.0 -trailers::** configures a WD80x3 board to use a mask of FF.FF.FF.00. Some systems require the broadcast option to enable routing.

The following example shows an interface entry with the broadcast argument:

```
wd:0::/dev/wd_0:netmask 255.255.255.0 -broadcast 137.65.208.255 -trailers::
```

The broadcast argument represents an IP address of 137.65.208.*xx*, where *xx* is the local address for a system.

The interface IP address for remote systems is in the **/etc/inet/hosts** file, which is usually accessed from the **/etc/hosts** directory.

Changing Your TCP/IP Address

Run the following script to change your Internet address for TCP/IP:

1. Change to the **/etc/confnet.d** directory and run the command **./configure -i**. UnixWare asks several questions, including what your interface and LAN board are. If you have just one LAN board in your system, it will be the only one listed.

2. Enter your board, host name, IP address, and **ifconfig** parameters (ClassC defaults to a netmask of 0xffffff00 in the **/etc/confnet.d/inet/interface** file).

3. Make sure that your **/etc/hosts** table is correct. (Your system name and IP address should appear in **/etc/hosts**, as entered in step 2.)

4. Make sure that your **/etc/confnet.d/inet/interface** file is correct. If you have one LAN board installed (for example, an Ethernet NE2K) two lines at the bottom of the file should be uncommented (delete the #):

```
lo:0:localhost:/dev/loop::add_loop
ne2k:0:::/dev/ne2k_0:netmask 0xffffff00 broadcast 137.65.44.255 - trailers::
```

These lines depend on your IP address and the type of LAN board installed.

NOTE
If multiple lines exist on your LAN board, delete all but the last line in the example.

You must reboot the system for the changes to take effect.

Changing TCP/IP Interface from the Command Line

Once you've configured TCP/IP, your UnixWare system can communicate with other systems on your local network without changing its general interface. In the two following cases, you must run the **configure** command to change your network interface.

If your network uses subnets or if you have multiple networking boards in your system, use the following procedure to change your network configuration:

1. Log in as root or enter **su** to become the root.

2. Enter the following:

```
cd /etc/confnet.d
./configure -i
```

The system displays a list of your network boards.

3. Enter the menu item number of the board to configure. The system displays the Internet address.

4. If you are configuring your first network board, enter your computer name. If you are configuring your second network board, press the ENTER key only.

5. Type your Internet address if it differs from the address listed. You'll see a message similar to the following:

```
Configure host <hostname> with default Ethernet ifconfig options?
Info message is long (yes no ClassC BerkeleyC info, default: info)
```

Each option is described in Table 13-1. If necessary, review the Internet address classes.

6. If your system contains multiple network boards, UnixWare asks if you want to set up the system as a gateway. Enter **Yes**, **No**, or **Unchanged**.

7. To see the configuration you just modified, enter **ifconfig -a**.

8. Reboot the system.

Configuring TCP/IP with the sysadm Interface

You can handle many network service facilities via the sysadm interface. However, you can do so only from the root, if you are a system owner, or if you are a trusted assistant temporarily accorded the sysadm password.

To generate the Network Services Management menu, enter the command **sysadm network_services** from the command line and then click on the

OPTION	DESCRIPTION
Yes	Uses the default **ifconfig** options.
No	Indicates a non-Class C network. You will be prompted to enter your netmask and broadcast.
ClassC	Use when you are on a Class B network and you want to do Class C subnetting. This adds a netmask (ffffff00) and a broadcast Ethernet segment of 255 (xx.xx.xx.255). No trailers are added.
BerkeleyC	Use when you are on a BerkeleyC network. This adds a netmask and a broadcast Ethernet segment of 0 (xx.xx.xx.0). No trailers are added.
info	Use if you need online help.

TABLE 13-1. *ifconfig Options*

appropriate menu item. Menu selections of interest to network managers are discussed next.

> **TIP**
> To save time, bypass the Network Services Management menu and select the desired option from the command line. For example, enter **sysadm basic_networking**.

Configuring TCP/IP from the Internet Setup (Desktop)

This section shows how to set up TCP/IP networking on your system via the Internet Setup application in the Admin Tools folder. Using Internet Setup, you can perform any of these tasks:

- Specify your system's network address.

- Configure your system's netmask and broadcast address.

- Set up access to a DNS (Domain Name Service) server, NIS (Network Information Service) server, and default router.

- Configure your system for Unix-to-Unix Copy Program (UUCP) routing.

- Set up remote user access to your system or login account.

- Add entries to your **/etc/hosts** file.

- Browse a list of systems for a specified domain and copy an icon for the system to a folder.

With the exception of browsing and setting up remote access to a login account, all these activities require Change Internet Setup permissions.

Communication with other systems or remote networks requires you to configure access to a router or a DNS server.

Configuring Your System for TCP/IP Networking

If you did not enter a network address for TCP/IP during installation, the first time you click on Internet Setup you'll see the Configure Local System window, as shown in Figure 13-1. Enter the following values:

- **System Name**   This is the name of your system, according to UnixWare.

- **Network Address**   Enter the network address (you can obtain it from the network administrator).

■ **Comment**   This optional information identifies the remote system.

If you have access to a DNS server, you should also set these options:

■ **Domain Name**   Enter the name of your domain, with an extension such as **.com**, **.edu**, or **.gov**.

■ **Name Server**   Enter the name of your organization's primary DNS server.

■ **Network Address**   Enter the DNS server address.

A system netmask determines the network address segment representing the network ID and the system ID. Information must be routed correctly between multiple computer systems. For example, consider a Class B network whose network address is 132.106.204.101. The Class B style netmask defines the network ID as 132.106 and the system ID as 204.101. However, with a Class C style netmask the network ID would be 132.106.204.

A system broadcast address generates a broadcast system ID instead of a unique system ID. Since all systems on the network recognize this ID, messages can be broadcast to multiple systems.

When finished, the Internet Setup window will display your system's name and address in the Systems List.

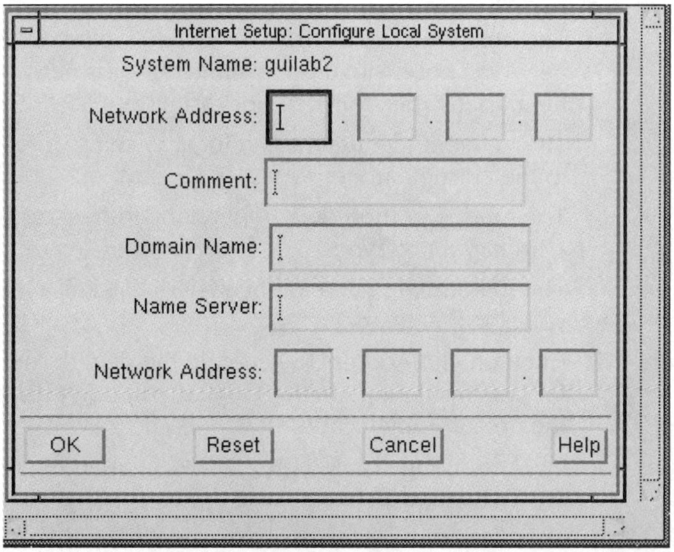

FIGURE 13-1.   *Configure Local System window*

Setting Up Routing

The Internet is a collection of individually operated and maintained physical networks. Each system that communicates with the Internet must have a unique address. You need a router to communicate with systems outside a given local area network. You may use a dedicated router or a specially configured UnixWare system. If you are using TCP/IP only to communicate with systems on a single local area network, you can skip this section on routing.

The router must be directly attached to your network. Networks using multiple routers need not specify a default router but may rely on the routers to determine the best path to transmit a given message. This is done by means of routing tables.

To configure your system for routing, you must be in the Internet Setup application. Choose Routing Setup from the Actions menu to generate the Routing Setup window. Set or change the fields described in Table 13-2 to set up the subnet mask and the default router.

Adding a Domain Name Service (DNS) Server

A DNS server is a specially configured system that knows about all systems in a given local domain. Furthermore, a DNS server will contact another server to obtain requested information for systems in a different domain.

FIELD	DESCRIPTION
Subnet Type	The network class (A, B, C, or Other). Select Other for networks not configured as standard class networks. Enter the netmask ID (hex format)—for example, 255.255.0.0.
Network ID	The network identifier in the local system address, according to the current Subnet Type.
System ID	The unique portion of your network address, according to the current Subnet Type.
Default Router	The full domain name of the system used as a router within your local network.
Network Address	Click on Get Address to generate the default router's address for systems configured for DNS. If you don't have DNS, enter the default router's address.
Update Routing Tables Using Broadcasted Info	Click to run the routed program, described in greater detail in the Command Reference.

TABLE 13-2. *Routing Setup Fields*

NOTE
If requested information is maintained on a geographically distant DNS server, your system may time-out before the requested information is transmitted. If this occurs, try to access the information again. Frequent users may apply the Copy to System List feature to save the system address in their local **/etc/hosts** file.

DNS servers let you manage the network "from the center." In other words, administrators need not store information about all other systems on the network in their **/etc/hosts** file.

To configure your system so it can access a DNS server, choose the DNS Access command from the Actions menu of Internet Setup. The DNS Access window appears, as shown in Figure 13-2. Enter the required information as described here:

- **Domain Name**   Enter the name of your domain, with an extension such as **.com**, **.edu**, or **.gov**.

- **Name Server**   Enter the name of your organization's primary DNS server.

- **Network Address**   Enter the address of the DNS server specified in Name Server.

- **DNS Servers**   Use the scroll bar to move up and down the server list.

FIGURE 13-2.   *The DNS Access window*

Click on Add to add the current entries in the Name Server and Network Address boxes into the scroll list.

Accessing a Network Information Service (NIS) Server

An NIS server is a specially configured system for centrally managing diverse administrative data in a network environment. For example, an NIS server may manage information for all users on a network. A request for information about a given user is passed along to the NIS server.

> ### NOTE
> The NIS server used to be called the "Yellow Pages," but was forced to change due to copyright restrictions. Most NIS commands from the command line still start with **yp**.

To configure a system for NIS access, use the NIS Access command from the Actions menu. Enter the NIS domain name and server name, using the list provided in the NIS Access window.

Viewing the Domain List

A system configured to access DNS can display a list of systems associated with a given organization. The Domain Listing displays a list of systems in a specific domain. By default, Internet Setup displays a list of systems in your local domain.

Starting from the Internet Setup window, here's how to display a Domain Listing:

1. Select Domain Listing from the View menu.

2. Enter the name of the domain to search in the Domain Name text box.

3. Click on Update Listing. Any existing subdomains for a given domain appear at the top of the Domain Listing. The icon representing a domain is different from the one representing a system.

4. Display a subdomain's contents by double-clicking on the subdomain entry. The results appear to the right of the subdomain entry. If desired, use the left and right arrows in the center of the window to explore the listings.

5. Search through the listings until you find the system you're looking for. Click on the system entry to invoke an action for that system.

The Systems List

The Systems List tracks the names of the systems that you can access without having to enter the Internet address.

To add a new entry to the Systems List, select New from the System menu. Enter the remote system name, the network address, and any commentary you wish to include. Click Add to accept the new system.

To view or change the properties of any system entry after it has been added, use the Properties command from the System menu.

To remove an entry from the Systems List, select the system name and use the Delete command from the System menu. You will have to confirm each deletion.

You also can copy any system entry from the Domain List to the Systems List. Then you don't have to rely on the DNS server to determine the address. To copy a system from the Domain Listing to the **/etc/hosts** file, select Copy to Systems List from the System menu.

Creating an Icon for a Remote System

You can create an icon for any remote system in the Systems List or the Domain Listing. You can later double-click on the icon to log in or drag and drop a file to it to transfer files to the remote system. Follow these steps:

1. Click on the desired system in the Systems List or the Domain Listing.

2. Select Copy to Folder from the System menu.

3. Click on the folder or Parent Folder to access the available folders and select the desired one.

4. Enter a name for the icon in the As field. The default name is the system name.

5. Click on Copy to generate a remote system icon in the folder.

Setting Up Remote User Access

The procedure described here configures a system so that users of other systems can log in to and copy files to and from the system without entering a password. Without a password, you can give administrative duties such as file backups and restores to a trusted user.

CAUTION
Be careful about giving other users these abilities. Users accorded access rights to your system are not asked for a password. They can access all your files and perform any system activity for which you have permission.

To set up local system access for remote users, select Remote User Access from the Actions menu in the Internet Setup application. This will generate the

```
┌─────────────────────────────────────────────────────┐
│          Internet Setup: Remote User Access          │
│  Remote System Name: ┌──────────────────────────┐    │
│                      │ asuw20                   │    │
│                      └──────────────────────────┘    │
│  Remove Password Restriction For: ○ Remote Users with Local Accounts│
│                                   ● Access to Your Personal Account │
│  ────────────────────────────────────────────────────│
│  Users on asuw20 Who May Freely Access Your Account   │
│   ● No One  ○ Self  ○ Specific Users                  │
│  ┌──────┐  ┌───────┐  ┌───────┐  ┌────────┐  ┌──────┐ │
│  │  OK  │  │ Apply │  │ Reset │  │ Cancel │  │ Help │ │
│  └──────┘  └───────┘  └───────┘  └────────┘  └──────┘ │
│  Specify which remote system users will log in from.  │
└─────────────────────────────────────────────────────┘
```

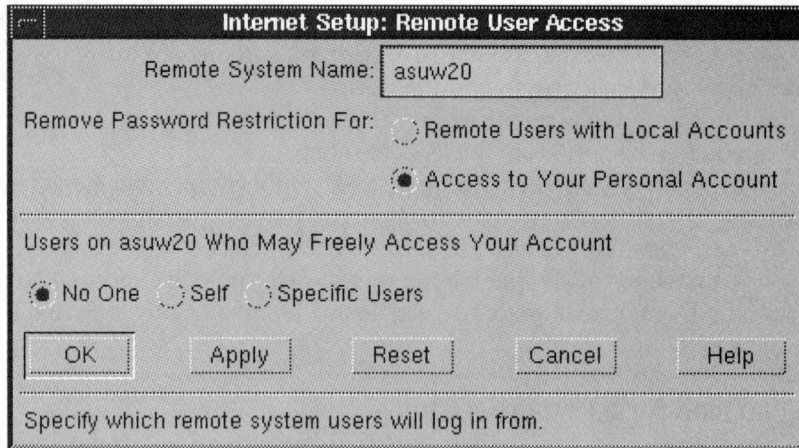

FIGURE 13-3. *The Remote User Access window*

window shown in Figure 13-3. The following list gives detailed information for
each field:

■ **Remote System Name**   The system name selected in the main Internet
Setup window. To configure local access for a different system, type over
the existing name and press the TAB key.

■ **Remove Password Restriction For**   The default value is Access to your
Personal Account, which configures remote user access to your login
account. According access rights to Remote Users with Local Accounts
requires Change Internet Setup permission. Remote users with an account
(of the same username) on your system can then log in and perform file
transfers without entering a password.

■ **Users on <*system name*> Who May Freely Access Your Account**   Choose
No One to not allow remote users to access their account or your account
without a password. Select Self if you want to log in from the remote
system using the same login ID. Choose Specific Users to select individual
accounts that can access your account. Or, choose All Users if you want
any remote user with an account on your system to be able to log in
without supplying a password. (The All Users option is available only if
you select Remote Users with Local Accounts in the Set Access Rights For
option.)

Setting Up UUCP File and Message Transfers

You can use the UnixWare UUCP facility to send and receive file transfers and electronic mail over dialup and TCP/IP networks.

To send UUCP messages, both your system and the remote system must be configured for UUCP transfers. Once this is done, you can use the Remote Access Desktop tool to send files to the remote system by way of the UUCP facility. Files sent to you through UUCP can be retrieved from the UUCP Inbox located in your Mailbox folder.

To set up UUCP transfers between a remote system and your local system, select the desired system and run UUCP Transfer Setup from the Actions menu. Set the desired options, as follows:

■ **System Name**   Displays the name of the current system in the Internet Setup window. Change the system name by typing over the existing name and pressing the TAB key.

■ **Network Address**   By default, the address of the current system is displayed. Changing the System Name blanks this address. With DNS, click on Get Address to get the network address. Otherwise, enter it manually.

■ **Current Status**   Accepting From indicates that UUCP file transfers are currently accepted for the selected system. Rejecting From indicates that UUCP file transfers are currently rejected.

Click on Accept to make the Internet Setup window add the system to the **/etc/uucp/Systems.tcp** file, or click Reject to make it remove the system from this file.

Dynamically Configuring TCP/IP with bootp

Usually when you set up TCP/IP on a UnixWare system, you first add your system name and IP address, and then you either add the names and the Internet address of all linked systems or you specify the domain name server that provides this information. Alternatively, you can specify route and netmask information to define routes to other networks.

A **bootp** server lets you configure basic TCP/IP information for a group of systems. As a result, by simply adding the server name to your system, you can get the remaining basic TCP/IP information you need to configure your system from the

bootp server. Later, you can obtain changed TCP/IP information from the **bootp** server. This way you can redefine information for many systems at once.

You can use **bootp** to configure TCP/IP In the following ways:

- ◼ **Configure a bootp server** To do this, edit configuration files from a Terminal window. There is no graphical interface.

- ◼ **TCP/IP Installation** When you install TCP/IP on your UnixWare system, TCP/IP checks for the presence of a **bootp** server. If it finds one, TCP/IP displays your Internet address, the name and address of the name server, and the names and addresses of router systems. You can accept or change this information.

- ◼ **Update bootp clients** If your network address, DNS server, router, or other TCP/IP information changes, you can obtain this information from the **bootp** server. Use the **/etc/inet/menu** command to read the **bootp** information and update your system.

To get updated TCP/IP information from a **bootp** server, follow these steps:

1. Open a Terminal window.

2. Enter **su** to become root.

3. Enter the **/etc/inet/menu** command to generate the Inet Setup Values window, shown in Figure 13-4.

4. Move the cursor to each field and press the F1 key to display the field description. Change values as you see fit, but you can't change the Node Name field from this window.

New values take effect after you reboot the system.

TCP/IP Serial Connections

UnixWare provides two methods for adding remote hosts that are not directly connected to the local area network. The Point-to-Point Protocol (PPP) uses telephone lines, direct connections, or other serial connections that support the standard UUCP (Unix-to-Unix Copy Program) file-transfer mechanism. Setting up PPP is fairly complicated and involves two separate procedures, one for the (incoming) host receiving calls and another for the (outgoing) host sending calls. Before you invoke these procedures, which are detailed in the system manual, be sure you understand their major functions. These functions are discussed next.

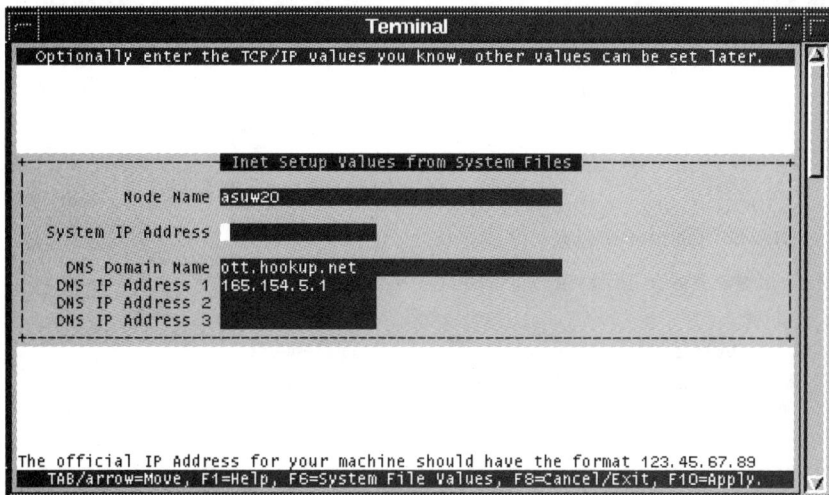

FIGURE 13-4.   *The Inet Setup Values window*

The Serial Line IP (SLIP) connection accesses remote TCP/IP sites without requiring UUCP. This section includes detailed procedures for configuring and disabling SLIP connections.

Configuring Incoming PPP Connections

Configuring the incoming Point-to-Point Protocol (PPP) connections requires the following general procedure (see the system manual for details):

1. Configure the incoming UUCP connections.

2. As the root user, issue the **pppconf** command and, from the PPP Configuration menu that appears, configure the PPP hosts.

3. Configure the incoming PPP parameters from the Configure Incoming PPP Parameters menu.

4. From the menu after that, add the incoming PPP setup.

5. The PPP Configuration menu will appear again. If you don't want authentication, exit. Otherwise, configure the authentication parameters before exiting.

6. Reboot the system.

Configuring Outgoing PPP Connections

Configuring the outgoing Point-to-Point Protocol (PPP) connections requires the following general procedures (see the system manual for details):

1. Configure the outgoing UUCP connections.

2. As the root user, issue the **pppconf** command and, from the menu that appears, configure the PPP hosts.

3. Quit the menu and reboot the system.

NOTE
An outgoing system does not require authentication.

Configuring SLIP Connections

Unlike PPP, Serial Line IP (SLIP) connections do not require a UUCP connection. To create a direct TCP/IP connection over a serial line, follow these steps:

1. Log in to UnixWare with the root account or issue the **su** command and the root password from the Terminal window.

2. Enter **pmadm -l** to determine whether there is an active port monitor (such as **ttymon**) running on the port to which you want to attach SLIP. If there is, change the SLIP port to one without a port monitor.

3. Physically link the serial ports on the local and remote hosts.

4. Add the remote host name and IP address to the local **/etc/hosts** file. Add the local host name and IP address to the **/etc/hosts** file on the subnet associated with the remote system.

5. Enter a **/usr/sbin/slattach** command such as the following:

```
/usr/sbin/slattach tty01 199.5.200.2 199.5.200.7 14400
```

This denotes the establishment of a connection via the COM2 (tty01) port from a local host with the IP address 199.5.200.2 to a remote host with the IP address 199.5.200.7 at a communication speed of 14400 baud.

Disabling SLIP Connections

To disable Serial Line IP (SLIP) connections, follow these steps:

1. Log in to the Desktop with the root account.

2. Open a Terminal window with root permission.

3. Issue the command **ps -ef | grep slattach** to obtain the PID (process ID) of the running slattach process.

4. Kill this process with the command **kill -9 PID**.

5. Enter a **/usr/sbin/route** command such as the following:

```
/usr/sbin/route delete 199.5.400.7 199.5.400.2
```

This command deletes a connection between a remote host with the IP address 199.5.400.7 and a local host with the IP address 199.5.400.2.

NFS Overview

Thanks to the File Sharing feature, a UnixWare system can share files and folders, called *share-items*, with other NFS-compatible systems.

Essentially, File Sharing lets you connect a remote file, folder (directory), or entire file system to a point in your file system. After you've connected a remote folder to your system, you can move down the directory structure to access all files and folders below that point in the remote system.

File Sharing is associated with workgroup computing. To share a folder containing files you would like several users to access, connect the folder to the file system on each user's computer. This way, each user can access these files even though there is only one physical copy of the files.

Using File Sharing

File Sharing is available on the Application Server or the Personal Edition with the optional NFS add-on package. Before using the File Sharing feature, you must configure your system for TCP/IP networking from the Internet Setup icon.

> **NOTE**
> File Sharing requires at least one of the Advertise Local Folders/Files or Connect to Remote Folders/Files permissions.

To give your system the ability to share files, double-click on File Sharing in the Networking folder. You'll see the File Sharing Setup window, shown in Figure 13-5.

From the File Sharing Setup window, you can view local share-items you made available (advertised) to other systems or remote share-items that other systems are advertising. The local share-items view must be active for you to advertise. Likewise, the remote share-items view must be active for you to access share-items

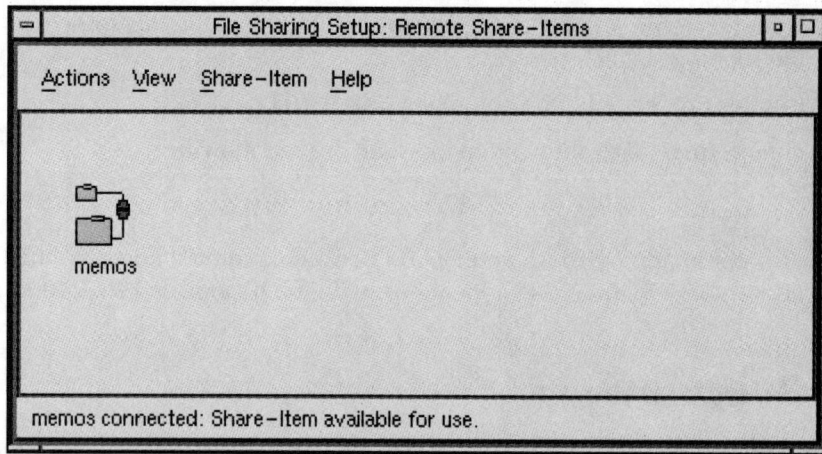

FIGURE 13-5. *The File Sharing Setup window*

advertised by other systems. To toggle back and forth between the two views, use the Remote and Local options from the View menu.

Starting NFS
NFS must be active on your system before you can share files with users on other systems. Usually NFS starts when you start UnixWare; however, sometimes NFS doesn't kick in.

To ensure that NFS is currently running, select Status from the Actions menu. You'll see the File Sharing: Status window, shown in Figure 13-6.

If the Start NFS button is disabled, it means NFS has already started. When NFS is running, YES appears next to the "advertise" and "connect" messages at the top of the window. You can share your share-items with remote systems and connect remote share-items to your system. The window also lists local folders used by remote systems.

If the Stop NFS button is disabled, it means NFS is not running. Click on Start NFS. A confirmation message appears in the lower-left corner of the window.

Managing Local Share-Items
Local share-items reside on your system but are made available to remote systems.

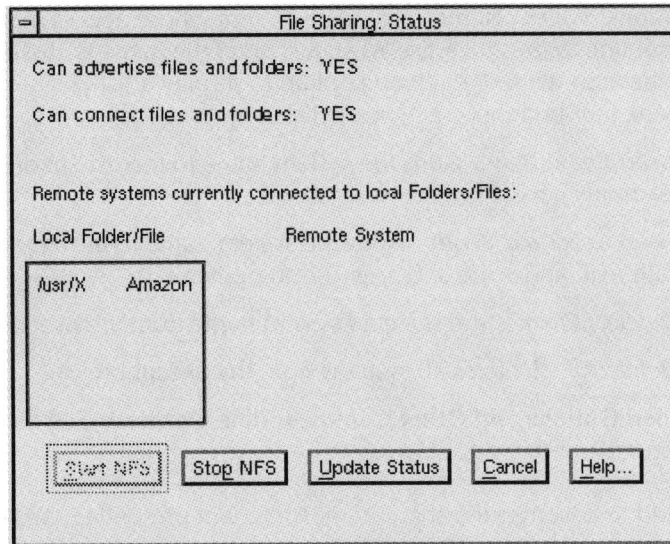

FIGURE 13-6. *The File Sharing: Status window*

To create a local share-item after starting NFS and accessing the Local
Share-Items window, select New from the Share-Item menu. The Add New
Share-Item Local window appears. Set the desired options, as follows:

■ **Folder/File to Share**   Enter the share-item name, or click on Find to
generate a list of share-items. Select the desired item and click on OK.

■ **Icon Name**   Enter the icon name identifying the share-item. By default,
the file or folder name is used as the icon name.

■ **Advertise When NFS Starts?**   Click on Yes to advertise the share-item
now and whenever NFS starts. Click on No to advertise the share-item
now only. NFS normally starts whenever you start UnixWare.

■ **Advertise as**   Click on Read Only to allow other systems to use but not
change or create files and folders associated with the share-item. Click on
Read and Write to allow full access to the share-item. Click on No Access
to allow access only to those systems in the Exceptions list below.

■ **Exceptions: System Name**   To add a system whose access permission is an exception to the Advertise As status, enter the name of the system to share the icon with, or click on Lookup to display a list of systems. Use the following four buttons to act on the list:

■ *Insert Read Only*   Adds the system name to the exception list with read-only access to the share-item.

■ *Insert Read and Write*   Adds the system name to the exception list with read and write access to the share-item.

■ *Delete*   Deletes the selected system name from the exception list.

■ *Delete All*   Deletes all systems from the exception list.

■ **Extended Options** *and* **Other Command-line Options**   See the manual for a description of these options.

Click on Add to advertise the share-item. An icon representing the advertised share-item appears in the Local Share-Items window, with the folder icon open.

Remove advertised share-items (local share-items) by unadvertising or deleting them. When you unadvertise or disconnect share-items, you merely disable them temporarily. Deleting share-items removes them from the list of share-items along with the associated icon. If a user subsequently wants to share that item, it must first be added to the share-item list.

NOTE
Access to the share-item, not the actual data, is removed from the local or remote system when you unadvertise.

NOTE
Before unadvertising or deleting a share-item, make sure that no remote users are accessing it. Otherwise, they may lose their current changes. Check the File Sharing Status window to see which local share-items remote systems are currently connected to.

To remove access to a local share-item, select one of these two commands:

■ **Unadvertise**   Use Unadvertise from the Actions menu to unadvertise the share-item. This makes the share-item unavailable to remote systems, but does not delete it from your File Sharing window. (If the share-item is advertised by default, the item is shared again when you reboot the system.)

■ **Delete**   Use Delete from the Share-Items menu to delete the share-item permanently from the File Sharing window.

Managing Remote Share-Items

A remote share-item resides on a different system, but you need access to it on your local system. To access a remote share-item after starting NFS and accessing the Remote Share-Items window, use the New command from the Share-Item menu. Then set the desired options, as follows:

■ **Remote System Name**   Enter the name of the system that contains the desired share-item and press the TAB key or click on Lookup to view a list of systems. Select a system from the list and click on OK.

■ **Show Available Share Items**   Click to display the list of share-items available from the remote system. Click on the share-item you want to use.

■ **Icon Name**   Displays the icon name identifying the share-item in the File Sharing window. Enter a new icon name or use the default name.

■ **Share-Item to Connect**   Displays the name of the selected share-item.

■ **Local Folder to Connect It To**   Enter the name of an empty folder on your system from which the contents of the share-item will be accessible, or click the Find Folder button to display a list of folders. If you specify a nonexistent folder, UnixWare asks you whether to create it when you click on Add. When the share-item is connected, access its contents by opening the folder specified in this field. When the share-item is not connected, this folder is empty (or will display its local contents if it was not originally empty).

> **CAUTION**
> Choose an empty folder; otherwise, the contents of the local folder become inaccessible when the remote share-item is connected.

■ **Connect Share-Item as**   Click on Read Only to access but not change the files and folders within the share-item, or click on Read and Write to allow full access to the share-item. (The remote share-item must be advertised as Read and Write for you to make this selection.)

■ **Connect When NFS Starts?**   Click on Yes to connect to the share-item now and whenever you start the system, or click on No to connect to the share-item now only.

- **Connection Is** Determines the connection type for broken connections. With Hard Waits, the connection is reestablished after the folder is reconnected. With Soft Waits, the system waits only a short time for a broken connection to be reestablished.

- **Other Command-line Options** See the manual for a description of **mount** command options.

Click on Add to use the share-item. An icon representing the remote share-item appears in the Remote Share-Items window. You now can open the specified local folder to access the remote share-item.

To make share-items advertised by another system (remote share-items) unavailable to users on your local system, use one of these commands:

- **Unconnect** Click Unconnect from the Actions menu to unconnect the share-item. This makes the share-item unavailable to users on your system but does not delete it from the File Sharing window.

- **Delete** Click Delete from the Share-Items menu to delete the share-item permanently from the File Sharing window.

Additional Services

Network administration can be a painstaking task. Among the tools available to ease the pain are Remote Procedure Call and the Network Information Service. Each is described in the following sections, including a section on other commands.

Remote Procedure Call Administration

Remote Procedure Call (RPC) administration increases network security and transparency. It configures administration files to execute the following tasks:

- Establish name-to-address mapping relationships with which applications can obtain transport-specific addresses independent of the transport mechanism actually used.

- Start server daemons (processes) when the system is booted.

- Prompt users for a network password when they log in to the system, increasing system security.

- Edit the **/etc/publickey** file, which identifies who may access secure RPC services.

- Start **ypdaemons** (Yellow-Pages daemons) associated with the Network Information Service described next.

The Network Information Service

The Network Information Service (NIS) is a distributed network lookup service, formerly known as the "Yellow Pages". It serves to identify and locate network objects and resources. It stores and retrieves files independently of the media and protocol used.

NIS contains domains, names that specify the hosts accessing a common set of maps, and administrative files obtained from files in the **/etc** directory. Each domain's set of maps is located on the directory **/var/yp/domainname** located on an NIS server, which may be a master server whose maps are updated upon demand or a slave server containing copies of the master server's maps. One master server is required. An NIS client runs processes that request maps from a server.

> **NOTE**
> A single machine may be both a server and a client.

The major NIS commands and utilities are described next.

The ypserv and ypbind Commands
The **ypserv** and **ypbind** commands are NIS server and binder processes. They have the following syntax:

```
ypserv
ypbind [ -ypset |-ypsetme ]
```

Both **ypserv** and **ypbind** are daemon processes typically activated at system startup. The **ypserv** command runs only on NIS server machines with a complete NIS database, whereas **ypbind** runs on both NIS servers and clients. The **ypserv** daemon's primary function is to access information in its local database of NIS maps. Communication to and from **ypserv** is done by means of RPC calls.

The following options are available for the **ypbind** command only:

- **-ypset**   Allows any user to call **ypset**. By default, no one can call **ypset**.

- **-ypsetme**   Only the root account on local machines may call **ypset**.

> *NOTE*
> The **ypbind** command must run on every machine running NIS client
> processes; in contrast, **ypserv** must be running somewhere on the
> network, but not necessarily on the same node. Both **ypbind** and
> **ypserv** support multiple domains. The **ypserv** process determines the
> domains it serves by looking for directories of the same name in the
> directory **/var/yp**. The **ypbind** process can also maintain bindings to
> several domains and their servers.

The ypwhich Utility
The **ypwhich** utility returns the name of the NIS server or map master. It has the
following syntax:

```
ypwhich [ -d [ ypdomain ] ] [ hostname ]
ypwhich [ -d ypdomain ] -m [ mname ]
```

The **ypwhich** utility tells which NIS server supplies the NIS name services to the
NIS client, or which is the master for a map. If invoked without arguments, it gives
the NIS server for the local machine. If *hostname* is specified, that machine is
queried to find out which NIS master it is using.
The following options are available:

- **-d [*ypdomain*]**   Uses *ypdomain* domain instead of the default domain.

- **-m *mname***   Finds the master NIS server for a map with the name *mname*.

The ypinit Utility
The **ypinit** utility builds and installs an NIS database. This utility is restricted to the
NIS administrator root account. It has the following syntax:

```
ypinit -c | -m | -s master-name
```

The **ypinit** utility sets up an NIS name service database on an NIS server. It can
set up a master or a slave server, or a client system. It asks a few self-explanatory
questions, and reports success or failure to the terminal. It sets up a master server
that is master to all maps in the database. This is the way to bootstrap the NIS
system. After doing so, you can remap the database-master server relationship. All
databases are built from scratch, either from information available to the program
at runtime, or from the ASCII database files in **/etc**. These files must be in the
traditional form, and not the abbreviated form used on client machines. An NIS

database on a slave server is set up by copying an existing database from a running server. The following options are available:

- **-c**   Sets up a client system.

- **-m**   Indicates that the local host is to be the NIS master.

- **-s *master-name***   Sets up a slave database based on the master database ***master-name***.

The yppoll Utility

The **yppoll** utility returns the current version of the map at the NIS server host. It has the following syntax:

```
yppoll [ -d ypdomain ] [ -h host ] mapname
```

The **yppoll** utility asks a **ypserv** process the order number and which host is the master NIS server for the named map ***mapname***. The following options are available:

- **-d *ypdomain***   Use ***ypdomain*** instead of the default domain.

- **-h *host***   Ask the **ypserv** process at the machine named ***host*** about the map parameters.

The yppush Utility

The **yppush** utility forces propagation of a changed NIS map. It has the following syntax:

```
yppush [ -v ] [ -d ypdomain ] mapname
```

The **yppush** utility copies a new version of the NIS name service map called ***mapname*** from the master NIS server to the slave NIS servers. It is normally run only on the master NIS server by the Makefile in **/var/yp** after the master databases are changed. It first constructs a list of NIS server hosts by reading the NIS map **ypservers** within the ***ypdomain***, or if the map is not set up, the local file is used. The following options are available:

- **-v**   Prints messages when each server is called, and for each response. The default is printing only error messages.

- **-d *ypdomain***   Specifies a ***ypdomain*** other than the default domain.

The ypset Utility

The **ypset** utility points **ypbind** at a particular server. It has the following syntax:

```
ypset [ -d ypdomain ] [ -h host ] server
```

In order to run **ypset**, **ypbind** must be initiated with the **-ypset** or **-ypsetme** options. The **ypset** utility tells **ypbind** to get NIS services for the specified **ypdomain** from the **ypserv** process running on the server. If the server is down, or is not running **ypserv**, this is not discovered until the NIS client process tries to get a binding for the domain. At this point, the binding set by **ypset** will be tested by **ypbind**. If the binding is invalid, **ypbind** will attempt to rebind for the same domain.

> **TIP**
> The **ypset** utility is useful for binding a client node that is not on a broadcast net, or is on a broadcast net not running the NIS server host. It also proves useful for debugging NIS client applications—for instance, where the NIS map only exists on a single NIS server host

The following options are available:

- **-h host**   Sets **ypbind**'s binding on host, instead of locally; **host** must be specified as a name.
- **-d ypdomain**   Uses **ypdomain** instead of the default domain.

The ypxfr Utility

The **ypxfr** utility transfers an NIS map from an NIS server to a host. It has the following syntax:

```
ypxfr options
```

The **ypxfr** utility moves an NIS map in the default domain for the local host to the local host by making use of normal NIS services. It creates a temporary map in the directory **/var/yp/ypdomain**, fills it by enumerating the map's entries, fetches the map parameters (master and order number), and loads them. It then deletes old versions of the map and moves the temporary map to the real mapname.

If run interactively, **ypxfr** writes its output to the terminal. However, if it is started without a controlling terminal, and if the log file **/var/yp/ypxfr.log** exists, it appends all its output to that file.

> **TIP**
> The **ypxfr** utility is most often run from the **crontab** file.

The major options include:

- **-f**   Forces the transfer to occur even if the version at the master is not more recent than the local version.

- **-d** *ypdomain*   Specifies the domain *ypdomain* other than the default domain.

- **-h** *host*   Gets the map from the *host*, regardless of what the map says the master is.

- **-s** *ypdomain*   Specifies a source domain *ypdomain* from which to transfer a map that should be the same across domains.

Other Commands

The **share** command makes a local resource available for mounting by remote systems. The **shareall** command shares multiple resources. The **unshare** command makes local resource unavailable for mounting by remote systems. The **unshareall** command unshares multiple resources. The **nfsping** command checks the status of NFS daemons. The **nfsstat** command generates Network File System statistics. Each command is described next.

The share Command
The **share** command makes local resource available for mounting by remote systems. Only a privileged user can execute this command.

The **share** command makes a resource available for mounting through a remote file system of type **fstype**. The default file system type is the first file system type listed in the file **/etc/dfs/fstypes**. When invoked with only a file system type, **share** displays all resources shared by the given file system to the local system. When invoked with no arguments, **share** displays all resources shared by the local system. When sharing a resource, the optional **-d** flag describes the resource being shared.

The shareall Command
The **shareall** command shares multiple resources. Only privileged users can execute this command and the related **unshareall** command.

The **shareall** command without arguments shares all resources from the designated file, which contains a list of **share** command lines. The hyphen (-) denotes that the **share** command lines are obtained from the standard input. If neither a file nor a hyphen is specified, the default file is **/etc/dfs/dfstab**. Resources may be shared among file systems specified in a comma-separated list as an argument to **-F**.

The unshare Command

The **unshare** command makes local resources unavailable for mounting by remote systems. Only a privileged user can execute this command.

The **unshare** command makes a shared local resource unavailable to file-system type **fstype**. The default file system type is the first one listed in the file **/etc/dfs/fstypes**.

The unshareall Command

The **unshareall** command unshares multiple resources. Only privileged users can execute this command and the related **shareall** command. The **unshareall** command has the following syntax:

```
unshareall [-F fstype[,fstype ... ]]
```

The **unshareall** command unshares all currently shared resources. The **-F** flag is used to designate the distributed file system types.

The nfsping Command

The **nfsping** command checks the status of NFS daemons. It has the following syntax:

```
nfsping [-a | -s | -c | -o name ]
```

nfsping allows any user to check the status of the NFS daemons and to see if they are running. The **nfsping** command is similar to the TCP/IP ping command. The following options are available:

- **-a** Checks that all NFS daemons (**nfsd**, **biod**, **rpcbind**, **mountd**, **lockd**, **statd**, **bootparamd**, and **pcnfsd**) are running.

- **-s** Checks that the **nfsd**, **rpcbind**, **mountd**, **lockd**, and **statd** NFS daemons are running.

- **-c** Checks that the **biod**, **rpcbind**, **lockd**, and **statd** NFS daemons are running.

- **-o name** Checks that the specified NFS daemon is running.

NOTE
Only one option may be used at a time.

The nfsstat Command

The **nfsstat** command generates Network File System statistics. It has the following syntax:

```
nfsstat options
```

The **nfsstat** command displays statistical information about the NFS and RPC interfaces to the kernel. It can also be used to reinitialize this information. The **nfsstat** command is similar to the TCP/IP **stat** command. The following options are available:

- **-c**   Displays clients information.

- **-s**   Displays servers information.

- **-n**   Displays NFS information for both the client and server.

- **-r**   Displays RPC information.

- **-z**   Zero (reinitializes) statistics.

> *CAUTION*
> The **-z** option is available only to privileged users. It may be combined with any of the other options listed above to zero particular sets of statistics after printing them.

The Simple Network Management Protocol (SNMP)

The Simple Network Management Protocol (SNMP) is used to monitor, troubleshoot, and control TCP/IP networks. It is a simple protocol that applies the User Datagram Protocol (UDP). UDP transmits data faster than TCP/IP.

SNMP systems are divided into two categories, management stations that issue queries and agents that are queried. UnixWare allows the same host to perform as a management station or an agent. The agents are implemented as daemon processes and use three files:

- The **/etc/inet/snmpd.conf** file containing information such as the types of software used, the system location, and the name of a person in charge.

- The **/etc/inet/snmpd.comm** file containing information listing from whom the agent will accept queries and the type of access allowed.

■ The **/etc/inet/snmpd.trap** file containing a list of stations to be informed in case of abnormal events.

The management stations may issue the commands described next.

SNMP Commands

The following paragraphs describe the commands that retrieve information from SNMP systems.

The getone Command
The **getone** command retrieves variables from an SNMP entity. This command is an SNMP application to retrieve a set of individual variables from an SNMP entity using a GET request. The arguments are the entity's address, the community string for access to the SNMP entity, and the fully qualified variable name(s) expressed as either dot-notation or the variable name as it appears in the MIB document.

The getid Command
The **getid** command retrieves system Management Information Base variables from an SNMP entity. This command is an SNMP application that retrieves the variables **sysDescr.0**, **sysObjectID.0**, and **sysUpTime.0** from an SNMP entity. The arguments are the entity's address and the community string needed for access to the SNMP entity. The primary purpose of this application is to illustrate the use of SNMP library routines.

The getmany Command
The **getmany** command retrieves classes of variables from an SNMP entity. This command is an SNMP application that retrieves classes of variables from an SNMP entity. The arguments are the entity's address, the community string for access to the SNMP entity, and the variable class name(s). The variable class name is expressed as an object identifier in either dot-notation or as the MIB variable from the Management Information Base document. **getmany** retrieves the variable class by first calling the SNMP entity with the variable class name to get the first variable in the class.

The snmpstat Command
The **snmpstat** command shows network status using SNMP. It has the following syntax:

```
snmpstat options
```

The **snmpstat** command symbolically displays the contents of various network-related data structures. Major options include:

- **-t** Shows the complete transport endpoint table.

- **-r** Shows the routing table.

- **-a** Shows the address translation table.

- **-i** Shows the status of active interfaces.

- **-S** Shows the SNMP status.

The setany Command

The **setany** command retrieves and sets variables in an SNMP entity. This command issues a GET request to get the current values of variables to be set, then performs a SET request on these variables. The arguments are the entity name or address in Internet dot notation, the community name for access to the SNMP entity, and a triplet for each variable to be set consisting of the variable name in dot notation.

CHAPTER 14

Using a UnixWare Machine as a NetWare Server

Perhaps the biggest advantage of UnixWare compared to other Unix systems is the ease with which people can connect to NetWare. Chapter 3 showed how easy it is for UnixWare users to access basic NetWare services. This chapter shows how easily the system owner can access the full range of NetWare services.

Configuring NetWare Networking Protocols

UnixWare provides push-button access to NetWare networking protocols. The sections that follow first give you the terminology associated with the various protocols, then tell how to use NetWare Setup to configure your network and the appropriate protocols.

Protocol Terminology

This section presents the following protocols: Internetwork Packet eXchange (IPX), Sequenced Packet eXchange (SPXII), Routing Information Protocol (RIP), Service Advertising Protocol (SAP), and Network Core Protocol (NCP).

Internetwork Packet eXchange (IPX)

The *Internetwork Packet eXchange (IPX)* is a Novell communications protocol that transports data between network devices. It is the main protocol used to transfer data from UnixWare to a NetWare server.

IPX simply sends the packet from the source to the destination. It does not wait for acknowledgment that the packet was received. However, if the destination does not respond within a predefined time period, IPX retransmits the packet.

IPX forms the base for the other NetWare protocols discussed in this section. To configure NetWare for communications with UnixWare, you must specify the IPX address and the maximum *hops*, the number of systems through which data, such as a file, can transfer from the source to the destination as shown in the "Using NetWare Setup" section later in this chapter. The default maximum is 16.

IPX Address   An IPX address contains three parts: the network address, the node address, and the socket address. The four-byte network address denotes a given network socket. All network devices attached to a socket share the same network address. The six-byte node address denotes individual network nodes. The node address for an Ethernet network adapter is set at the factory. The two-byte socket address denotes the operation to be performed on the packet which arrives at a given node. A sample IPX address follows:

```
01010393 (Net) 000000000000 (Node) 0451 (Socket)
```

Sequenced Packet eXchange (SPXII)

The *Sequenced Packet eXchange (SPXII)* protocol uses the IPX protocol to send and receive packets. SPXII assures that packets are received in order, resequencing them if necessary. It performs extensive error verification on the data. Applications using SPXII do not need to determine packet size because the SPXII driver handles packet size for the application. When setting up NetWare, you will need to turn on SPXII and provide configuration data, such as the maximum number of SPXII connections and sockets. (Specific steps for installing NetWare are beyond the scope of this book.)

Routing Information Protocol (RIP)

The *Routing Information Protocol (RIP)* provides routing information for forwarding packets within a network. Each server broadcasts its routing table to all other networked servers periodically, by default once a minute.

Service Advertising Protocol (SAP)

The *Service Advertising Protocol (SAP)* requires each server to advertise across the network its name, its server type (such as file server), and its network address. This information is stored upon reception in each server's Server Information Table. Network clients use this feature to determine which services are available and then find the server address. Later in this chapter you will see how to configure the Service Advertising Protocol.

Network Core Protocol (NCP)

The *Network Core Protocol (NCP)* is a proprietary set of procedures for controlling client requests such as enabling and disabling a connection and processing directories and files. NCP checks packets for errors. Fortunately, you need only familiarize yourself with these terms; UnixWare takes care of the details.

Using NetWare Setup

Use the NetWare Setup icon to configure IPX when installing additional network boards or to reconfigure IPX for LAN boards.

> **CAUTION**
> Setting many of the following options requires general networking knowledge and familiarity with NetWare.

The NetWare Setup icon is located in the Networking folder within Admin Tools. When you double-click this icon, the NetWare Setup window appears; the first five options are shown in Figure 14-1. The bottom of the window includes a message area.

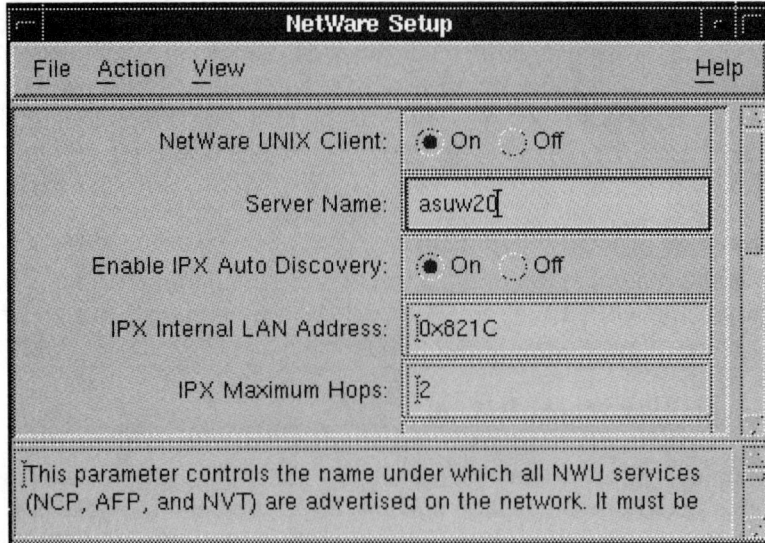

FIGURE 14-1. *The NetWare Setup window*

Here is a summary of the fields in this window:

- **NetWare UNIX Client** Click On to start the NetWare UNIX Client when booting UnixWare, provided that UnixWare is connected to NetWare. See the "NetWare UNIX Client (NUC)" section later in this chapter for more information. Click Off if UnixWare is not connected to NetWare or to avoid starting the NetWare UNIX Client when booting UnixWare.

- **Server Name** Enter the server name to be configured.

- **Enable IPX Auto Discovery** This option (enabled by default) detects various characteristics of the linked NetWare network. After checking the network boards, this option turns off. When adding boards after the initial installation, turn this option on, shut down your system, insert the new board, and restart the system.

- **IPX Internal LAN Address** Enter the address of your internal LAN (up to eight characters), for example, 00110454. This address is used for communication between the UnixWare system and network boards. This field must contain a correct address for the logical LAN configuration (the specific socket for your Internet address) to become active.

■ **IPX Maximum Hops**   Enter the maximum number of systems through which data, such as a file, can travel from the source to the destination (not counting the source and the destination). For example, 3 hops means the file travels through a maximum of five nodes. The default value for this field is 16.

The remaining options (which don't appear in the screen shown in Figure 14-1) are described here:

■ **Logical LAN Configuration**   Click to display the Logical LAN dialog box. You'll see more about this in the next section, "Configuring Your Logical LAN."

■ **Sequence Packet eXchange**   This option, also known as SPXII, configures the number of SPXII sockets. (The "Configuring SPXII" section later in this chapter gives more information.) Each socket represents a remote SPXII connection. The default is 100; the minimum is 5; the maximum is 1024.

■ **Service Advertising Protocol**   Click On to advertise your applications to others. By default, this option is turned off. See the "Configuring SAP" section later in this chapter.

■ **Network Management**   Click to enable NetWare Protocol Stack (NPS) network management. See the "Managing Your Network" section later in this chapter.

■ **Diagnostics Daemon**   Click On to run diagnostics. This option is turned off by default. This daemon fulfills diagnostic requests from other network applications. For example, a diagnostics application can query each network node for configuration information using the IPX Configuration Request Packet, and the diagnostics daemon responds by using an IPX Configuration Response Packet.

■ **Remote NUC Auto-Authentication**   This option allows you to authenticate automatically to a NetWare server. The default value is On. Click Off to suppress auto-authentication. See "Methods for Authenticating to a NetWare Server" later in this chapter for more information.

■ **Enable NetWare Single Login**   This feature provides single login capability when names and passwords are synchronized between a NetWare server and UnixWare. The default value is On. See the "NetWare UNIX Client (NUC)" section later in this chapter.

Configuring Your Logical LAN

A logical LAN consists of the IPX address used with a given network board. Each physical LAN board may be associated with a maximum of four logical LANs. Enabling the Logical LAN Configuration option in the NetWare Setup window displays a list of logical LANs. The LANs are numbered 1 through 8. A connection symbol appears next to an available LAN(s). When a LAN is not available, the symbol is crossed out.

When you select a LAN, you will see the NetWare Setup window shown in Figure 14-2. Here is a description of each field:

- **IPX LAN Device**   Click on the desired device, such as **/dev/wd_0**, the physical network board Ethernet NE2000.

- **IPX LAN Frame Type**   Click on the desired logical frame type, such as Ethernet II or 802.2.

- **IPX External Net Address**   Enter the ten-character number assigned by your network administrator in this text field, such as 0x89413000.

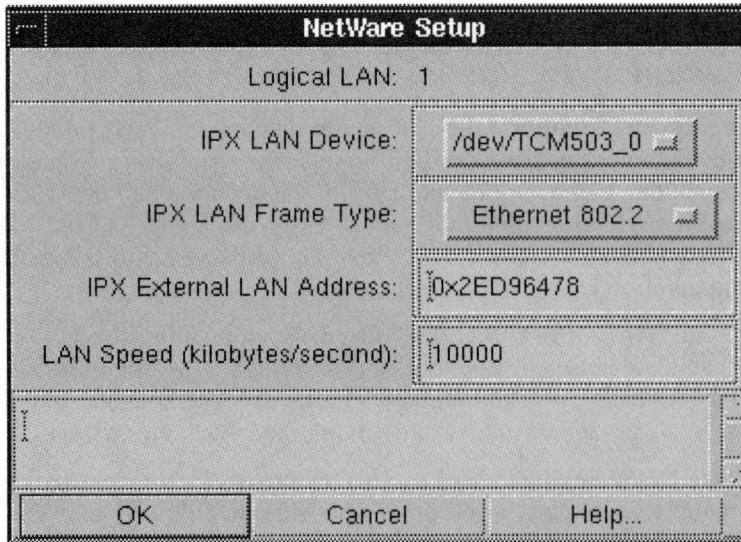

```
+------------------------------------------------------+
|  ....              NetWare Setup                     |
+------------------------------------------------------+
|                                                      |
|             Logical LAN:  1                          |
|                                                      |
|         IPX LAN Device:   [ /dev/TCM503_0  v ]       |
|                                                      |
|     IPX LAN Frame Type:   [ Ethernet 802.2  v ]      |
|                                                      |
|  IPX External LAN Address: [0x2ED96478       ]       |
|                                                      |
| LAN Speed (kilobytes/second): [10000         ]       |
|                                                      |
|  [                                          ]        |
|                                                      |
+------------------------------------------------------+
|    [  OK  ]      [  Cancel  ]      [  Help...  ]      |
+------------------------------------------------------+
```

FIGURE 14-2.   *The Netware Setup: Logical LAN configuration window*

■ **LAN Speed (kilobytes/second)**   Enter the transfer speed in kilobytes (KB). The default is 10000Kb. The speed depends on the network type; for example, an Ethernet II network is 10MB/sec.

Configuring SPXII

Clicking the Sequenced Packet eXchange option displays the Sequenced Packet eXchange window, shown here:

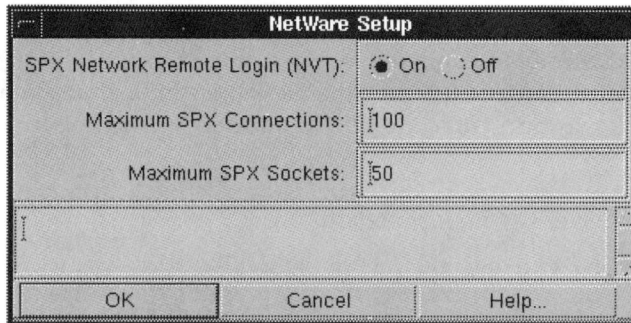

```
┌─────────────────────────────────────────────────────────┐
│                      NetWare Setup                        │
├─────────────────────────────────────────────────────────┤
│  SPX Network Remote Login (NVT):    ◉ On   ○ Off          │
│                                                           │
│      Maximum SPX Connections:    [100        ]            │
│                                                           │
│         Maximum SPX Sockets:     [50         ]            │
│                                                           │
│  [                                              ]         │
│                                                           │
├─────────────────────────────────────────────────────────┤
│      OK          │      Cancel      │      Help...        │
└─────────────────────────────────────────────────────────┘
```

The SPX Network Remote Login (NVT) field lets you enable or disable remote NVT logins. The other fields control the maximum number of connections for SPXII, and the maximum number of sockets simultaneously available for listening to incoming connect requests from other endpoints.

Configuring SAP

The Configuring the SAP (Service Advertising Protocol) option specifies the number of services to advertise. When you select the SAP option you generate a simple window with one field: the maximum number of services to advertise. The default is 3000.

Managing Your Network

To enable the network management feature, click on the Network Management option, which generates the Network Management window. Set the desired options:

■ **NUC Network Management**   Click On to enable NetWare UNIX Client management.

■ **Host Resource Network Management**   Click On to enable this feature.

■ **NPS Network Management**   Click On to enable monitoring of the NetWare for UNIX Management Protocol Stack. This allows data on IPX/SPX diagnostics to be collected from a protocol stack.

■ **Network Management Trap Time** Enter the trap time in this text field.
The default is 5 seconds. *Trap time* is how the system sends network event
and alert information to the network management console. Trap time
defines how much time the system can spend trying to synchronize signals.

Configuring IPX at the Command Line

The Using NetWare Setup procedure presented at the beginning of this chapter
showed you how to configure IPX from the Desktop. Although it is more
complicated, you may also configure IPX from the command line by following
these steps:

1. Log in or enter **su** to become root.

2. Enter **cd /etc** to access the **/etc** directory.

3. Using a text editor such as **vi**, edit the **NPSConfig** file.

4. Enter your system name and IPX network address located in the top 12
lines of the file. For example:

   nvt_server_name = *system name*
   server_name = *system name*
   internal_network = *address*
   LAN_1_network = *address*

5. Reboot the system

NetWare UNIX Client (NUC)

The NetWare UNIX Client (NUC) provides extensive NetWare services to
UnixWare users. It includes the NUC file system (NUCFS); the NetWare UNIX
Client Auto-Mounter (NUCAM); the NUC daemon (NUCD) and command line
utilities; NUC API (Applications Program Interface) requestor and API Calls; and the
NUC.NLM. The following sections describe these features in more detail.

NUC File System (NUCFS)

The NetWare UNIX Client File System (NUCFS) is a UnixWare network file system
providing NetWare file services. It enables UnixWare users to access files and
directories on remote NetWare servers transparently—in other words, as if they

were local UnixWare files. Key features of the NetWare Unix Client File System include its ability to operate in both the DOS partitions and the Unix partitions, its robust connection to NetWare servers, its support for the Packet Burst protocol, and the single login. These aspects are discussed next.

The DOS Name Space

The NUCFS can operate in the DOS name space or the Unix name space. When operating in the default DOS name space, the usual DOS limitations are in force.

- Filenames are restricted to a maximum of eight characters prior to the period, a maximum of three characters after the period (called the 8.3 rule), and only one period is allowed.

- File ownership may not be changed.

- Hard and symbolic file links are not available.

- Limited permissions are available.

The DOS name space maps the NetWare user's effective rights to UnixWare permissions and presents them in the owner permissions on UnixWare. It does not map group users.

The Unix Name Space

The Unix name space uses Owner, Group, and Other file and directory permissions, including read, write, and execute permissions. The Unix name space is used when NUC.NLM is installed on the NetWare server and the UNIX (NFS) name space is added to the volume.

Connections to NetWare Servers

The NUCFS enables the NetWare Server to maintain control information for each of its clients. This means that file mounts need not be redone if the connection from the server to the client is lost, for example if the server ceases to function. When the server is reestablished, the file system displays the auto-authentication panel. Once the authentication is completed, service to the client resumes.

NOTE
The NetWare single login function removes the need for authentication should the server cease to function. If the server is reestablished quickly, the client won't even know service was interrupted.

The Packet Burst Protocol

The Packet Burst protocol is a way of transmitting multipacket messages over the Internet. This protocol does not expect the receiver to acknowledge each transmitted packet.

The Single Login Feature

The single login facility enables users whose usernames and passwords are synchronized between UnixWare and a NetWare server to access either system with only one login. NUC attempts to use the UnixWare user's name and password to access NetWare servers on request.

NUC Auto-Mounter (NUCAM)

The NetWare UNIX Client Auto-Mounter (NUCAM) automatically mounts the NUCFS file system. It links UnixWare users to NetWare volumes via the Desktop or the command line. Double-clicking on the NetWare icon in the Desktop displays NetWare servers as folders. Double-clicking on one of these folders displays the auto-authenticator for users who are not yet authenticated to the NetWare server.

NUC Daemon (NUCD) and Command Line Utilities

The NUC daemon is a background process that starts multiple threads: **nucmessage**, **nwlogin**, **nucam**, **nucam_unmount**, and **slogin**. The following command line utilities enable users to access the NetWare servers and associated file systems:

UTILITY	DESCRIPTION
mount_nucam	Allows users to mount the **nucam** file system.
mount_nucfs	Allows users to mount the **nucfs** file system.
nlist	Displays a list of NetWare resources including servers, volumes, and users.
nwlogin	Provides users with login facilities to a NetWare server.
nwlogout	Provides users with logout facilities to a NetWare server.
nwprimserver	Allows users to access and set the primary NetWare server.
nwwhoami	Displays the NetWare server accessed by the user.
setpass	Allows users to change their password for a NetWare server.

NUC API Requestor and API Calls

The NUC requestor maps NetWare API (Applications Program Interface) calls to Network Core Protocol requests and vice versa. The requestor must keep a count of processes using a given connection and maintain the connection as long as any process is using it. The API calls come from a C library of function calls, providing a host application interface to NetWare. Service options include Connection, Synchronization, and Auditing.

NUC.NLM

NUC.NLM is software that extends the Network Control Protocol to enable Unix name space information on NetWare volumes. This software first became available under Netware 3.11. The network administrator can choose between a NetWare mode or a Unix mode. The NetWare mode provides traditional NetWare access mechanisms such as trustee assignments, and maps NetWare rights to UnixWare permissions. The Unix mode provides access from UnixWare as well as from NetWare. UnixWare features such as permissions are mapped to the corresponding NetWare features. Because the physical files reside on NetWare volumes, access rights are determined by the effective rights of the NetWare-authenticated users.

Authenticating to NetWare Servers

The process of authenticating to a NetWare server establishes a connection between a given UnixWare computer and the NetWare server. This process must be completed before UnixWare users can access NetWare files or printers.

CAUTION
Although UnixWare users can access NetWare printers once the authentication process is complete, they must first mount any required NetWare volume before accessing NetWare files and directories.

Methods for Authenticating to a NetWare Server

There are three ways to authenticate to a NetWare server. The choices are the Auto-Mounter, the NetWare Access icon, or the command line.

Using the Auto-Mounter

To authenticate to a NetWare server using the auto-mounter, open the NetWare icon and double-click on the desired NetWare server. If you aren't already authenticated to that server, the Authenticate window appears, asking you to enter your name and password. If your login name and password are synchronized between the UnixWare and NetWare Server, and NetWare Single Login is enabled, authentication is automatic. Otherwise, you must enter your login and password to authenticate to a NetWare server.

Using the NetWare Access Icon

To authenticate to a NetWare server using the NetWare Access icon, first double-click the NetWare Access icon in the Networking folder. Click on the desired NetWare server to generate an Authenticate window. If your login name and password are synchronized between the UnixWare and NetWare server, and NetWare Single Login is enabled, authentication is automatic. Otherwise, you must enter your login and password to authenticate to a NetWare server.

Using the Command Line

Use the following steps to authenticate to a NetWare server from a Terminal window:

1. Double-click on the Applications folder at the UnixWare Desktop.

2. Double-click on Terminal in the Applications folder.

3. Enter **nwlogin** *fileserver/username*, where *fileserver* denotes the desired server and *username* denotes the user logging in.

4. Enter the **nwlogout** command to log out of a NetWare server.

Mounting and Unmounting NetWare Volumes

To access files and directories on a NetWare volume, first mount the NetWare volume to a directory on a UnixWare file system. You may use the **mount** command plus arguments.

> **NOTE**
> When running UnixWare, NetWare volumes are automatically mounted using the auto-mounter through the NetWare icon, or by accessing the **/.NetWare/servername/volume name** directory. Clicking on the NetWare icon displays the authentication panel unless you are already authenticated to that NetWare server. Authentication to the NetWare server is necessary to transfer into **/.NetWare/servername/volume name** on the command line.

To mount a NetWare volume from the command line, you must first become superuser, then authenticate to the desired NetWare server with the **nwlogin** command, like this

```
nwlogin servername/username
```

Then enter

```
mount -F nucfs servername/volume: /path
```

where **servername** denotes the server, **volume** denotes the volume, and **path** denotes the mount point on your local system. For example, to mount the volume Sys from the NetWare server NWs (assuming the local directory already exists), enter the following:

```
mount -F nucfs NWs/Sys: /NWs/Sys
```

This command directs UnixWare to mount the NetWare volume Sys on server NWs onto the **/NWs/Sys** directory. The NetWare volume will be mounted on a UnixWare directory as a **nucfs** file system.

To unmount a volume you use the **umount** command, like this:

```
umount pathname
```

where **pathname** denotes the directory previously specified as the mount point for the volume.

To unmount all NetWare server volumes, enter this:

```
umount -F nucfs
```

For more information on the **mount** command, see Chapter 10.

File and Directory Rights and Permissions

The full use of NetWare from UnixWare stations requires knowledge of UnixWare commands for NetWare servers, NetWare and UnixWare filenames, and the process for copying files from UnixWare to NetWare and NetWare access control, both with and without NUC.NLM.

UnixWare Commands for NetWare Servers

The UnixWare File and Edit menu commands can access NetWare servers. Recall that the NUC.NLM facility provides two access modes. The Unix mode attempts to invoke Unix filenaming and access syntax on NetWare files. This mode supports Unix file attribute commands. The NetWare mode does not support most Unix file attribute commands.

Filename Conventions

It is important to remember that NetWare obeys DOS rules for naming files, and UnixWare has its own conventions.

DOS filenames contain one to eight characters, an optional period, and then zero to three characters (known as the 8.3 rule). Characters may be letters (DOS does not distinguish between capital letters and lowercase letters), numbers, or special characters. The following characters may not be used in DOS filenames:

    * / [ ] : < > + = ; ' "

UnixWare filenames contain one to 255 characters, may not contain a slash or a null character, and do distinguish between capital letters and lowercase letters.

Copying Files from UnixWare to NetWare

Because NetWare filenames are more restrictive than UnixWare filenames, you must be careful when copying files from UnixWare to NetWare, or the filename can change. If NUC.NLM is not running on your system, you must watch for filename truncation and conversion. The system will not always warn you dynamically.

The NUC.NLM product converts UnixWare filenames to NetWare filenames on the NetWare server but does not change the filenames on UnixWare itself. Conversion includes transforming lowercase letters to uppercase, dropping DOS special characters, truncating filenames to meet the DOS 8.3 rule, and generating one or more digits to avoid duplicate filenames with existing NetWare files.

NetWare Access Control

This concluding section describes access control of NetWare files with and without NUC.NLM.

If NUC.NLM is not active on a NetWare server, you cannot change the access control attributes of NetWare files. The account displaying File Properties is shown as the owner, and its primary group name is shown as the group, regardless of the actual file ownership. The **chmod** command is restricted to according execute permission.

If NUC.NLM is active on a NetWare server, UnixWare file ownership depends on the corresponding NetWare file or directory Access Control right. Not all NetWare access rights can be seen from UnixWare. The **chmod** command again is restricted to according execute permission.

CHAPTER 15

Electronic Mail

Mail services provide electronic communications between users on the same system, or between systems linked over a network. UnixWare makes it particularly easy for users to send and receive mail electronically from the Desktop. At the click of a mouse, users can access the popular Message Handling Service (MHS) associated with NetWare. UnixWare also offers powerful System V Unix commands, which are accessible from the Terminal window.

Using the Desktop to Set Up Mail Services

The Desktop provides an easy-to-use interface for reading incoming mail and sending outgoing mail. You may create aliases for a single user or for a group of users to ease the burden of typing. Finally, by pushing a few buttons, you can customize the mail interface.

All Unix mail programs process incoming mail and store it in a mailbox, usually in the **/var/mail** file. UnixWare provides a basic, default mail system. However, you can easily improve and extend this system from the Mail Setup window. For example, you can assign a single name to a group of remote computers in order to process their mail.

Files and Directories

UnixWare uses the following files and directories for processing mail:

- **/bin/mail**   This program is used for mail routing and serves as a back-end to the Desktop mailer.

- **/etc/mail/namefiles**   This file contains a partial list of alias files and directories referenced by the **mailalias** command. The default values are the alias file **/etc/mail/names** and the mailing list directory **/etc/mail/lists.**

- **/var/mail**   This subdirectory contains each user's mailbox and mail log files.

- **/etc/mail/mailsurr**   This file is used internally by the **/bin/mail** program.

Using the Mail Setup Window

This section describes how to customize your Unix mail system. Many of the tasks described here require permission to change Mail Setup, as discussed in Chapter 8. The system owner automatically has permission.

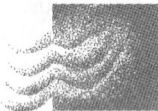

> **CAUTION**
> Files in the **/etc/mail** directory are generated by the program, which means manual changes could be lost at any time.

Double-click on the Mail Setup icon in the Admin Tools folder to display the UNIX Mail Setup window, as shown in Figure 15-1.

Setting Basic Mail Variables
The Basic Mail Setup category shows the most commonly changed UnixWare mail variables.

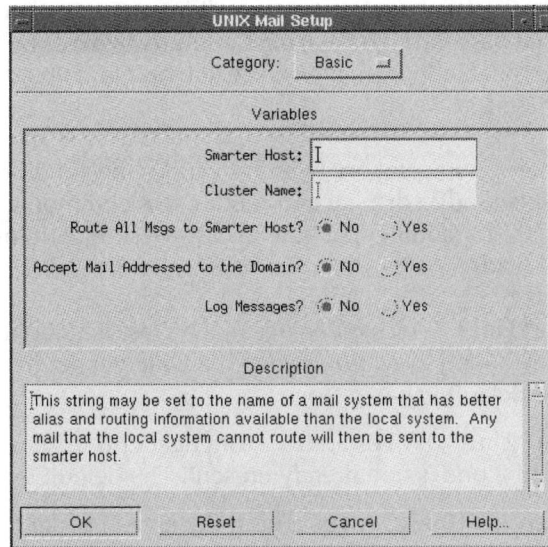

FIGURE 15-1. *The UNIX Mail Setup window*

NOTE
Clicking on a variable label generates information about it in the
Description box at the bottom of the window.

The options in the Basic category are as follows:

- **Smarter Host**   A *smarter host* is an external mail server that routes mail
  from your system to a destination that your system does not recognize. This
  destination may be inside or outside of your network.

- **Cluster Name**   If desired, enter a name to represent a closely coupled set
  of systems called a *cluster*. All mail delivered to client systems may appear
  to come from a single server.

- **Route All Msgs to Smarter Host?**   Click on Yes if you want all mail not
  destined for users on other systems to be sent to the smarter host. This host
  will route each message to its correct destination.

- **Accept Mail Addressed to the Domain**   Click on Yes to accept mail
  addressed to the local domain if a system's name is not specified.

■ **Log Messages?**   Click on Yes to store all incoming and outgoing mail messages that pass through **/bin/mail** in the **/var/mail/log** file. The **/var/mail/errors** file logs mail errors. Click on No if you don't want to store mail messages.

The Extended Mail Setup category (which includes the variables in the Basic Mail Setup category) is used to display and modify less commonly used mail variables, such as those for adding a debug level to your mail. It includes the following additional fields:

■ **Add a "Date" Line?**   A Yes specifies that a Date header line be automatically added to outgoing mail if a Date header line is not already present. The default value is No.

■ **Add a "From" Line?**   A Yes adds a From header line automatically to outgoing mail if one is not already present. The default value is No.

■ **Add a "Received" Line?**   A Yes adds a Received header line automatically to outgoing mail if one is not already present. The default value is No.

■ **Debug Level**   Enter a number to represent the debug value (0 for no debugging and 9 for maximum debugging) to generate information about unsuccessful mail messages. The information is stored in **/tmp/MLDBG***process id*, where ***process id*** is the process identification of the **/bin/mail** program. The default is 0.

■ **"Remote From:" String**   Enter the string to be sent in the From header line that replaces your system name or the smarter host name.

TIP
Using this variable may improve security because the message won't contain your system name or smarter host name.

■ **Failsafe Forwarding System**   Enter the name of the system that stores your system's **/var/mail** directory. Set this variable when sharing a **/var/mail** directory with several systems using NFS and other networked file systems. If the system containing the **/var/mail** directory is down, the mail is stored temporarily and will be delivered when the directory becomes available again.

■ **Delete Empty Mail Files?**   Click on Yes to display a menu and direct the system to delete empty mailboxes automatically.

> **TIP**
> Using the Delete Empty Mail Files option saves disk space and
> simplifies your directory structure.

- **Domain Name**   Enter the mail domain name if it differs from your default
  domain name.

- **Mailsurr Env Var's**   Enter a comma-separated list of environment
  variables for the **mailsurr** commands.

- **Mailsurr Mailcnfg Var's**   Enter a comma-separated list of *mailcnfg*
  variables for the **mailsurr** commands.

- **Compile Mailsurr File?**   Click on Yes to recompile **/etc/mail/mailsurr** to
  obtain the latest version if **mailsurr** changed since it was last compiled.
  The default is No.

- **Add a "Message ID:" Line?**   Click on Yes to add a message identification
  string to the Header field. The default is No.

- **Convert to 7-Bit Headers?**   Click on Yes to convert incoming 8-bit
  headers to 7-bit headers. The default is No.

- **Convert to 7-Bit MIME?**   Click on Yes to convert incoming messages to
  7-bit MIME (Multipurpose Internet Mail Extensions). The default is No.

- **Convert non-MIME to MIME?**   Click on Yes to convert to MIME. This
  allows additional character sets, audio, video, and other data to be added
  to mail messages. The default is No.

- **Add a "To" Line?**   Click on Yes to add a To field to the header if one is
  absent from the incoming mail. The default is No.

Setting Up the UnixWare MHS Gateway

This section describes how to set up the UnixWare side of the MHS (Message
Handling Service) gateway from your Desktop. The UnixWare MHS gateway is a
set of programs that allows UnixWare and NetWare mail to send and receive
messages from an MHS mail system. To accomplish this, the gateway translates
between the Internet RFC822 mail format and the MHS SMF71 mail format. This
gateway places SMF71 messages into the MHS incoming mail queue and retrieves
SMF71 messages destined for UnixWare from an outgoing mail queue.

Use the gateway to exchange messages between a UnixWare mail system and an MHS mail system. Only a single MHS gateway is required per site.

CAUTION
The **/etc/mail** directory is programmatically generated; changes could be lost at any time. If you need to edit the **mailsurr** file, edit the **mailsurr.proto** file and run the **createSurr** program.

TIP
Configure a single MHS gateway per site to reduce administrative overhead. Use a production system (Application Server version) instead of a desktop system (Personal Edition version) to reduce the chance of system failure. If you assign a gateway to a desktop system and the gateway goes down, mail will be rejected.

Configure the other systems to send mail going to an MHS address to the single UnixWare system running the gateway. For example, set smarter hosts to point to the MHS gateway system. Non-UnixWare systems can access the gateway by forwarding mail to the gateway system.

CAUTION
The following procedures require familiarity with NetWare MHS or NetWare Global MHS. Many functions described here can be done only by the NetWare MHS gateway system site administrator.

Configuring MHS
An MHS gateway, configured on a NetWare file server, manages incoming and outgoing mail through NetWare and UnixWare. The MHS host automatically routes incoming mail to a drop box (gateway directory) on a server. UnixWare retrieves this mail from the server and transfers it to individual systems.

The MHS gateway administrator must configure MHS from both NetWare and UnixWare. From the NetWare MHS server side, the administrator must set up an MHS gateway on the server containing the NetWare MHS host and set up a gateway account on the MHS host NetWare file server. From the UnixWare side, the administrator of the UnixWare system on which the MHS gateway resides must run MHS Setup at one UnixWare system for each gateway.

Setting Up the NetWare Side of an MHS Gateway
To set up the NetWare side of an MHS gateway, the NetWare administrator must perform these tasks in this order:

  1. Make sure that the appropriate NLMs are installed on the NetWare file server (see Chapter 14 and the NLM Installation and Administration manual).

2. Create a new gateway on the MHS host, using gateway version 71 or SMF71, depending on your MHS software.

3. Set up an account on the MHS host if one is not already available.

4. Set up MHS routes for users who will be sending and receiving MHS mail through the gateway.

5. Name the directory containing the mail folder **/mhs**.

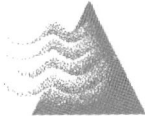

TIP
For more information on configuring the NetWare side of the MHS gateway, see your Novell MHS documentation.

Setting Up the UnixWare Side of an MHS Gateway

To set up the UnixWare side of an MHS gateway from a UnixWare system, double-click on the MHS Setup icon in the Admin Tools folder, and then enter values for each field, using Table 15-1 (and your network administrator) as a guide.

NOTE
Change the variable DEBUG to MHSLOGIN in the **/usr/lib/setup/MHS_Setup/setup.def** file.

Once MHS mail is set up, mail sent to an MHS address goes through the gateway to the MHS mail system. See your Desktop User Handbook for more information about MHS Mail and Unix Mail.

The Internet Gateway field deserves some special attention. If your system is configured with a domain name, the name entered in the Internet Gateway field is treated as a subdomain. For example, enter **mhs** to send Unix mail to the domain **mhs.Novell.COM** by way of the MHS gateway if your system's domain is Novell.COM. To reach users in a domain, mail must be addressed to **user@mhs.novell.com**, where **user** is the login ID of the user receiving the mail. If your system was configured without a domain name, the Internet Gateway field contains a special name that routes mail through the gateway. For example, to route Unix mail sent to mhs through the MHS gateway, enter **mhs**.

Scheduling the Gateway with cron

The cron program schedules commands to run at specified time. Cron itself begins during system startup in the transition from single-user to multiuser mode. The cron process gets its instructions for executing programs from a "cron table" file **crontab**. You should never edit the **crontab** file directly. Instead, the **crontab** program is

FIELD NAME	DESCRIPTION
MHS Gateway	The name of the MHS gateway configured on your MHS mail server.
Internet Gateway	The name for your MHS gateway in Unix. The suggested name is **mhs**.
MHS File Server	The name of the NetWare server containing the MHS directory. The UnixWare MHS gateway expects the NetWare side of the gateway to be on the named server.
MHS Volume	The name of the NetWare server containing the MHS directory, usually the sys volume.
MHS Login	The name of the login account on the NetWare server used to access the MHS gateway directory.
MHS Password	The password for the MHS login. After exiting this variable, a window appears in which you enter the password a second time. Enter your password again to ensure accuracy.
Poll Frequency	The number of times per hour the gateway will be checked for incoming MHS mail. Enter 0 to turn off the gateway. To set the poll frequency to a positive value, all other fields in the window must be filled in.

TABLE 15-1.   *Fields in the MHS Mail Setup Window*

used to change the configuration file **crontab**. Use the cron process to schedule correctly the MHS gateway. Follow these steps:

1. Double-click on Applications in the Desktop.

2. Double-click on Terminal to open a Terminal window.

3. Enter the following two lines:

```
su -mhsmail
crontab -s
```

4. Add the lines:

```
1,30 * * * * /usr/lib/surrcmd/smfsched
* * * * * /usr/lib/mail/surrcmd/smf-poll
```

to poll the gateway once a minute.

Using Your Mailbox

Your personalized mailbox is located on the Desktop. It collects your saved mail messages. When you open your mailbox for the first time, you see only a UUCP Inbox icon. This icon represents a folder for files that were transferred from a remote system to your system via UUCP (the Unix-to-Unix Copy Program, discussed shortly).

The Mail Window

The Mail window lists messages that were sent to you. It includes information about the message subject, time of sending, size, and whether the message has been read. Use this window to save your messages, delete them, or print them without first reading them.

Double-click on the Mail icon in the Applications folder to see the Mail window, shown in Figure 15-2. The Mail window contains the following information for each mail message:

- **No** The order in which each message was received.

- **Status** An *R* tells you that the message has been read, an *N* that the message is new and has not been read, and a *U* that the message hasn't been read but isn't new.

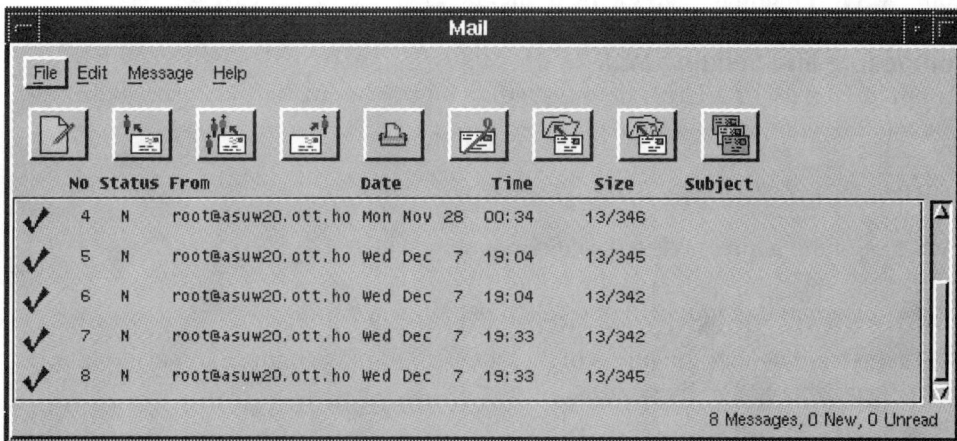

FIGURE 15-2. *A typical Mail window*

- **From**   The ID of the user who sent the message.
- **Date**   The date the message was sent.
- **Time**   The time the message was sent.
- **Size**   The number of lines and characters in the message.
- **Subject**   The message subject.

Reading Mail

To read a mail message, double-click on the Mail icon in the Applications folder and then double-click on the appropriate mail message in the Mail window.

TIP

To open and read several messages at once, press and hold down the CTRL key as you click the left mouse button on the messages you want to open. Choose the Read command from the Message menu to display a window for each message.

To delete the message, use the Delete command from the Edit menu.

You can print a hard copy of the message with the Print Message command in the File menu.

To save a message after you read it, choose Save Message from the File menu. Your mail message is automatically included in your Mailbox in the **SavedMail.ml** file.

When you finish reading and processing a message, select the Next command from the View menu to read the next one, or use the arrows in the tool bar.

Composing and Sending Mail

Determine the user's address before sending him or her mail. MHS user addresses take the following general format:

username@system.domain

Each part of the address has a specific meaning:

- ***username*** uniquely defines each user in a system.
- ***system*** defines the name of the organization; this name can have multiple parts separated by periods.
- ***domain*** indicates the type of organization, such as **edu** for an educational institution, or **com** for a commercial organization.

When you compose a message you are either replying to someone else's message, forwarding a message, or creating a brand-new message. Choose the appropriate command from the Message menu:

COMMAND	FUNCTION
Reply to Sender	Replies to the sender without repeating the original message.
Reply to Sender (Att.)	Replies to the sender with a copy of the original message.
Reply to All	Replies to people on the From and Cc list, without repeating the original message.
Reply to All (Att.)	Replies to people on the From and Cc list with a copy of the original message.
Forward	Forwards the mail to another user with a copy of the original message.
Compose	Creates a new mail message.

When you choose one of these commands, you'll see the Mail: Compose Message window, shown in Figure 15-3. Enter the appropriate information in these fields:

- **To**   Enter the recipients' names and addresses or aliases, separated by a space.

- **Subject**   Enter a message subject name to identify the message in the recipient's incoming mail box.

- **Cc**   Enter the names of other recipients, separated by a space, whom you want to receive copies. (Cc originally stood for "carbon copy" in the secretarial pools of long ago when carbon paper was still used.)

- **Bcc**   Enter the names of recipients, separated by a space, to receive copies. Other recipients are not notified that Bcc recipients received copies. (Bcc stands for "blind carbon copies," or copies that the recipient of the original letter wouldn't know about.)

The rest of the window shows the message area where you compose the message. You may use the Text Editor, described in Chapter 3. You also can drag and drop a text file onto the window pane.

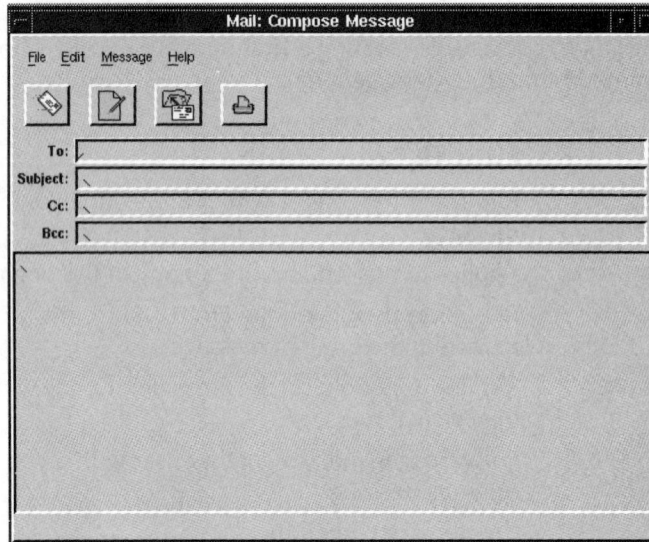

FIGURE 15-3. *The Mail: Compose Message window*

When your message is complete, use the Send command from the Message window. The following message should appear at the bottom of the screen: "The Message has been sent."

TIP
Because there is no unsend option, before sending a critical message to its recipient first send it to yourself. Send it to the recipient only after rereading and verifying your message.

If you get part of the way through composing a message, but can't finish it for some reason, use the Save Unsent command from the File menu. This will store the unsent message in the **UnsentMessage** file, which you can open when ready to resume typing your message.

NOTE
The **UnsentMessage** file is always overwritten and can contain only one message at a time.

Working with Aliases

As you have probably noticed, mail names and addresses can be cumbersome, hard to enter, and easy to forget or mistype. Not to worry; UnixWare supports *aliases*, or short names that represent longer addresses. Included are procedures for creating, modifying, and deleting aliases.

> **NOTE**
> An alias can identify a single user or a group of users. A single user can have multiple aliases.

Creating Aliases

Aliases save you from typing long addresses or several names every time you send mail. You can set up aliases for individuals, groups, and groups of groups; regardless of how many users will share an alias, you create a mail alias from the Alias Manager found in the Mail application. Follow these steps:

1. Choose the Alias Manager item from the File menu. You'll see a window showing the list of current aliases.

2. Enter the alias name in the Name field, and the mail address(es) in the Address field. An address can be multiple addresses (or other aliases) separated by a blank space.

3. Click on the Apply command in the Edit menu.

The new alias will appear in the username list. An icon showing a single person represents an individual alias, while an icon showing two people represents a group alias.

If you need to change an existing alias, click on the alias and change the Name or Address as needed. This will create a new alias. To delete the old one, use the Delete command from the Edit menu.

Customizing Mail

The mail application lets you customize various features of the mail system. This section summarizes the options for both reading mail and sending mail.

Read Options

To customize how mail messages open on your Desktop, click on the Mail Options command in the File menu. The resulting window contains just one field called Double-click Opens Message in. Click on Open Reader to reuse an open window or New Reader to open a new window for each new mail message.

Once you have read a message, you can determine the portion of a mail message header you wish to display. Use the Read Mail Options command from the File menu. Choose from the following options:

- **Header** Specifies the type of message header displayed: the Brief option displays only selected fields, Full displays all header fields.

- **Brief Header Shows** Specifies header items to be displayed as you read a message. Select from Cc, Content-Length, Content-Type, Date, and From.

Send Options

There are two options available for sending messages. To change these options, start in the Compose Message window, and choose the Compose Options command from the File menu. The Compose Options window contains these two options:

- **Save Copy of Outgoing Mail** Click on On to save each message you send automatically (UnixWare saves the messages in a file called **SentMail.ml** located in your Mailbox folder). Click on Off if you don't want to save messages automatically.

- **Signature** Enter the text that will act as your signature at the end of each message you send, such as your full name and phone number. The signature may contain any number of lines.

NOTE
The same options are available with the Sender Properties command in the File menu from the main Mail window.

Receiving Files from a Remote System: The UUCP Inbox

The Unix-to-Unix Copy Program (UUCP) is a sophisticated, powerful facility for transferring files between Unix systems, executing commands on a remote system, and sending mail to remote users. By way of the UUCP Inbox icon in the Utilities folder, you can receive files from a remote system using UUCP. Here's how:

1. Double-click on the UUCP Inbox icon in the Utilities folder.

2. Double-click on the icon associated with the remote sender.

3. Click on the file and copy it to the desired location.

NOTE
If the remote system was configured with Internet Setup, the file is transferred to the sender-designated folder on the local system.

Handling Mail via the Command Line

Although it is convenient to handle most of your mail via the Desktop, sometimes you may want the extra control afforded by the command line. This section examines basic aspects of the widely used **mail** and **rmail** commands and associated files. It concludes with a section on using the more sophisticated **xmail** command.

The mail Command Family

The **mail** and **rmail** commands are used for reading, sending, and forwarding mail. The associated **mailcheck** command verifies whether mail has been received. The **mailconfig** file initializes information for the mail service.

The default file for saving mail is **$HOME/mbox**. If **$HOME/mbox** is a directory, the file **$HOME/mbox/mbox** is used.

The mail and rmail Commands
The **mail** and **rmail** commands read mail or send mail to users. The syntax varies with the function.

Sending and Forwarding Mail   Use this syntax to send and forward mail:

```
mail [ -tw ] recipient ...
rmail [ -tw ] recipient ...
mail -F recipient ...
```

The last form is used to forward mail. A **_recipient_** is usually a username or alias. When recipients are named, mail assumes a message is being sent (except for the **-F** option). It reads from the standard input up to an end-of-file (CTRL-D) or a line containing a single period sent from a terminal device. **mail** then adds the message to the **mailfile** for each recipient.

The following command-line arguments affect sending mail:

- ■ **-t** Adds a To: line to the message header for each recipient.

- ■ **-w** Sends a letter and returns you to the command line without waiting for delivery confirmation.

An undeliverable letter is returned to the sender with diagnostics indicating the location and nature of the failure. If mail is interrupted during input, the message is added to the **dead.letter** file for editing and retransmission.

Reading Mail Use this syntax for reading mail:

```
mail [ -ehpPqr ] [ -f file ]
```

The following command-line arguments affect reading mail:

- ■ **-e** Suppresses mail printing. An exit value of 0 indicates that the user has mail; 1 indicates no mail.

- ■ **-h** Displays a window of headers instead of the latest message. The display is followed by the ? prompt.

- ■ **-p** Prints all messages without prompting for disposition.

- ■ **-P** Prints all messages with all header lines displayed, instead of the default selective header line.

- ■ **-q** Terminates mail after interrupts. By default, an interrupt terminates only the message being printed.

- ■ **-r** Prints messages in first-in, first-out order.

- ■ **-f *file*** Specifies the named file (such as **$HOME/mbox**) instead of the default **mailfile**.

In the absence of command-line arguments, **mail** prints a user's mail messages in last-in, first-out order. When a user logs in, available mail is usually indicated. When **mail** is active, the user is notified of any new mail.

The mailcheck Command
The **mailcheck** command checks for mail. It has the following syntax:

```
mailcheck [ -Z ]
```

If **mailcheck** finds mail it prints the message "You have mail" on standard output. **mailcheck** is commonly used in a person's **$HOME/.profile** as follows: **mailcheck 2>/dev/null**. This prints a message only when there is mail.

The mailcnfg File
The **/etc/mail/mailcnfg** file provides initialization information for the **mail** and **rmail** commands. This file must be created initially by the administrator. Each entry in **mailcnfg** consists of a line in the following form:

```
Keyword = Value
```

These are the major *keyword* definitions:

- ADD_DATE   If a message originating on the local machine has no Date: header and ADD_DATE has a *value*, this header will be added.

- ADD_FROM   If a message originating on the local machine has no From: header and ADD_FROM has a *value*, this header will be added.

- ADD_RECEIVED   If a message is received that has no Received: header and ADD_RECEIVED has a *value*, this header will be added.

- NOCOMPILEDSURRFILE   Normally, **mail** creates a compiled version of the surrogate file **/etc/mail/Cmailsurr** whenever the surrogate file or configuration file changes, and then uses the compiled version. However, setting this variable to any value causes **mail** to ignore the compiled surrogate file.

Interactive Mail

The more sophisticated **mailx** utility is available with every Unix system. It is more powerful than the **mail** command and somewhat more difficult to master. Only the basics are presented here. System administrators should take the time to master this command and the Message Handling Service (MHS) that accompanies NetWare. It is discussed in the next section.

The mailx Utility
The **mailx** utility provides an interactive message-processing system. When reading mail, **mailx** provides commands for saving, deleting, and responding to messages. When sending mail, **mailx** allows you to edit, review, and modify the message as it is entered. It processes supplementary code set characters according to the locale specified in the LC_CTYPE environment variable.

Many remote features of **mailx** require that incoming mail be stored in a standard file (mailbox) for each user. The mailbox is the default location for mail to be read by **mailx**. As **mailx** reads messages, it flags them for removal to a secondary file for storage. The default filename is **mbox**, and by default it is located in the user's **home** directory. Messages remain in storage until disposed of. Users can access a secondary file via the **-f** option of the **mailx** command. The same commands process primary file messages and secondary file messages. This gives rise to the notion of a "current mailbox."

The **mailx** command has the following syntax:

```
mailx [options] [recipient ...]
```

Command-line options start with a dash (-). Any other arguments are assumed to be destinations (***recipients***). If no recipients are specified, **mailx** attempts to read messages from the mailbox. These are the major command-line options:

- **-f [*filename*]**   Reads messages from the designated filename instead of **mailbox**. The default filename is **mbox**.

- **-F**   Records the message in a file specified after the first recipient. Overrides the record variable, if set.

- **-n**   Does not initialize from the system default **mailx.rc** file.

- **-N**   Does not print initial header summary.

- **-s *subject***   Sets the Subject header field.

- **-t**   Reads the To:, Cc:, and Bcc: headers found on standard input to determine the recipient list.

- **-u *user***   Read user's mailbox if it is not read-protected.

- **-U**   Converts UUCP-style addresses to Internet standards. Overrides the *conv* environment variable.

- **-V**   Prints the **mailx** version number and exits.

When reading mail, **mailx** is in command mode. It displays a header summary of the first several messages and then prompts for regular commands. When sending mail, **mailx** is in input mode.

When the command line does not specify a subject, **mailx** prompts for one. Recipients listed on the command line may be one of three types: login names, shell commands, or alias groups. Login names may be any network address, including mixed network addresses. An attempt is made to return undeliverable mail to the sender's mailbox.

Once in the **mailx** program, commands take this form:

```
[ command ] [ msglist ] [ arguments ]
```

At startup, **mailx** tries to execute commands from the optional system-wide file (**/etc/mail/mailx.rc**) to initialize certain parameters. Next it tries to execute commands from a private startup file (**$HOME/.mailrc**) for personalized variables. With the exceptions noted below, regular commands may appear within startup files. The most common use of a startup file is to set up initial display options and alias lists.

CAUTION

The startup file may not contain the following commands: **!**, **bedit**, **bvisual**, **Copy**, **edit**, **followup**, **Followup**, **hold**, **mail**, **prerve**, **reply**, **Reply**, **shell**, and **visual**. An error in a startup file causes the remaining lines in the file to be ignored. The **.mailrc** file is optional, and must be constructed locally. See the manual for a description of **mailx** commands.

The following environment variables are taken from the execution environment and may not be changed within **mailx**:

- **HOME=*directory***   The user's home directory.

- **MAIL=*filename***   The name of the initial mailbox file to read. The default is the standard system mailbox **/var/mail/*username***.

- **MAILRC=*filename***   The name of the startup file. Default is **$HOME/.mailrc**.

The following variables are major internal **mailx** variables. They may be imported from the execution environment or set via the **set** command at any time. The **unset** command erases variables.

- **DEAD=*filename***   Specifies the file for saving incomplete letters in case of untimely interrupt. Default is **$HOME/dead.letter**.

- **MBOX=*filename***   Specifies the file for saving messages that already have been read. The **xit** command overrides this function, as does saving the message explicitly in another file. The default file for saving mail is **$HOME/mbox**. If **$HOME/mbox** is a directory, the file **$HOME/mbox/mbox** is used. In this case, **$HOME/mbox** is a Multi-Level Directory, as required by the Enhanced Security Utilities. Consequently, multiple versions of **$HOME/mbox** will be maintained automatically, one for each security level at which mail is saved.

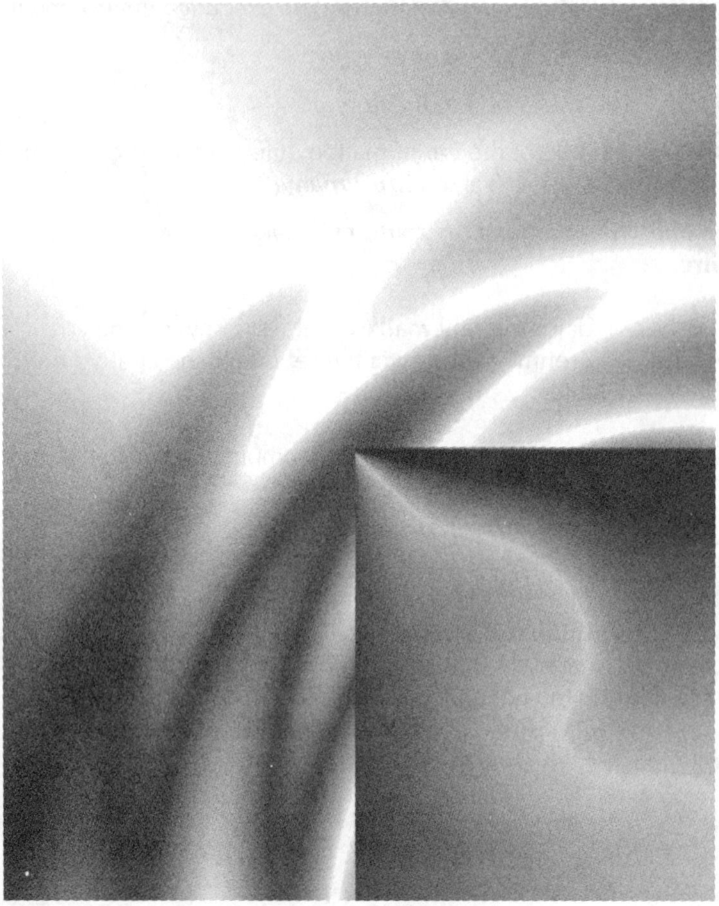

APPENDIX A

Device Management

A major system administration responsibility is device management, which simply means adding, modifying, reserving, or deleting devices and device groups. UnixWare devices include the following: floppy diskettes (that use the **/dev/dsk** directory for their block devices and the **/dev/rdsk** directory for their character devices), hard disk drives, CD-ROM drives, and tape drives. The names of floppy disk drives are constructed as follows:

```
fx {5h | 5d9 | 5d8 | 5d4 | 5d16 | 5q | 3h | 3d} [t]
```

where *x* specifies the drive number. The option **t** specifies that the device uses the complete floppy diskette; when absent the device does not use the first cylinder.

This is the complete list of diskette specifications:

- **5h** High density 1.2MB, 5 1/4-inch
- **5d9** Double density 360KB, 5 1/4-inch
- **5d8** Double density 320KB, 5 1/4-inch (8 sectors/track)
- **5d4** Double density 320KB, 5 1/4-inch (4 sectors/track)
- **5d16** Double density 320KB, 5 1/4-inch (16 sectors/track)
- **5q** Quad density 720KB, 5 1/4-inch
- **3h** High density 1.44MB, 3 1/2-inch
- **3d** Quad density 720KB, 3 1/2-inch

UnixWare supports the following tape devices:

- **c0s0** non-retensioning rewinding device
- **c0s0n** non-retensioning non-rewinding device
- **c0s0r** retensioning rewinding device
- **c0s0nr** retensioning non-rewinding device

Managing Devices

UnixWare allows authorized personnel to manage devices from the command line, the sysadm interface, or the Desktop.

Using the Command Line

You'll use the **putdev** command to add a new device to the Device Database (DDB), modify a device's attributes, or remove a device from the DDB. The **mknod** command makes a special file or device. The **getdev** command lists devices defined in the Device Database based on criteria. The **devattr** command lists device attributes.

Adding Devices

The **putdev** command adds a new device to the Device Database (DDB), modifies an existing device's attributes, or removes a device entry from the DDB. It also lets you append new values to attributes that take value-lists (separated by commas), and remove specific values from value-lists. The **putdev** command has the following syntax:

```
putdev device -a alias [secdev=value] [attribute=value [...]]
```

adds a device to the DDB using the specified attributes.

> **NOTE**
> The device must be referenced by its alias, which must be unique throughout the DDB. The alias is limited to 64 characters and should contain only alphanumeric characters and any of the following special characters: . (period), _ (underscore), $ (dollar sign), and - (hyphen).

The following describes the variables used with the **putdev** command shown above:

- **device**   Designates the absolute pathname or alias name of the device whose attribute is to be added, modified, or removed. If **device** is a pathname, then the attributes of the alias to which it maps are updated.

- **alias**   The unique name by which a device is known. No two devices in the database may share the same alias name.

- **attribute**   Designates a device attribute to be added, modified, or deleted. This prevents an accidental modification or deletion of a device's alias from the DDB.

- **value**   Designates the value to be assigned to a device's attribute. If any of the values are invalid, then **putdev** fails and prints an error message.

> **NOTE**
> Whenever the attributes in a Device Database file are updated, the old version of the file is saved to a file with the capital letter "O" prefixed to the filename.

> **CAUTION**
> If errors occur when modifying device attributes, recover old versions of the Device Database files.

These are the major device attributes that can be defined (see the manual for a complete list):

- **cyl** Used by the command specified in the **mkfscmd** attribute.

- **desc** A description that will be associated with this device (such as a floppy diskette).

- **dpartlist** The list of disk partitions associated with this device.

- **dparttype** The type of disk partition represented by this device. Used only if **type=dpart**. It should be either **fs** (for file system) or **dp** (for data partition).

- **erasecmd** The command string that, when executed, erases the device.

- **fmtcmd** The command string that, when executed, formats the device.

- **fsname** The file system name on the file system administered on this partition, as supplied to the **/usr/sbin/labelit** command.

- **mkfscmd** The command string that, when executed, places a file system on a previously formatted device.

- **gap** Used by the command specified in the **mkfscmd** attribute.

- **mountpt** The default mount point to use for the device.

- **nblocks** The number of file system blocks administered on this partition.

- **ninodes** The number of file sytem inodes administered on this partition.

- **norewind** The name of the character special device node that allows access to the serial device without rewinding when the device is closed.

- **pathname** Defines the pathname to an inode describing the device (used for non-block or character device pathnames, such as directories).

- **type** A token representing inherent qualities of the device. Standard types include: 9-track, ctape, disk, directory, and diskette.

- **volname** The volume name on the file system administered on this partition, as supplied to the **/usr/sbin/labelit** command.

- **volume** A text string that describes any instance of a volume associated with this device. The **volume** attribute should not be defined for devices that are not removable.

The **mknod** command, which is restricted to privileged users, makes a special file or device. It has the following syntax:

```
mknod name b | c major minor
mknod name p
```

The argument **name** specifies the special file to be created. The argument **b** indicates a block-type special file, whereas **c** indicates a character-type file. **major** and **minor** specify device numbers which may be either decimal or octal. The assignment of device numbers is specific to each system. The second format is used to create a named pipe.

Removing Devices and Deleting Attributes

The **putdev -d** command removes a device or deletes device attributes. It has the following syntax:

```
putdev -d device [attribute [...]]
```

The **-d** option removes a **device** entry from the DDB when executed without the **attribute** argument. If the **attribute** argument is specified, the attribute and its value are deleted from the device entry.

> **NOTE**
> To remove a device first run the **devnm** command (described later in this section) to determine on which device the root file system is mounted.

Changing Attribute Values

The **putdev -m** command modifies device attributes. It has the following syntax:

```
putdev -m device attribute=value [attribute=value [...]]
```

You use this command to modify a **device** entry in the DDB using the specified attribute values. If a specified attribute does not exist in the device entry, **putdev** adds it to the entry. **putdev** also modifies attributes that already have a value with the value specified.

Listing Devices

The **getdev** command lists devices defined in the Device Database based on specified criteria. It has the following syntax:

```
getdev [-ae] [criteria [ ... ]] [device [ ... ]]
```

getdev generates a list of devices that match certain **criteria**. These criteria include a list of attributes (given in expressions) and a list of devices. If no criteria are given, all devices are included in the generated list.

Devices must satisfy at least one criteria in the list (see **-a** option). Devices defined on the command line that match the criteria are included in the generated list.

> **NOTE**
> The **-e** flag specifies that the list of devices defined on the command line becomes a set of devices to be excluded from the list.

The criteria argument may be specified with any of the following four expression types:

- **attribute=value**   Selects all devices for which the attribute is defined and is equal to value.

- **attribute!=value**   Selects all devices for which the attribute is defined and does not equal value.

- **attribute:***   Selects all devices for which the attribute is defined.

- **attribute!:***   Selects all devices that do not have the attribute defined.

getdev takes the following options and arguments:

- **-a**   Specifies that the list of devices that follows on the command line must match all criteria to be included in the list generated by this command. The flag has no effect if no criteria are defined.

- **-e**   Specifies that the list of devices following on the command line should be excluded from the list generated by this command.

> **NOTE**
> The flags **-a** and **-e** have no effect if no devices are defined.

- **criteria**   Defines the criteria that a device must match to be included in the generated list. The criteria should be given in expressions.

- **device**   Defines the devices that should be included or excluded (based on the command options) in the generated list. This can be the pathname of the device or the device alias.

Listing Attributes
The **devattr** command lists device attributes. It has the following syntax:

```
devattr [-v] device [attribute [ ... ]]
```

devattr displays the values for a device's attributes. The display can be presented in two formats. When run without the **-v** option, **devattr** shows only the attribute values. When run with **-v**, **devattr** shows the attributes in the format ***attribute=value*[,*value ...*]**. When no attributes are given on the command line, all attributes for the specified device are displayed in alphabetical order by attribute name. If attributes are given on the command line, only those are shown and they are displayed in command line order.

devattr takes the following options and arguments:

■ **-v**   Specifies verbose format, where attribute values are displayed in an ***attribute=value*** format.

■ ***device***   Defines the device for which attributes should be displayed. This value can be the absolute pathname of the device or the device alias. If the provided value is an absolute pathname, **devattr** gets the device alias name to which the pathname maps, and displays all the attributes defined for that alias.

■ ***attribute***   Defines which attributes should be shown. The default is to show all attributes for a device.

Using the sysadm Interface

Execute **sysadm storage_devices** to access the storage device management menu from the command line. Then execute the **devices** option to access the Device Alias and Attribute menu and select the desired option.

Managing Device Groups

Devices are often grouped for ease of management. The **/etc/dgroup.tab** file is the device group database.

Using the Command Line

The **putdgrp** command edits a device group table or deletes a device group or a device from a group definition. The **listdgrp** command generates the list of devices composing a group.

Creating a Device Group
The **putdgrp** command edits a device group table. It has the following syntax:

```
putdgrp dgroup [device [...]]
```

putdgrp modifies the device group table by creating a new device group. It also can change group definitions by adding or removing a device from the group definition.

When **putdgrp** is executed without a device specification, it adds the specified group name to the device group table if it does not already exist.

When **putdgrp** is executed with both a *dgroup* and a device specification, it adds the given device name (or names) to the group definition. If the **device** group does not exist, it creates the group and adds the specified devices to that new group.

putdgrp takes these options and arguments:

- ◼ *dgroup*   Specifies a device group name.
- ◼ *device*   Specifies the pathname or alias of the device that is to be added to or deleted from the device group.

For example, the following command:

```
putdgrp floppies
```

adds a new device group, **floppies**. The following command:

```
putdgrp floppies diskette2
```

adds a device **diskette2** to the device group, **floppies**.

Removing a Device Group

The **putdgrp -d** command deletes a device group or a device from a group definition. It has the following syntax:

```
putdgrp [-d] dgroup [device [...]]
```

where *dgroup* and *device* are the same as described just above. For example,

```
putdgrp -d floppies
```

deletes the device group called **floppies**. The following command:

```
putdgrp -d floppies diskette2
```

deletes the device **diskette2** from the device group called **floppies**.

Generating a List of Group Members

To generate the list of devices composing a group enter this:

```
listdgrp group_name
```

This is an example of how to use this command:

```
# listdgrp mydisk
mydiskx
mydisky
sysdiska
#
```

The group **mydisk** contains three members: **mydiskx**, **mydisky**, and **sysdiska**.

Managing Device Reservations

Device reservations prevent other users from accessing the specified devices while the requestor is using them. It is important to free a device reservation as soon as possible to enable others to access it.

Using the Command Line

The command **devreserv** reserves devices for exclusive use and lists the devices that have been reserved. The command **devfree** releases devices from exclusive use.

Reserving a Device

The command **devreserv** reserves devices for exclusive use. It has the following syntax:

```
devreserv [key [devicelist ...]]
```

TIP
When the device is no longer required, use **devfree** to release it.

devreserv reserves at most one device per *devicelist*. Each list is searched in linear order until the first available device is found.

CAUTION

If a device cannot be reserved from each list, the entire reservation fails.

The command **devreserv** used without arguments lists devices that are currently reserved, and the keys to which they are reserved. When **devreserv** is executed with only the key argument, it lists the devices currently reserved to that key.

devreserv takes the following arguments:

- *key* Designates a unique key on which the device will be reserved. The key must be a positive integer.

- *devicelist* Defines a list of devices searched to find an available one. The list must be formatted as a single argument to the shell.

TIP

Processes that utilize the device reservation capability cannot access a device until the reservation has been canceled. However, processes that do not use device reservation may use reserved devices since they do not check for its reservation status.

The command

```
$ devreserv
```

with no arguments lists all devices currently reserved, as shown in the following example:

```
disk1 2423
diskette1 10658
ctape1 10658
```

Freeing a Device

The command **devfree** releases devices from exclusive use. It has the following syntax:

```
devfree key [device [...]]
```

TIP

Request exclusive use of a device with the command **devreserv**.

When **devfree** is invoked with only the key argument, it releases all devices reserved for that key. When called with key and device arguments, **devfree** releases the specified devices that have been reserved with that key.

devfree takes the following arguments:

■ **key**   Designates the unique key on which the device was reserved.

■ **device**   Defines the device to be released from exclusive use. This can be the device pathname or the device alias.

NOTE
The commands **devreserv** and **devfree** manage device availability on a system. They do not limit device access but serve to centralize bookkeeping. Processes that do not use **devreserv** ignore device reservations.

APPENDIX B

File System Check Program Errors

This appendix presents errors that may arise when running the **fsck** program. The **fsck** (for **f**ile **s**ystem **c**heck) program checks the file system and generates various error messages at each phase of its operation. Unless you have run it with the **-y** option (not recommended), it waits for your response before continuing its operation.

General Errors

These three error messages may appear in any phase of **fsck**. In general you should regard them as fatal, stop the program, and investigate the cause of the problem.

CANNOT SEEK: BLK B (CONTINUE?)
The request to move to a specified block number B in the file system failed. You can respond to "Continue?" with either no or yes.

- **No**   Terminates the program, and is the recommended response.

- **Yes**   Attempts to continue to run the file system check program. Often, however, the problem persists. The error condition does not allow a complete check of the file system. Run **fsck** again to recheck the file system.

CANNOT READ: BLK B (CONTINUE?)
The request for reading a specified block number B in the file system failed. You can respond to "Continue?" with either no or yes.

- **No**   Terminates the program, and is the recommended response.

- **Yes**   Attempts to continue to run file system check program. Often, however, the problem persists. The error condition does not allow a complete check of the file system. Run **fsck** again to recheck the file system.

CANNOT WRITE: BLK B (CONTINUE?)
The request for writing a specified block number B in the file system failed. The disk may be write-protected. You can respond to "Continue?" with either no or yes.

- **No**   Terminates the program, and is the recommended response.

- **Yes**   Attempts to continue to run file system check program. Often, however, the problem persists. The error condition does not allow a complete check of the file system. Run **fsck** again to recheck the file system.

Errors in the Initialization Phase

This phase checks the command syntax. Before performing the file system check, **fsck** sets up certain tables and opens some files. It terminates on encountering initialization errors.

Errors in Phases 1 and 1B—Check Blocks and Sizes

Phase 1 checks the inode list. This section lists each of the error or warning messages that may be generated in Phase 1, and notes the problems that each error message may indicate.

UNKNOWN FILE TYPE I=I (CLEAR?)

The mode word of the inode I suggests that it is not a named pipe, special character inode, regular inode, or directory inode. You can respond to "Clear?" with either no or yes.

- **No** Ignores the error condition. Responding with no is appropriate only if the user intends to take other measures to fix the problem.

- **Yes** Deallocates inode by zeroing its contents. This may invoke the UNALLOCATED error condition in Phase 2 for each directory entry pointing to this inode.

LINK COUNT TABLE OVERFLOW (CONTINUE?)

An internal table containing allocated inodes with a link count of zero is full. You can respond to "Continue?" with either no or yes.

- **No** Terminates the program (the recommended response).

- **Yes** Continues with the program. This response means a complete file system check is not possible. Run **fsck** again to recheck the file system.

B BAD I=I

Inode I contains block number B with a number lower than the number of the first data block in the file system or greater than the number of the last block in the file system. This error condition may invoke the EXCESSIVE BAD BLKS error condition in Phase 1 if inode I has too many block numbers outside the file system range. This error condition invokes the DUP/BAD error condition in Phase 2 and Phase 4.

EXCESSIVE BAD BLKS I=I (CONTINUE?)

There are too many (usually more than 10) blocks whose number is lower than the number of the first data block in the file system or greater than the number of the last block in the file system associated with inode I. You may respond to "Continue" with either no or yes.

- ■ **No**   Terminates the program (the recommended response).

- ■ **Yes**   Continues with the program. This response means a complete file system check is not possible. Run **fsck** again to recheck the file system.

B DUP I=I

Inode I contains block number B, already claimed by another inode. This error condition may invoke the EXCESSIVE DUP BLKS error condition in Phase 1 if inode I has too many block numbers claimed by other inodes. This error condition invokes Phase 1B and the BAD/DUP error condition in Phase 2 and Phase 4.

EXCESSIVE DUP BLKS I=I (CONTINUE?)

There are too many (usually more than 10) blocks claimed by other inodes. You can respond to "Continue?" with either no or yes.

- ■ **No**   Terminates the program (the recommended response).

- ■ **Yes**   Continues with the program. This response means a complete file system check is not possible. Run **fsck** again to recheck the file system.

DUP TABLE OVERFLOW (CONTINUE?)

An internal table containing duplicate block numbers is full. You can respond to "Continue?" with either no or yes.

- ■ **No**   Terminates the program (the recommended response).

- ■ **Yes**   Continues with the program. This response means a complete file system check is not possible. Run **fsck** again to recheck the file system.

POSSIBLE FILE SIZE ERROR I=I
The inode I size does not match the actual number of blocks used by the inode. This is only a warning. The **-q** option suppresses this message.

DIRECTORY MISALIGNED I=I
The directory inode size is not a multiple of 16. This is only a warning. The **-q** option suppresses this message.

PARTIALLY ALLOCATED INODE I=I (CLEAR?)
Inode I is neither allocated nor unallocated. Phase 1B: Rescan for More DUPS When a duplicate block is found in the file system, the file system is rescanned to find the inode that previously claimed that block. When the duplicate block is found, the **B DUP I=I** message is printed. (It's discussed next.) You may respond to "Clear" with either no or yes.

- **No** Ignores the error condition. Responding with no is appropriate only if the user intends to take other measures to fix the problem.

- **Yes** Deallocates inode by zeroing its contents. This may invoke the UNALLOCATED error condition in Phase 2 for each directory entry pointing to this inode.

B DUP I=I
Inode I contains block number B, which is already claimed by another inode. This error condition invokes the BAD/DUP error condition in Phase 2. Inodes with overlapping blocks may be determined by examining this error condition and the DUP error condition in Phase 1.

Errors in Phase 2–Check Pathnames

Phase 2 removes directory entries pointing to bad inodes found in Phase 1 and Phase 1B. This section covers the error messages that Phase 2 may generate.

ROOT INODE UNALLOCATED. TERMINATING
The root inode (always inode number 2) has no allocate mode bits. This error condition indicates a serious problem and stops the program.

ROOT INODE NOT DIRECTORY (FIX?)

The root inode (usually inode number 2) is not a directory inode type. You can respond to "Fix?" with either no or yes.

- ■ **No**   Terminates the program since **fsck** will be unable to continue.

- ■ **Yes**   Changes the root inode type to directory. If the root inode data blocks are not directory blocks, a very large number of error conditions are produced.

DUPS/BAD IN ROOT INODE (CONTINUE?)

Phase 1 or Phase 1B found duplicate blocks or bad blocks in the root inode (usually inode number 2) for the file system. You can respond to "Continue" with either no or yes.

- ■ **No**   Terminates the program.

- ■ **Yes**   Ignores the DUPS/BAD error condition in root inode and attempts to continue running the file system check. If root inode is not correct, this may result in a large number of other error conditions.

I OUT OF RANGE I=I NAME=F (REMOVE?)

A directory entry F has an inode number I greater than the end of the inode list. You can respond to "Remove?" with either no or yes.

- ■ **No**   Ignores the error condition. Responding no is appropriate only if the user intends to take other measures to fix the problem.

- ■ **Yes**   Removes duplicate or unallocated blocks.

UNALLOCATED I=I OWNER=O MODE=M SIZE=S
MTIME=T NAME=F (REMOVE?)

A directory entry F has an inode I without allocate mode bits. The owner O, mode M, size S, modify time T, and filename F are printed. If the file system is not mounted and the **-n** option was not specified, the entry is removed automatically if it points to an inode whose character size is 0. You can respond to "Remove?" with either no or yes.

- ■ **No**   Ignores the error condition. Responding no is appropriate only if the user intends to take other measures to fix the problem.

- ■ **Yes**   Removes duplicate or unallocated blocks.

DUP/BAD I=I OWNER=O MODE=M SIZE=S
MTIME=T DIR=F (REMOVE?)

Phase 1 or Phase 1B found duplicate blocks or bad blocks associated with directory entry F, directory inode I. The owner O, mode M, size S, modify time T, and directory name F are printed. You can respond to "Remove?" with either no or yes.

- **No**   Ignores the error condition. Responding no is appropriate only if the user intends to take other measures to fix the problem.

- **Yes**   Removes duplicate or unallocated blocks.

DUP/BAD I=I OWNER=O MODE=M SIZE=S
MTIME=T FILE=F (REMOVE?)

Phase 1 or Phase 1B found duplicate blocks or bad blocks associated with file entry F, inode I. The owner O, mode M, size S, modify time T, and filename F are printed. You can respond to "Remove?" with either no or yes.

- **No**   Ignores the error condition. Responding no is appropriate only if the user intends to take other measures to fix the problem.

- **Yes**   Removes duplicate or unallocated blocks.

BAD BLK B IN DIR I=I OWNER=O MODE=M SIZE=S
MTIME=T

This message occurs only when the **-D** option is used. A bad block was found in DIR inode I. Error conditions looked for in directory blocks are nonzero padded entries, inconsistent **.** and **..** entries, and embedded slashes in the name field. This error message means that the user should subsequently either remove the directory inode if the entire block looks bad or change (or remove) those directory entries that look bad.

Errors in Phase 3—Check Connectivity

Phase 3 is concerned with the directory connectivity seen in Phase 2. This section covers the error message that may be generated in Phase 3.

UNREF DIR I=I OWNER=O MODE=M SIZE=S MTIME=T (RECONNECT?)

The directory inode I was not connected to a directory entry when the file system was traversed. The owner O, mode M, size S, and modify time T of directory inode I are printed. **fsck** forces the reconnection of a nonempty directory. You can respond to "Reconnect?" with either no or yes.

- **No** Ignores the error condition. This invokes the UNREF error condition in Phase 4. Responding no is appropriate only if the user intends to take other measures to fix the problem.

- **Yes** Reconnects directory inode I to the file system in the directory for lost files (usually **lost+found**). This may invoke a lost+found error condition if there are problems connecting directory inode I to **lost+found**. This invokes the CONNECTED information message if link was successful.

SORRY. NO lost+found DIRECTORY

There is no **lost+found** directory in the root directory of the file system; **fsck** ignores the request to link a directory in **lost+found**. This invokes the UNREF error condition in Phase 4, and indicates a possible problem with access modes of **lost+found**.

SORRY. NO SPACE IN lost+found DIRECTORY

There is no space to add another entry to the **lost+found** directory in the root directory of the file system; **fsck** ignores the request to link a directory in **lost+found**. This invokes the UNREF error condition in Phase 4. Clean out unnecessary entries in **lost+found** or make **lost+found** larger.

DIR I=I1 CONNECTED. PARENT WAS I=I2

This is an advisory message indicating a directory inode I1 was successfully connected to the **lost+found** directory. The parent inode I2 of the directory inode I1 is replaced by the inode number of the **lost+found** directory.

Errors in Phase 4—Check Reference Counts

Phase 4 checks the link count information seen in Phases 2 and 3. This section discusses the various error messages that Phase 4 may generate.

UNREF FILE I=I OWNER=O MODE=M SIZE=S MTIME=T (RECONNECT?)

Inode I was not connected to a directory entry when the file system was traversed. The owner O, mode M, size S, and modify time T of inode I are printed. If the **-n** option is omitted and the file system is not mounted, empty files are cleared automatically. Nonempty files are not cleared. You can respond to "Reconnect?" with either no or yes.

- **No**   Ignores this error condition. This invokes a CLEAR error condition later in Phase 4.

- **Yes**   Reconnects inode I to file system in the directory for lost files (usually **lost+found**). This can cause a lost+found error condition in this phase if there are problems connecting inode I to **lost+found**.

SORRY. NO lost+found DIRECTORY

There is no **lost+found** directory in the root directory of the file system; **fsck** ignores the request to link a file in **lost+found**. This invokes the CLEAR error condition later in Phase 4. This error message may indicate a problem with permissions of **lost+found**.

SORRY. NO SPACE IN lost+found DIRECTORY

There is no space to add another entry to the **lost+found** directory in the root directory of the file system; **fsck** ignores the request to link a file in **lost+found**. This invokes the CLEAR error condition later in Phase 4. If you get this error message, check the size and contents of **lost+found**.

LINK COUNT FILE I=I OWNER=O MODE=M SIZE=S
MTIME=T COUNT=X SHOULD BE Y (ADJUST?)

The link count for inode I, which is a file, is X but should be Y. The owner O, mode M, size S, and modify time T are printed. You can respond to "Adjust?" with either no or yes.

- **No**   Ignores the error. Responding no is appropriate only if the user intends to take other measures to fix the problem.

- **Yes**   Replaces link count of file inode I with Y.

LINK COUNT DIR I=I OWNER=O MODE=M SIZE=S
MTIME=T COUNT=X SHOULD BE Y (ADJUST?)

The link count for inode I, which is a directory, is X but should be Y. The owner O, mode M, size S, and modify time T of directory inode I are printed. You can respond to "Adjust?" with either no or yes.

- **No**   Ignores the error. Responding no is appropriate only if the user intends to take other measures to fix the problem.

- **Yes**   Replaces link count of file inode I with Y.

**LINK COUNT F I=I OWNER=O MODE=M SIZE=S
MTIME=T COUNT=X SHOULD BE Y (ADJUST?)**

The link count for F inode I is X but should be Y. The filename F, owner O, mode M, size S, and modify time T are printed. You can respond to "Adjust?" with either no or yes.

- **No**   Ignores the error. Responding no is appropriate only if the user intends to take other measures to fix the problem.

- **Yes**   Replaces link count of file inode I with Y.

**UNREF FILE I=I OWNER=O MODE=M SIZE=S
MTIME=T (CLEAR?)**

Inode I, which is a file, was not connected to a directory entry when the file system was traversed. The owner O, mode M, size S, and modify time T of inode I are printed. If the **-n** option is omitted and the file system is not mounted, empty files are cleared automatically. Nonempty directories are not cleared. You can respond to "Clear" with either no or yes.

- **No**   Ignores the error condition. Responding no is appropriate only if the user intends to take other measures to fix the problem.

- **Yes**   Deallocates the inode by zeroing its contents.

**UNREF DIR I=I OWNER=O MODE=M SIZE=S
MTIME=T (CLEAR?)**

Inode I, which is a directory, was not connected to a directory entry when the file system was traversed. The owner O, mode M, size S, and modify time T of inode I are printed. If the **-n** option is omitted and the file system is not mounted, empty directories are cleared automatically. Nonempty directories are not cleared. You can respond to "Clear?" with either no or yes.

- **No**   Ignores the error condition. Responding no is appropriate only if the user intends to take other measures to fix the problem.

- **Yes**   Deallocates the inode by zeroing its contents.

**BAD/DUP FILE I=I OWNER=O MODE=M SIZE=S
MTIME=T (CLEAR?)**

Phase 1 or Phase 1B found duplicate blocks or bad blocks associated with file inode I. The owner O, mode M, size S, and modify time T of inode I are printed. You can respond to "Clear?" with either no or yes.

- **No** Ignores the error condition. Responding no is appropriate only if the user intends to take other measures to fix the problem.

- **Yes** Deallocates the inode by zeroing its contents.

BAD/DUP DIR I=I OWNER=O MODE=M SIZE=S
MTIME=T (CLEAR?)
Phase 1 or Phase 1B found duplicate blocks or bad blocks associated with directory inode I. The owner O, mode M, size S, and modify time T of inode I are printed. You can respond to "Clear?" with either no or yes.

- **No** Ignores the error condition. Responding no is appropriate only if the user intends to take other measures to fix the problem.

- **Yes** Deallocates the inode by zeroing its contents.

FREE INODE COUNT WRONG IN SUPERBLK (FIX?)
The actual free inodes count does not match the count in the superblock of the file system. If the **-q** option is specified, the count will be fixed automatically in the superblock. You can respond to "Fix?" with either no or yes.

- **No** Ignores the error. Responding no is appropriate only if the user intends to take other measures to fix the problem.

- **Yes** Replaces count in superblock by actual count.

Errors in Phase 5—Check Free List

Phase 5 checks the free block list. This section covers the error messages that may be generated in Phase 5.

EXCESSIVE BAD BLKS IN FREE LIST (CONTINUE?)
The free block list contains too many (usually more than 10) blocks whose value is less than the first data block in the file system or greater than the last block in the file system. This error condition will always invoke the BAD BLKS IN FREE LIST error condition later in Phase 5. You can respond to "Continue?" with either no or yes.

- **No** Terminates the program.

- **Yes** Ignores the rest of the free blocks list and continues execution of **fsck**.

EXCESSIVE DUP BLKS IN FREE LIST (CONTINUE?)

The free block list contains too many (usually more than 10) blocks claimed by inodes or earlier parts of the free block list. This error condition will always invoke the BAD BLKS IN FREE LIST error condition later in Phase 5. You can respond to "Continue?" with either no or yes.

- ■ **No** Terminates the program.
- ■ **Yes** Ignores the rest of the free blocks list and continues execution of **fsck**.

BAD FREEBLK COUNT

The free block count in a free-list block is greater than 50 or less than 0. This error condition will always invoke the BAD FREE LIST condition later in Phase 5.

X BAD BLKS IN FREE LIST

X blocks in the free block list have a block number lower than the first data block in the file system or greater than the last block in the file system. This error condition will always invoke the BAD FREE LIST condition later in Phase 5.

X DUP BLKS IN FREE LIST

X blocks claimed by inodes or earlier parts of the free-list block were found in the free block list. This error condition will always invoke the BAD FREE LIST condition later in Phase 5.

X BLK(S) MISSING

X blocks unused by the file system were not found in the free block list. This error condition will always invoke the BAD FREE LIST condition later in Phase 5.

FREE BLK COUNT WRONG IN SUPERBLOCK (FIX?)

The actual free block count does not match the count in the superblock of the file system. You can respond to "Fix?" with either no or yes.

- ■ **No** Ignores the error condition. Responding no is appropriate only if the user intends to take other measures to fix the problem.
- ■ **Yes** Replaces count in superblock by actual count.

BAD FREE LIST (SALVAGE?)

This message is always preceded by one or more Phase 5 information messages. If the **-q** option is specified, the free block list will be salvaged automatically. You can respond to "Salvage?" with either no or yes.

- **No**   Ignores the error. Responding no is appropriate only if the user intends to take other measures to fix the problem.

- **Yes**   Replaces actual free block list with a new free block list. The new free block list will be ordered according to the gap and cylinder specs of the **-s** or **-S** option to reduce time spent waiting for the disk to rotate into position.

Errors in Phase 6—Salvage Free Block List

This phase reconstructs the free block list. It has one possible error condition that results from bad blocks-per-cylinder and gap values. It may generate the following warning message:

DEFAULT FREE BLOCK LIST SPACING ASSUMED
This advisory message indicates one of the following: the blocks-to-skip (gap) is greater than the blocks-per-cylinder, the blocks-to-skip is less than 1, the blocks-per-cylinder is less than 1, or the blocks-per-cylinder is greater than 500. The values of 7 blocks-to-skip and 400 blocks-per-cylinder are used.

Errors in Cleanup Phase

After checking a file system, **fsck** performs a few cleanup functions. The cleanup phase displays advisory messages about the file system and its status.

Cleanup Phase Messages X files Y blocks Z free
This advisory message indicates that the file system contained X files using Y blocks leaving Z blocks free in the file system.

* * * * * BOOT Unix (NO SYNC!) * * * * *
This advisory message indicates that a mounted file system or the root file system has been modified by **fsck**. If the Unix system is not rebooted immediately without **sync**, the work done by **fsck** may be undone by the in-core copies of tables the Unix system keeps. If the **-b** option was specified and the file system is root, a reboot is automatically done.

* * * * * FILE SYSTEM WAS MODIFIED * * * * *
This advisory message indicates that **fsck** modified the current file system.

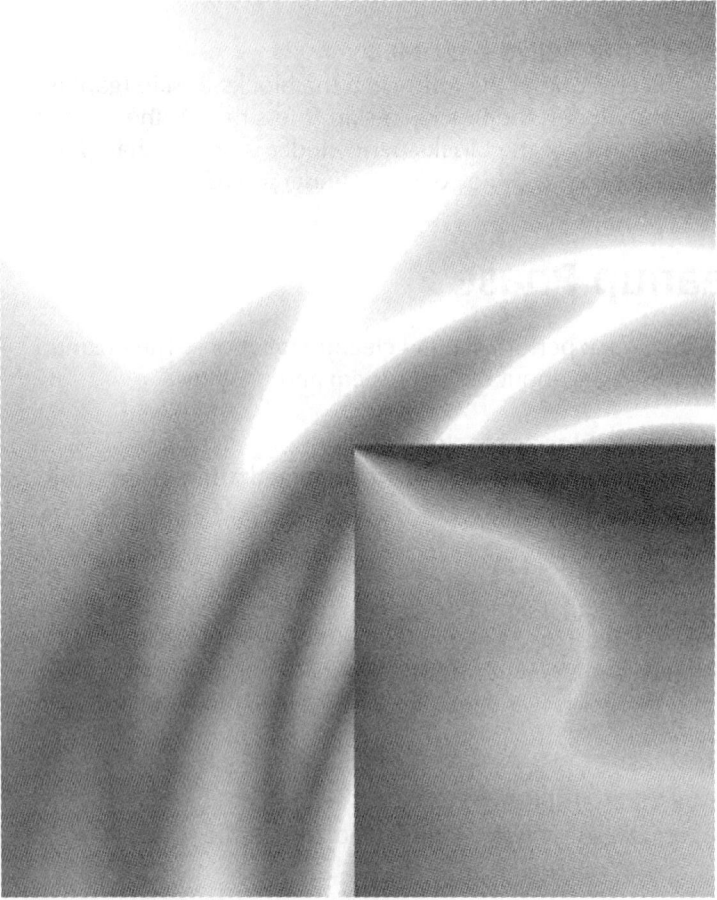

A P P E N D I X C

Installing UnixWare
and MS Windows

This appendix provides step-by-step instructions for installing the Personal Edition or Application Server. You can use this appendix as a checklist for installing UnixWare or refer to it for specific installation procedures. This appendix also includes instructions for installing Windows on top of UnixWare.

Before installing UnixWare, you have to perform a few basic steps. These steps include attaching and configuring hardware peripherals, backing up system data, and recording networking configuration information.

CAUTION
Don't forget to back up your software, including its operating system, before you install UnixWare.

The Installation Procedure

To begin the installation, follow these steps:

1. Boot your computer according to the current operating system. (For example, if you are running an earlier version of UnixWare, click the Shutdown icon or enter **shutdown -i6**.)

2. Press the reset button or turn off your computer, then wait a few seconds and turn it back on. If your computer is currently off, turn it on.

3. Insert the Install Diskette into disk drive 1. The Install Diskette contains the software for starting the installation. Later the installation may call for CD, cartridge tape, or network device.

Depending on your hardware, you may be prompted to change existing BIOS or SCSI settings. Because these prompts are external to UnixWare, wait until the UnixWare 2.0 installation screen appears before pressing any keys.

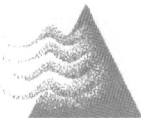

> *TIP*
> Press the SPACEBAR to interrupt the boot sequence. You will get the shell prompt (#). After examining it, type **go** and press the ENTER key. You can press the ALT-SYSREQ keys and then type **H** to change to the debugging mode. Return to the Install screen by pressing ALT-SYSREQ and then pressing F1.

4. Identify your monitor type (if you are prompted to) and then press the ENTER key. If your monitor is not attached via a VGA or compatible video adapter, you are asked if you are using a color monitor.

5. A welcome message appears. Press the ENTER key once you have read the welcome message.

> *NOTE*
> If prompted for it, insert the Install Diskette, called Diskette 2 of 2 and press the ENTER key. Having to insert a second diskette is more common with 5 1/4-inch diskettes than with 3 1/2-inch diskettes.

The Keyboard Type

Next, select your keyboard type. The keyboard type usually corresponds to the language spoken and/or country of residence. Each of the following cases gives you the choice of two keyboard types:

■ Italian keyboard type is Italian (IBM 142) for an IBM 142 keyboard, or Italian otherwise.

■ Japanese keyboard type is Japanese (AX) or Japanese (A101).

■ For United States keyboard types, select US (Latin I) to generate ASCII or non-ASCII (special) keyboard characters, or select US (ASCII) to generate only ASCII keyboard characters.

■ In Japanese locales, the US (Latin I) and US (ASCII) selections are the same.

When prompted either to "install Host Bus Adapter Drivers" *or* to "Continue Installation," first remove the Install Diskette.

Installing Host Bus Adapter (HBA) Diskettes

Insert the HBA (Host Bus Adapter) diskette (or diskettes, as required) or select Continue Installation. The installation process determines which device drivers on the diskette are needed.

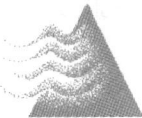

TIP
If the installation later fails because the hard disk could not be found, repeat the installation using HBA diskette(s).

The Host Bus Adapter Drivers diskette is provided with UnixWare 2.0. Some system configurations include additional HBA diskettes from Novell or third-party vendors.

CAUTION
Do not press any keys before the system displays an appropriate message. If you do, you may interfere with the loading of hardware and software device drivers.

Follow the prompts for removing the HBA diskette and perhaps installing another one.

Using the DCU to Handle Device Driver Configuration

The Device Configuration Utility (DCU) is an advanced system administration tool for viewing and changing UnixWare device driver configuration data. DCU is described in Chapter 7.

Select whether to enter the DCU and then press the ENTER key.

UnixWare can detect what most hardware is and automatically configure the required software device drivers without your having to invoke the DCU. But you may need to access the DCU to perform the following operations:

■ Determining the available hardware components on a given system, especially if the system has configured device drivers.

■ Assigning device driver parameters for hardware devices (such as non-SCSI CD-ROMs) that UnixWare cannot automatically detect.

■ Preventing the installation software from loading device drivers that are not needed.

■ Changing the system device driver configuration.

Verifying the Hardware Configuration

The system verifies the hardware configuration. Wait until the Select Installation Method screen appears to tell you that the verification is complete. If an error occurred in installing the hardware or configuring the software, follow the online instructions for correcting it. For example, UnixWare lists all software device drivers with conflicting settings. If there is a conflicting setting, record this information and, when prompted, reboot or shut down your system. Then follow these instructions:

■ If the displayed device driver settings are the same as the hardware settings, your hardware has been configured incorrectly. Reconfigure your hardware to use nonconflicting parameters, including IRQ and memory address.

■ If the displayed device driver settings differ from the hardware settings, repeat the UnixWare installation and use the DCU to reconfigure the device drivers.

Selecting the Installation Method

To perform a network installation, go to the next step. To install from media (CD-ROM or cartridge tape), insert the medium, select Install from CD-ROM or Install from Tape, and press the ENTER key.

If the media type you want to install from is not displayed, check for one of these potential problems:

■ The power on the CD-ROM or cartridge tape drive may be turned off. To fix this problem, turn on the power, reboot the system, and repeat the installation.

■ The CD-ROM or cartridge tape drive may not be properly connected to your system. To fix this problem, connect and power up the external unit, reboot the system, and repeat the installation.

■ UnixWare did not detect the CD-ROM or cartridge tape drive. To fix this problem, reboot the system and insert HBA diskette(s) when prompted. If the problem persists, repeat the installation and invoke the DCU to assign the device driver parameters for the CD-ROM or cartridge tape drive.

Performing a Network Installation

To perform a network installation, first specify whether you are installing from an IPX/SPX or a TCP/IP Install Server. Then press the ENTER key and follow the prompts for network installation.

When prompted, insert the Network Installation Utilities diskette into Drive 1 and press the ENTER key. When prompted, enter the system node name. If the computer has a name, enter it. Otherwise (with the help of your system or network administrator if necessary), select a name unique to the network. Confirm the name by pressing the ENTER key.

When prompted, select the networking hardware from the menu that lists supported networking cards. An asterisk marks the currently selected networking card. After making your selection, press the ENTER key.

NOTE
If your networking card is not listed, then you must reboot your system and install from media.

Configure the network hardware parameters. Depending on the selected networking card, you are prompted for the interrupt vector (IRQ), I/O address range, memory address range, cable type, and/or EISA slot number. After verifying your selections, press the F10 key to confirm them.

When prompted, enter the appropriate networking data:

■ In an IPX/SPX network installation, you are prompted for the Install Server name. By default, the name of the "closest" Install Server on your network is displayed. A number in square brackets indicates the number of network hops from the Install Server to the system being installed. A menu lists other configured Install Servers on your network. An asterisk denotes the current selection. To select another Install Server, press the F2 key or the TAB key. Press the ENTER key to confirm your selection.

■ In a TCP/IP network installation, you are prompted for the following parameters: system IP address, netmask, Router IP address, and Server IP address. Default values for these parameters may be displayed; a blank denotes any parameter the installation software cannot detect. Press the TAB key to move the cursor to the field to change. (If the current field contains an invalid value, the cursor will not move to the next field.) Enter a correct value. Review the entries, and press the F10 key to confirm and exit the menu.

Upgrading from a Previous UnixWare Release

This step first determines whether you are performing a nondestructive installation or a destructive installation. A nondestructive installation preserves existing user and configuration files; a destructive installation destroys them. Once the installation is complete, the files are merged, unneeded packages are removed, and online data-manager media is provided as required.

If prompted, select whether to attempt a nondestructive installation, to attempt a destructive installation, or to cancel the installation. If the installation software determines that the active partition contains UnixWare 2.0 or a version of UnixWare that can be upgraded to UnixWare 2.0, you are prompted to perform a nondestructive or destructive installation, or to cancel the installation. If the installation software detects a version of Unix that cannot be upgraded to UnixWare 2.0 in the active partition, you are prompted to continue the installation or to cancel it. If the installation software does not detect a Unix operating system in the active partition, then you must perform a destructive installation or cancel the installation.

The next step describes a nondestructive installation. To do a destructive installation, skip to the following section.

Performing a Nondestructive Installation

Use the Choose merge options menu to specify whether to combine system configuration files. Some system configuration files (called *volatile files*), such as

/etc/passwd, are overwritten during the installation process unless you decide to combine them. You'll see more about merging files shortly.

If your system contains any obsolete packages (such as UnixWare 1.1 packages superseded by UnixWare 2.0 packages), the Obsolete Packages menu appears and asks whether to remove them and continue the installation or cancel the installation.

If your previous system included the Online Data Manager product and you did not remove it before starting the installation, insert the UnixWare 2.0 Online Data Manager media or cancel the installation. If so prompted, you must insert the Online Data Manager media to install UnixWare 2.0. For more information, see the UnixWare Installation Handbook. Then enter the date and time.

Merging Device Driver Files
When performing a nondestructive installation, you must decide whether to merge the **/etc/conf** files.

The UnixWare 2.0 installation software attempts to determine the necessary device drivers for your hardware. During a nondestructive installation, you are asked whether to merge additional device drivers from your previous system into the **/etc/conf** directory. To save space, do not merge these device drivers. When needed, you can copy the saved information from the **/etc/inst/save/user** directory.

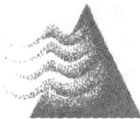

> *TIP*
> If the system won't boot after merging the **/etc/conf** files, reboot UnixWare using the **unix.old** file, move **unix.old** to **unix**, and do another nondestructive installation.

Performing a Destructive Installation

There are two procedures that are available only for destructive installation: configuring disk partitions and setting the system node name.

> *CAUTION*
> To perform a nondestructive installation when the Destructive Installation menu is displayed, select Cancel Installation and Shut Down System, set the active partition to the previous UnixWare partition and then repeat the installation.

Configuring Disk Partitions
You have three choices. You can dedicate the entire primary hard disk to UnixWare, partition the disk for multiple operating systems, or cancel the

installation. If you want to keep other installed operating systems or install additional operating systems, partition your disk and assign a partition for UnixWare from the Disk I Partitions menu. After viewing and/or changing your disk partition, press the F10 key.

You can view or change the partitions of a first or second hard disk by selecting View or Change Disk Configuration from the Install menu. If you select this menu, the four disk partitions are displayed. This menu is also used for advanced disk configuration operations (such as adding partitions, deleting partitions, selecting the active partition, changing the partition size, viewing/changing file systems, deciding whether to overwrite your system boot code, and selecting whether to perform a surface analysis).

Use the following procedure to change a partition type:

1. Move the cursor to the type field for the partition you are changing.

2. Press the F2 key to display the partition choices. Use the TAB key or the UP ARROW and DOWN ARROW keys to cycle through the choices and select the desired partition type (Unix System, pre-5.0 DOS, DOS, other, unused, or system partition).

3. Press the ENTER key to confirm your selection and exit from the Choose Type menu. The new partition type is displayed.

To change the partition status (from inactive to active or vice versa), move the cursor to the status field and press F2. To change the size of a partition, move the cursor to the % field or the cylinders field, enter the new value, and press F10 to confirm.

Entering the System Node Name

The procedure for entering the system node name is available only for destructive installation.

When prompted, enter the system node name. The system node name must be between 3 and 35 characters long and can include only the following letters and characters: A through Z, a through z, period (.), at (@) sign, dollar sign ($), underscore (_), or dash character. Using periods and at signs is discouraged. Use the existing computer name, if there is one. If your computer is not networked, its name is only restricted by these naming conventions. Select a unique name for a networked computer (with the help of the network or system administrator if necessary).

Entering the Date and Time

Enter the date, time, and time zone. Use the TAB key or the arrow keys to move to the desired field set.

To set the Timezone field, press the F2 key to display the Continent menu. Use the arrow keys or the TAB key to select the Continent. Then press the ENTER key to display a list of time zones. Use the arrow keys or the TAB key to select a time zone. Then press the ENTER key to confirm. Finally, press the F10 key to complete the date and time zone entry.

The Install Menu Screen

The Install Menu screen lets you view or change installation options, including package selection and file system configuration, and begin installing UnixWare on your hard disk. If you want to, you can cancel or restart the installation. Typically, most users want to modify the installed set of packages and partition a second hard disk, if one is available. For example, in order to view the UnixWare online manuals, you must install the DynaText document browser and the Personal Edition Documentation or Application Server Documentation package. To install them, access the View or Change Package Selection command from the Install menu.

NOTE
In a multimachine computing environment, you can install these packages on one machine and configure other networked machines to access them.

Once you are satisfied with the installation setup, select Accept All Settings and Install Now. Default values are used for options not set explicitly, and then the installation begins.

The View or Change Package Selection Option
The View or Change Package Selection option displays the package list for your version of UnixWare. Asterisks denote packages to be installed. To install a particular package, move the cursor to it with the arrow keys and press the SPACEBAR to select (or deselect) it. Press the F1 key to obtain more information about individual packages.

Press the F5 key to install all packages except the OS Multiprocessor Support package.

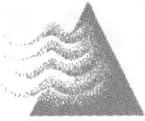

> **TIP**
> On multiprocessor systems, install the OS Multiprocessor Support package. This package is usually not installed if your UnixWare partition is less than 300MB.

Some packages depend on other packages. If you modify the list of packages and do not select a prerequisite package, an error message appears and tells you which packages are missing.

When installing the Advanced Platform Support package, UnixWare displays an additional menu prompting for the platform type. See the system manual for more information about this option.

The Accept All Settings and Install Now Option

Selecting the Accept All Settings and Install Now option begins installation of UnixWare on your hard disk. The installation time depends on the hardware and on the packages being installed. The software installation of default packages takes about forty minutes on a 33 Mhz 486 with 16MB of RAM. The following takes place during the installation:

■ The installation software verifies the requested partition and file system configuration. If no problem is detected, installation proceeds without any other prompts. Otherwise, an error message is displayed and you return to the Install menu to make corrections as described in the next section.

■ UnixWare software is copied to your system. An information gauge shows the percentage of files installed.

■ The UnixWare operating system kernel (the program that makes sure your system hardware and UnixWare applications can communicate) is created.

Troubleshooting Setup Inconsistencies

If the installation software detects an error in the selected configuration options, it displays an error message in red and returns you to the Install menu to correct the error. This section describes several error messages and tells you how to correct the errors.

Partition Error

A partition error message indicates that an active Unix partition for UnixWare of at least 80MB was not defined. Use the following procedure to correct this problem:

1. Check if you have loaded the correct driver from the HBA diskette. You may have to load a driver provided by your computer vendor.

2. From the Install menu, select View or Change Disk Configuration.

3. From the Disk Configuration menu, select Disk 1 Partitions.

4. On the Disk 1 Partitions screen, update the partition information to make the active partition a Unix partition of at least 80MB.

File System Error

A file system error message indicates that the total size of the file systems exceeds the active partition size. To correct this problem, reduce the size of one or more file systems. Usually the total size of the file systems equals the partition size. However, you must leave sufficient space if you want to add additional file systems after installation.

To update the file system configuration, follow these steps:

1. From the Install menu, select View or Change Disk Configuration.

2. From the Disk Configuration menu, select File Systems.

3. On the File Systems screen, reduce the file system sizes to make the total size less than or equal to the partition size.

Insufficient Space Error

An insufficient space message appears when there is not enough disk space to install UnixWare. Three solutions are available:

- **Install fewer packages**   Select View or Change Package Selection from the Install menu and install fewer packages as described previously.

- **Assign a larger Unix partition and/or increase file system sizes**   Select View or Change Package Selection from the Install menu. Then follow the instructions in the Viewing/Changing Disk Configuration section later in this appendix.

- **Cancel the UnixWare installation**   Select Cancel Installation from the Install menu.

Final Steps Before Reboot

If so prompted, insert the specified HBA diskette. If you have multiple HBA diskettes, you are prompted to insert the HBA diskettes in reverse order.

If so prompted, identify your multiprocessor platform. If you install the OS Multiprocessor Support package, the software attempts to determine your platform type and displays a message if it cannot do so. After reading the message, press the F5 key and either install multiprocessor support or choose a platform type from the displayed list of supported multiprocessor platforms.

CAUTION

If you select multiprocessor support, you must enter the correct platform type. Failure to do so may prevent you from booting the system, in which case you'll have to reinstall UnixWare.

If you have a platform support module (PSM) diskette for a multiprocessor platform not listed on the Choose Platform Support Module menu, select Add-on Platform Support Module Diskette and, when prompted, insert the PSM diskette.

When all files are installed, you will be prompted to reboot the system. Remove any diskette in the boot drive, and press ENTER to confirm.

TIP

If the system does not reboot and displays a message that the CD-ROM is not empty, power down the system.

Final Installation Steps

The following sections describe the installation process after the software is installed and the system is rebooted.

Configuring Your Network Interface Cards

Select and configure the network interface cards for your system. Then press the F10 key.

NOTE

These screens are only displayed if you installed the Network Interface Card Support (nics) package. (The nics package is installed by default.)

Select the available network interface types from the Network Interface Card Selection window. Enter the number of cards (the maximum is four) for each network interface type.

The Network Interface Card Configuration screen is displayed and prompts you for the hardware parameter settings for each network card type. Typical parameters include the cable type, interrupt vector (IRQ), memory address range, and I/O address range.

Selecting TCP/IP Network Parameters

Enter the TCP/IP networking software parameters and confirm by pressing the F10 key.

NOTE
These screens appear only if you have installed the Internet Utilities (inet) package, which is installed by default.

For each networking card, you are prompted for:

- Your system Internet Protocol (IP) address, netmask, and Broadcast address.
- Your local router IP address.
- The DNS domain name and the IP address for a maximum of three DNS servers.
- Your network frame type.

NOTE
If a BOOTP server is configured on your network, some or all of the fields may be assigned default values.

When installing multiple networking cards, you will be asked the node name and device handle for each networking card. You should enter these parameters now, but also may do so later via the Internet Setup icon in the Networking folder under Admin Tools (or the **/etc/inet/menu** utility), in which case you must reboot the system.

TIP
Contact your network administrator to determine the appropriate values for your system.

Configuring NIS (Application Server only)

With the left and right arrow keys, specify whether you want to configure Network Information Services (NIS) now. Then highlight Apply and press the ENTER key.

NOTE
Before displaying these screens you must explicitly select the Network Information Service (nis) package from the Package Selection screen. This package comes with the Application Server. Personal Edition users can purchase the NFS add-on product.

If you configure NIS now, you are prompted to choose the type of NIS system (master, slave, or client) and its NIS domain name. Master and client systems are prompted for the system node name of the NIS servers (master or slave) in the network. When installing a slave server, you are prompted for the name of its master server.

Selecting Your Locale

Select the country and language preference, highlight Apply, and press the ENTER key.

> **NOTE**
> These prompts are only displayed if you installed the Language Supplement (ls) package, which is installed by default.

UnixWare prompts for the system user's country of residence. Use the left or right arrows to cycle through the country choices. The answer determines locale-specific characteristics such as collation sequence and the characters that signify yes and no in "yes/no" prompts.

The system asks if you want to support only related locales (for example, when selecting the United States related locales include the United Kingdom, Australia, and Canada English) or to support all locales. Selecting all locales is recommended if your system supports users who speak different languages.

Selecting the Mouse Type

As part of this step, you select the mouse type, configure the mouse, and test it.

Select the mouse type. Specify the type of mouse you are using: Serial Mouse (the default), Bus Mouse, PS/2-compatible mouse, or No Mouse. Enter the number associated with your mouse type and press the ENTER key.

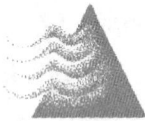

> **TIP**
> If your serial mouse came with a PS/2 adapter (a device that allows the mouse to be plugged into a computer's PS/2 port) and your computer has a PS/2 mouse port, install the mouse as a PS/2 mouse.

> **TIP**
> Set up your mouse as soon as possible. You can set up or change the mouse configuration at any time. To do so, log in as root and issue the **/usr/bin/mouseadmin** command, which prompts for information about the mouse.

Configure your mouse. If you selected No Mouse, proceed to setting up accounts. Otherwise, answer the prompts for the mouse you selected.

- If you selected Serial Mouse, specify the serial port your mouse is connected to and the number of buttons on your mouse. By default, the port used is **tty00** (on a DOS system, **tty00** is known as COM1 or LPT1) and the number of buttons is two.

- If you selected Bus Mouse, specify the mouse's interrupt vector and the number of buttons on it.

- If you selected a PS/2 mouse, specify the number of buttons on it.

After answering these questions, the blinking message "Loading mouse driver" appears in the center of the help bar at the bottom of the screen. This message means that the mouse driver is loading and should not be interrupted.

Testing Your Mouse

After you select a mouse, UnixWare checks if the mouse can communicate with your computer. When so prompted, press the ENTER key to begin the test. Then move the mouse and check whether the cursor on the screen moves. Press any mouse button to end the test.

If the test is not successful within 15 seconds, the message "ERROR: Mouse Not Detected" is displayed. Return to the Mouse Selection screen and do one of the following: select a different mouse type, select No Mouse, or select to shut down the computer so you can check your hardware.

Setting Up Accounts

Setting up accounts involves the following procedures: Setting up the owner, root, and sysadm accounts; assigning the owner name and password; assigning the root password; and assigning the sysadm password.

Setting up the owner, root, and sysadm Accounts

UnixWare supports multiple users. A user login ID and password are required for access to a UnixWare system. You are prompted for the login and passwords for three important UnixWare accounts:

■ **owner** The system owner, or owner, performs administrative tasks from the Desktop. Tasks include adding new user accounts and managing the network.

■ **root** The root account performs administrative tasks from the UnixWare command line. This account can access any file on the system.

■ **sysadm** The sysadm account performs administrative tasks using the Operations, Administration, and Maintenance character-based menu interface.

Enter the system owner login and password, the root password, and the sysadm password. If you performed a nondestructive installation, you are not prompted for the owner login, owner password, or root password. If you did not install the OA&M package, or if you performed a nondestructive installation of the OA&M package, you are not prompted for the sysadm package.

Assigning Your Owner Name and Password

Set up the owner's account. Enter the following login identification information for the system owner:

■ **Owner's name** Enter the owner's full (first and last) name.

■ **Owner's login ID** Enter the owner's login ID. Common entries are the first name or initials.

■ **Owner's user number** The default user number is the first unassigned number greater than 100. For a new installation, use 101. Each new user account should have a unique user number. A given user should have the same user number on each machine in a network. This is not only easier to remember, it simplifies setting permissions to files and directories.

> **CAUTION**
> Once assigned, a user number should not be changed. If it is, you may run into permission problems because the old number is still associated with your files and directories.

Enter the owner's account password when so prompted. Don't forget it! Assign the password using these guidelines:

■ Each password must contain six or more characters. (Only the first eight characters are significant.)

■ Each password must contain two or more alphabetic (upper- or lowercase) characters, and one or more numeric or special characters.

■ Avoid easy-to-guess passwords such as your name, nickname, initials, or those of friends, family, or pets.

Enter your new password and press the ENTER key. When so prompted, enter your password a second time and press the ENTER key to confirm.

If the two entries do not match, reenter the password. After three trials, an error message is displayed. The owner will be prompted for a password when the login ID is first used.

Assigning the root Password

When so prompted, enter the root password and follow the same procedure as you did for assigning the owner password (described in the previous section). The root account has full system privileges. Use it for advanced system administration activities.

Assigning the sysadm Password

When so prompted, enter the sysadm password and follow the same procedure as you did for assigning the owner password (described previously in the "Assigning Your Owner Name and Password" section. The sysadm account is created when the OA&M package is installed. It is used to perform system administration tasks through the sysadm user interface.

Preparing to Use Your System

After you have responded to all the prompts, the system boots and displays the login prompt. You should now do the following:

■ Create emergency recovery diskettes used for repairing a damaged hard disk and restoring data from emergency recovery tapes, which you must create. Chapter 10 gives more information about backing up your system.

■ UnixWare 2.0 provides an enhanced graphical Desktop. If you performed a nondestructive installation, determine where your UnixWare 1.1 applications now reside.

TIP
The **/usr/X/adm/README.UW2.0** file lists all system files that have been moved. A **README.UW2.0** file in each user's home directory lists the folders and icons that have moved.

TIP
Inform other users on your system that UnixWare was upgraded to Release 2.0 and tell them to read the **README.UW2.0** file in their home directory.

■ Perform all necessary system administration tasks, such as setting up and configuring TCP/IP networking for dialup connections, mail, printing, and Internet access as described in Chapter 13.

Now UnixWare is ready to go!

Installing MS Windows 3.1 On a Unix System

The procedure for installing MS Windows 3.1 is somewhat lengthy, whether you install a personal copy, a shared version, or a network version. However, these three procedures are quite similar: master one and you have mastered the other two.

Installing a Personal Copy of Windows 3.1

The following procedure installs a personal copy of MS Windows 3.1 on a UnixWare system, starting from the Desktop. The procedure is somewhat long because neither a regular user, nor MS Windows has write permission for the C: directory.

1. Access the Applications folder window and then double-click on the MS Windows Setup icon to open a DOS window configured for Windows installation.

2. Insert MS Windows Disk 1 in the appropriate drive (here assumed to be A:), type **A:\SETUP** and press ENTER.

3. If the screen displays a warning message referring to the file SUBST.EXE, type **C** to continue.

4. Wait, perhaps even a few minutes, while the Setup program checks the hard disk for a previous version of MS Windows.

5. At the prompt, type **c** for a custom setup.

6. The default drive and directory is displayed. Press BACKSPACE to clear this entry and then type **D:\WINDOWS** to specify the required drive and directory.

> **CAUTION**
> This step is mandatory because only **root** has write access to drive C:.

7. The MS Windows installation program will show you the current hardware configuration. To change a field, select Change System Settings, and choose the appropriate value.

8. Be sure your keyboard type is "Enhanced 101 or 102 key and Non U. S." (the only type supported by UnixWare).

9. Set the Network to "Novell NetWare (shell version 3.26 or greater)".

> **CAUTION**
> If you are running Novell NetWare and IPX, select Novell NetWare and enter the shell version, which may be obtained by running the Novell command NVER.

10. Specify the Display to "DOS Merge Windows/X." If it is not listed, click on Other, enter **C:\usr\lib\merge\windows**, and locate the driver in the new list.

11. Set the Mouse field to "DOS Merge Mouse." If it is not listed, click on Other and enter **C:\usr\lib\merge\windows**.

12. Insert additional floppy disks as requested (a total of six).

13. Click on the Make the modifications later option and then click on Don't Save. Because you are installing MS Windows under UnixWare and not under DOS, MS Windows must not modify either your AUTOEXEC.BAT or your CONFIG.SYS file. You will manually modify your AUTOEXEC.BAT file.

14. Install a printer driver by selecting the proper printer type, clicking first on Install, and then Connect. Select LPT1.DOS from the ensuing Ports box.

15. Exit Zoom mode by pressing the SCROLL LOCK key. This displays the UnixWare Desktop window in addition to the DOS window.

16. Create or modify an AUTOEXEC.BAT file with a PATH statement that includes D:\WINDOWS. (Chapter 3 shows you how to do so with the UnixWare editor.)

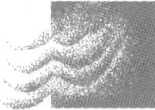

> **CAUTION**
> Always make a backup copy before editing the AUTOEXEC.BAT file. All entries in the PATH statement, except for the first one, must be preceded by a semicolon (;), and then D:\.

Installing MS Windows 3.1 in a Shared Environment

When MS Windows is installed in a shared environment, several users can access it simultaneously, provided that they have not violated Microsoft's licensing agreement. The installation procedure requires the **root** password. It is similar to the procedure for installing a personal copy of the software, with some important changes:

- Before starting, follow the steps in the "Adding Write Permissions" section (which follows shortly) to write MS Windows on the shared UnixWare directory **/usr/ldbin**, which DOS refers to as C:\USR\LDBIN or J:.

- When invoking the SETUP command, use **A:\SETUP /A** instead of **A:\SETUP**.

- Use **J:\WINDOWS** when specifying the required drive and directory.

This procedure installs the shared copy of MS Windows. Then follow the steps given under the "Completing a Shared or Network Installation" section presented below. Finally, follow the steps in the "Removing Write Permissions" section.

Installing MS Windows 3.1 in a Network Environment

When MS Windows is installed in a network environment, several users can access it simultaneously, provided that they have not violated Microsoft's licensing agreement. Use the same process provided for the single-user environment, except use **O:\WINDOWS:** as the required drive and directory.

This procedure installs the network copy of MS Windows. Then run the steps given in the "Completing a Shared or Network Installation" section below. Finally, follow the steps given in the "Removing Write Permissions" section.

Completing a Shared or Network Installation

Complete a shared or network Windows installation for each user with the following procedure:

1. Copy the necessary Windows files to each user's local directory with the **SETUP /N** command.

2. Edit the PATH statement in the AUTOEXEC.BAT file to include both the shared MS Windows directory and the user's personal MS Windows directory. Remember, if you are installing MS Windows applications on a shared drive, you will have to execute the steps given in the "Adding Write Permissions" section, and then follow the steps in the "Removing Write Permissions" section once the installation is complete.

3. Using the **winxcopy** command, copy the Windows/X display drivers to the shared Windows directory (you must have write permission) with a command such as **winxcopy j:\windows**.

4. Install Windows applications to the shared directory.

NOTE
For personal installations, specify D: as the installation drive. This installs the Windows applications in your home directory. To open these applications by clicking on their icon, you must associate them from the Icon Setup box.

Adding Write Permissions

UnixWare normally accords write permission on the C: drive to the **root** account only. This procedure accords write permission on the C: drive to other accounts. Steps 4 and 5 accord write permission on the **/usr/bin** file as a prerequisite to installing shared or network user versions of MS Windows. As soon as the software installation is complete follow the steps given in the "Removing Write Permissions" section below. Otherwise you have opened the door to a potentially serious security violation.

1. Access the Applications window and double-click on the Terminal icon to generate the command line.

2. In response to the prompt, type **su** and then press ENTER.

3. In response to the prompt, type the root password and then press ENTER.

4. Type **cd /usr** and then press ENTER.

5. Type **chmod 777 ldbin** and then press ENTER. (This allows all accounts full privileges on the **/usr/ldbin** file.)

6. Press CTRL-D to return to the regular prompt.

Removing Write Permissions

UnixWare normally accords write permission on the C: drive to the **root** account only. However, as you've seen in the previous sections, on occasion it is necessary to relax this restriction, temporarily. This procedure reinstates the normal situation. Be sure to execute it as soon as possible. Otherwise you have opened the door to a serious security violation.

1. Access the Applications window and double-click on the Terminal icon to generate the command line.

2. Enter **su** and the root password.

3. Type the following:

```
cd /usr
chmod 755 ldbin
```

This returns you to the "normal" situation, in which only the root account has write privileges on the **/usr/ldbin** file.

4. Press CTRL-D to return to the regular prompt.

APPENDIX D

Setting Up Modems and Other Serial Communications

Along with local area networks, serial communications is a major method for networking Unix systems. The following types of serial communications are widely used:

■ **Dumb terminals** Often the most economical way of running character-based applications is by connecting several dumb terminals to the serial ports on a single computer.

■ **Telephone communications** UnixWare supports high-speed serial connections over a variety of lines to remote systems.

■ **Direct connections** Cable can connect two systems via their serial ports, provided that they are in the same building.

> *NOTE*
> Whereas TCP/IP is usually used with connectionless networks, such as Ethernet, UnixWare supports TCP/IP over serial connections. PPP (Point-to-Point Protocol) and SLIP (Serial Line Internet Protocol) provide serial interfaces to the Internet.

To configure serial communications, you can use the UnixWare graphical interface (Dialup Setup) or standard text editors such as **vi** to edit configuration files in the **/etc/uucp** directory. Both methods are described in this appendix.

Configuring Serial Communications with Dialup Setup

Use Dialup Setup to configure communications with remote systems and dumb terminals via direct connections or modems.

> *NOTE*
> To use Dialup Setup, you must have permission to change Dialup Setup, as discussed in Chapter 8.

To use Dialup Setup, double-click on the Dialup Setup icon in the Networking folder in the Admin Tools folder. You'll see an empty window from which you can add a dialup device or a remote system entry. When you add a new dialup device or system, you can display it on the Desktop as a named icon.

When you add a remote dialup system entry, it adds a line of text in the Dialup Setup window, as shown in Figure D-1. To iconize the remote dialup system entry, drag the text line onto an open folder. The remote dialup system icon carries the name of the remote system—hookup, for example.

Use the remote system icon to log on to a remote dialup system and transfer files between the remote dialup system and the local UnixWare system. Before logging on to a remote system from either Dialup Setup or the remote dialup system icon, you must first add a dialup device.

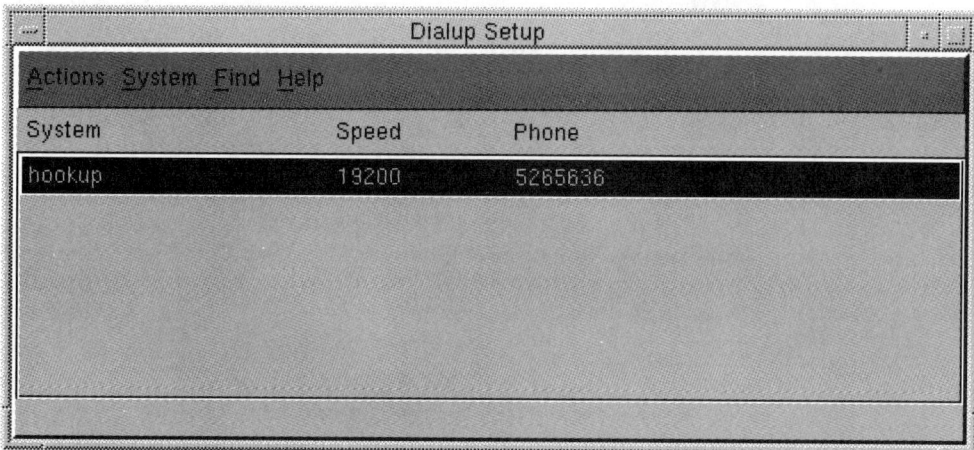

FIGURE D-1. *The Dialup Setup window*

Working with Dialup Devices

A dialup device entry represents a connection to a modem or to another directly connected computer system or terminal. UnixWare requires you to add and configure these devices before connecting to remote dialup systems or terminals.

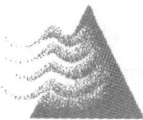

> **TIP**
> When connecting a dumb terminal directly to a serial port, configure the port as Direct and Incoming. The login prompt appears after you connect the terminal to the serial port and press the ENTER key from that terminal.

Adding a Dialup Device Entry
Starting from the Dialup Setup window, follow these steps to add a dialup device entry:

1. Select Setup Devices from the Actions menu. You'll see the Devices window. This window is empty until you add a device.

2. Choose New from the Device menu to display the Add New Device window, as shown in Figure D-2.

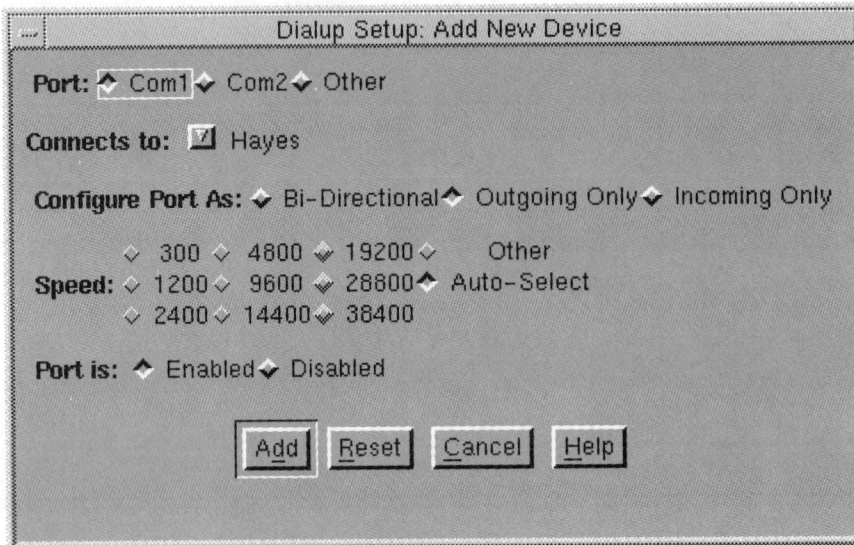

FIGURE D-2. *The Add New Device window*

3. Set the Port field—COM1, COM2, or Other, depending on which port is cabled for dialup. If you select Other, you must enter the port's device name. (If the device is not in the **/dev** directory, you must create an entry with the **mknod** command.)

4. Select the appropriate device type in the Connect to: field.

5. Configure the port as Bi-Directional, Outgoing Only, or Incoming Only. Bi-Directional establishes connections to the port in both directions. Outgoing Only is for calls that only go out. Incoming Only just allows incoming calls. (Bi-Directional and Incoming start a ttymon port monitor that listens for incoming call requests.)

6. Click on Add to add the device and close the window. An icon representing the port is displayed in the Devices window.

Modifying, Deleting, or Copying a Dialup Device

After you've added a dialup device, the following commands are available from the Devices menu:

- **Copy to a Folder**   Click here to copy the device icon to a folder. You'll see the Copy to Folder window. Select the folder to receive the copy of the device, and then click on Copy. After adding a device icon to a folder, double-click on it to access that device for remote login.

- **Delete**   Click here to delete the device.

- **Properties**   Click here to view or change device properties. You'll see the Device Properties window with information for the selected entry. Change any options, then click on OK.

Setting Up Access to a Remote Dialup System

If you know the remote system's name and have added a dialup device, you can configure a remote dialup system icon to make it easy to log in and transfer files to the remote system.

> *CAUTION*
> The system must be accessible by modem, or must be directly connected to your system via a serial port.

To add a remote dialup system, follow this procedure:

1. Start from the Dialup Setup window and select New from the System menu. This will display the Add New System window, as shown in Figure D-3. Then set each field, as described here:

- **System Name**   Enter the name of the remote system.

- **Connect Via**   Click on either Modem or Direct, depending on which device was used to connect to the remote system.

- **Speed**   Click on the speed of your modem or port. Click on Auto-Select if you don't know the speed. For a direct connection, click on 19200.

- **Phone Number**   Enter the telephone number to call. (This field is not available for direct connection.) Including a dash (–) in a phone number entry generates a four-second pause. Including an equal sign (=) means the system waits for an outside dial tone. For example, the entry 9=6135265636--1335 tells the modem to dial 9, wait for an outside dial tone, dial 6135265636, wait 8 seconds, and then dial 1335.

```
┌─────────────────────────────────────────────────────────────────┐
│ ┌─┐                Dialup Setup: Add New System                   │
│ └─┘                                                               │
│ ┌───────────────────────────────────────────────────────────────┤
│ │ CATEGORY:  ⌐⌐ Basic Settings                                    │
│ ├───────────────────────────────────────────────────────────────┤
│ │                                                                 │
│ │                                                                 │
│ │         System Name: │⌐_____│                   │
│ │         Connect Via: ⌃ Modem ⌄ Direct                          │
│ │                                                                 │
│ │                  ⌄ 300  ⌄ 4800 ⌄ 19200 ⌄   Other              │
│ │         Speed: ⌄ 1200 ⌄ 9600 ⌄ 28800⌃ Auto-Select             │
│ │                  ⌄ 2400 ⌄ 14400 ⌄ 38400                        │
│ │                                                                 │
│ │         Phone Number: │⌐_____│                  │
│ │                                                                 │
│ │                                                                 │
│ ├───────────────────────────────────────────────────────────────┤
│ │         │ Add │  │ Reset │  │ Cancel │  │ Help │               │
│ │                                                                 │
│ │ Enter the System name to dial.                                  │
│ └───────────────────────────────────────────────────────────────┘
```

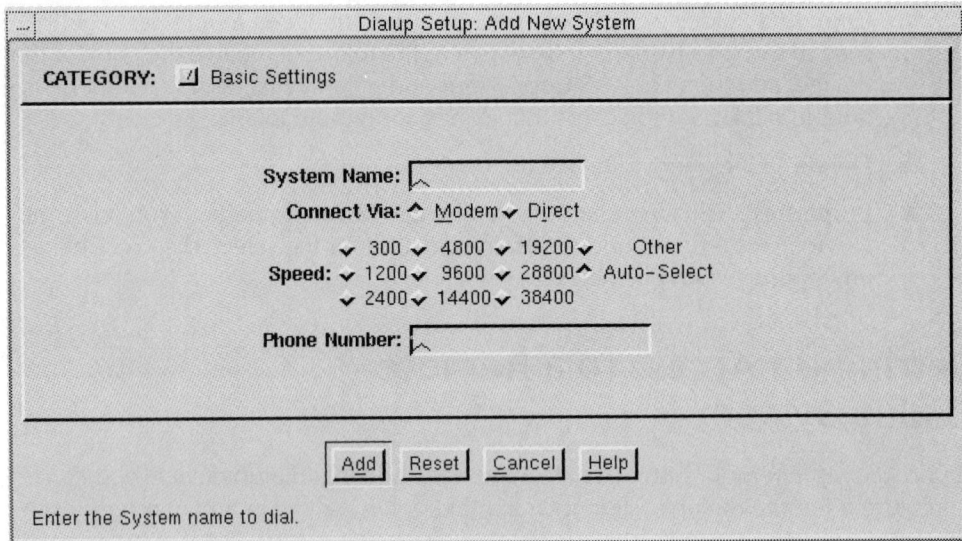

FIGURE D-3. *The Add New System window*

2. Click on Add to add a remote system and close the window.

3. Once you have added the remote system, click on CATEGORY next to Basic Settings, and select Login Sequence.

4. Click on Login Sequence. This entry is usually optional but is required for file transfers to the remote system. The login sequence defines the dialog between your system and the remote system for transferring a file to the remote system. The Prompt defines the remote system statement; Response defines your system response.

5. Complete the login sequence (Prompt and Response) and click on the Add button next to the Current Login Sequence box. You may use several Prompt/Response lines. Consider the following typical dialogue:

PROMPT	RESPONSE
in:--in	nuucp
word:	nuucp password on remote system

Here, your system expects the remote system to send the letters in: (the last part of login:). If your system doesn't receive this prompt, it sends a newline and looks for in: again. The system responds to in: by sending **nuucp** (to login as **nuucp**). When the remote system responds with word: (for password:), your system sends the password for the remote **nuucp** login. Then the remote system may receive remote file transfers.

Using Serial Communications Configuration Files

You may use any ASCII text editor such as **vi** to modify configuration files directly. Most of these files are located in the **/etc/uucp** directory.

The configuration files described in this section include:

- **Systems** Describes the linked remote systems.
- **Devices** Describes the serial ports used for modem and direct communications and names the devices linked to each port.
- **Dialers** Describes the dialup devices connected to your serial ports. This information includes the required chat scripts for linking your system to modems and other devices.

These configuration files are part of the Service Access Facility (SAF) and are found in the **/etc/saf** directory.

Adding Remote Systems

Adding a system name via the Dialup Setup window creates an entry in the **/etc/uucp/Systems** file. The following system entry describes a system named hookup that is accessible via a dial-out modem:

```
hookup Any ACU Any 5265636
```

The system name, hookup, is used with communications commands such as **cu** and **uucp**. The first Any specifies that the system is available at any time. The ACU (Automatic Call Unit) specifies that you can access the system via a modem. The **Devices** file must contain at least one ACU entry, as discussed in the next section. The second Any specifies that any supported line speed may be used to call the system. The 5265636 is the telephone number of the remote system.

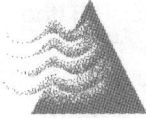

> **TIP**
> The **/etc/uucp/Systems** file contains a description of each field.

Adding Serial Devices

Adding a device via the Devices window creates an entry in the **/etc/uucp/Devices** file. The following device entry describes an automatic call unit (such as a modem) connected to the COM2 port:

```
ACU tty01,M - Any hayes
```

The **ACU** represents a dial-out modem, which can be used to connect any remote system over telephone lines. The second field specifies that the ACU be connected to the COM2 port (**/dev/tty01**), which can be opened without waiting for a carrier (,M). The dash in the third field is a placeholder telling you to ignore that field. This field is used only if the dialer and the modem were separate devices attached to separate ports. The **Any** specifies that any supported line speed may be used to call the system. The word **hayes** tells you that the modem is Hayes-compatible, which is represented by an entry in the Dialers field.

> **TIP**
> The **/etc/uucp/Devices** file contains a description of each field.

Adding Dialer Entries

Dialers and other serial communications devices are contained in the **/etc/uucp/Dialers** file. This file contains entries for Hayes and other popular modems. The key parts of Dialers entries are chat scripts describing the dialogue between UnixWare and the modem that establishes the connection.

The following Dialers entry is associated with a basic Hayes-compatible modem:

```
hayes ,-, "" \M\dAT\r\c OK\r ATDT\T\r\c CONNECT \r\m\c
```

Initiating a connection to a remote system over a Hayes modem launches the following activities:

■ UnixWare sends an AT signal to the modem to check if it is ready.

■ After the modem replies OK, UnixWare sends an ATDT signal to request that the modem dial a number and the telephone number.

■ After making the connection, the modem responds CONNECT. UnixWare may now send data to the remote system.

This example used the following control codes:

■ **\c**   No new line

■ **\d**   Delay two seconds

■ **\m**   Turn off CLOCAL flag

■ **\M**   Turn on CLOCAL flag

■ **\r**   Carriage-return

■ **\T**   Use the phone number supplied in the Systems file

Add your own dialers by coding additional entries in the Dialers file.

NOTE
The **/etc/uucp/Dialers** file contains a description of each field and the valid control codes.

Using Other Configuration Files

In addition to the systems, devices, and dialers files, several other files are useful for configuring serial communication. Files found in the **/etc/uucp** directory are used to poll remote systems, set permissions delimiting remote systems' operations on your system, and define dialer abbreviations.

Short descriptions of the **/etc/uucp** configuration files follow. More detailed descriptions are found in the Applications Server system manual and within the file documentation.

■ **Permissions**   Specifies login, file access, and command-execution permission that remote computers have to your system.

■ **Config**   Allows you to set the parity and charsize parameters used by the **cu** command. For example, the default parity value is 7, but you can change it to 8. You can change these parameters or delete them if necessary.

TIP
You can override these parameters by using the **-i**, **-o**, and **-b**
arguments to the **cu** command.

- **Dev/config**   Configures basic networking over a TCP/IP connection.

- **Sysfiles**   Allows you to create other files to store Systems, Devices, and Dialers information. Useful for separating systems and devices that use different network connections.

- **Limits**   Limits the maximum number of basic networking daemons active at any time for file transfers (**uucico**), remote execution (**uuxqt**), and schedules for contacting remote systems (**uusched**).

- **Dialcodes**   Allows you to specify abbreviations for telephone numbers.

- **Poll**   Specifies when to poll remote systems. You can add a system name and the time it may be contacted.

- **Grades**   Defines the job grades assigned to queued communications to remote systems. This allows you to set priorities for file transfers.

Monitoring Incoming Serial Communications

When you add a device through Dialup Setup that allows incoming calls or bi-directional connections, an entry is added to the **/etc/saf/ttymon1/_pmtab** file. This entry starts a daemon process that listens for incoming calls on the port and provides a prompt for a user to log in over the modem or direct connection.

The following is a sample entry (it appears here on two lines because of typesetting considerations):

```
tty01:u::reserved:reserved:login:/dev/tty01:bhr:0:/usr/bin/shserv
    :60:auto:ldterm:login\: :::::#
```

This entry starts a ttymon process that listens for connection requests on the COM2 port (**/dev/tty01**). The transmission speed is negotiated (auto). Once the connection is established, the system presents a login prompt (**login\:**).

Few people would want to create such entries manually. However, you might want to modify it. For example, you could hard-code a particular line speed instead of using auto (line speeds appear in the **/etc/ttydefs** file) or you could change the login prompt.

Using Dumb Terminals

To add a dumb terminal to your UnixWare system, create a device entry, as described earlier in this appendix, and connect the terminal to a serial port.

The number of dumb terminals that you can link to your system is determined by your hardware configuration. Serial port boards are available to add 8, 16, or more ports.

Although UnixWare does not limit the number of linked terminals, the Personal Edition supports a maximum of two users logged in at the same time. In contrast, the Application Server supports an unlimited number of users logged in simultaneously.

Dumb terminals do not support the Desktop or graphical applications. They do support the Unix shell and character-based applications.

Configuring Dumb Terminals

Effective use of dumb terminals requires configuring your user environment. You must set the terminal type and the PATH to your applications. You also can add items like the default text editor.

The easiest way to add this information is by opening the **.profile** file in the user's home directory and adding lines for TERM, PATH, and EDITOR to the file. The following is an example:

```
PATH=$HOME/bin:$PATH:/usr/bin;export PATH
TERM=wyse150;export TERM
EDITOR=vi;export EDITOR
```

The terminal type is set to a wyse150 character terminal. A **bin** directory in the user's home directory is added to the path, as well as a **bin** in the **/usr2** directory that can contain shared character-based applications. The text editor is set to **vi** by default.

Directories within the **/usr/lib/terminfo** directory contain definitions for different terminal variables. For example, you could replace **wyse150** with the name of another **terminfo** file. Assigning the correct terminal definition enables you to run applications such as **vi** that need to control the entire screen.

A Desktop user account who logs in to UnixWare from a dumb terminal will see a prompt to start the Desktop. Enter **n** (no) to see a shell command prompt and then start a UnixWare shell session.

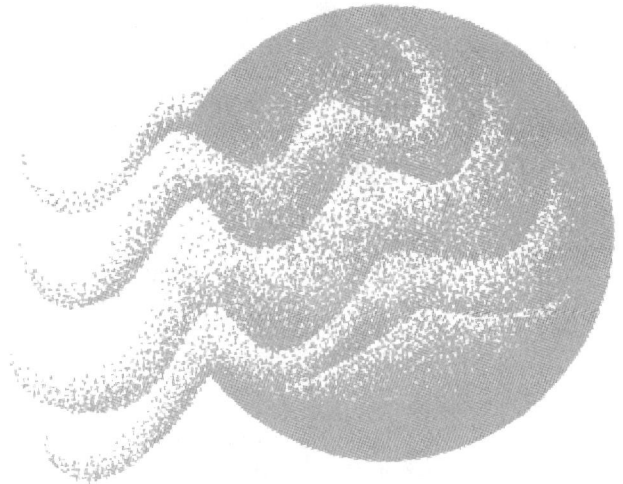

Index

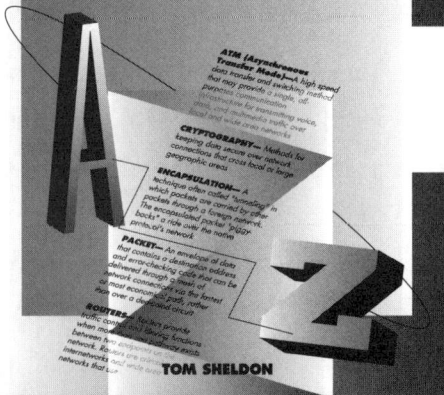

Yo Unix!

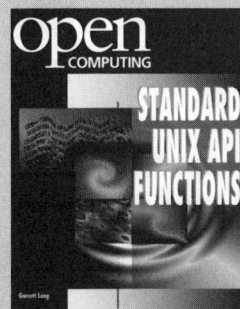

ORDER BOOKS DIRECTLY FROM OSBORNE/McGRAW-HILL

For a complete catalog of Osborne's books, call 510-549-6600 or write to us at 2600 Tenth Street, Berkeley, CA 94710

Call Toll-Free: 1-800-822-8158
24 hours a day, 7 days a week in U.S. and Canada

Mail this order form to:
McGraw-Hill, Inc.
Customer Service Dept.
P.O. Box 547
Blacklick, OH 43004

Fax this order form to:
1-614-759-3644

EMAIL
7007.1531@COMPUSERVE.COM
COMPUSERVE GO MH

Ship to:

Name _____

Company _____

Address _____

City / State / Zip _____

Daytime Telephone: _____
(We'll contact you if there's a question about your order.)

ISBN #	BOOK TITLE	Quantity	Price	Total
0-07-88				
0-07-88				
0-07-88				
0-07-88				
0-07-88				
0-07088				
0-07-88				
0-07-88				
0-07-88				
0-07-88				
0-07-88				
0-07-88				
0-07-88				

Shipping & Handling Charge from Chart Below		
Subtotal		
Please Add Applicable State & Local Sales Tax		
TOTAL		

Shipping & Handling Charges

Order Amount	U.S.	Outside U.S.
Less than $15	$3.50	$5.50
$15.00 - $24.99	$4.00	$6.00
$25.00 - $49.99	$5.00	$7.00
$50.00 - $74.99	$6.00	$8.00
$75.00 - and up	$7.00	$9.00

Occasionally we allow other selected companies to use our mailing list. If you would prefer that we not include you in these extra mailings, please check here: ❑

METHOD OF PAYMENT

❑ Check or money order enclosed (payable to Osborne/McGraw-Hill)

❑ AMERICAN EXPRESS   ❑ DISCOVER   ❑ MasterCard   ❑ VISA

Account No. ☐☐☐☐☐☐☐☐☐☐☐☐☐☐☐☐

Expiration Date _____

Signature _____

In a hurry? Call 1-800-822-8158 anytime, day or night, or visit your local bookstore.

Thank you for your order

Code BC640SL

Save 60%

Realize the Promise of Open Computing

The open computing era will reward both the individuals and the organizations that can put their knowledge to use and harness the potential of interoperable systems. Build your knowledge through the in-depth features, industry news, comprehensive product reviews, and technical insights in every issue of *Open Computing*. Subscribe Today!